Gregor Lersch

Manchen wird es sicher überraschen, dass zwei Floral Designer zu einem gemeinsamen Buchprojekt gefunden haben, von denen jeder bislang eher seinen eigenen Weg gegangen ist. Denn die Philosophien im Umgang mit floraler Gestaltung haben sich doch recht deutlich voneinander unterschieden. Schließlich wollte der von Klaus Wagener propagierte Lifestyle mit der Pflanze – zumindest aus meiner Sicht – nicht so recht zu meinem Credo für eine intensive Beziehung zwischen Mensch und Pflanze passen.

Dass Klaus Wagener und ich uns dennoch zu diesem Schritt entschlossen haben, zeigt, wie groß Respekt und Anerkennung der fachlichen Leistung des jeweils anderen sind. Genau dies hat sich auch im Laufe der Zusammenarbeit bestätigt. Aufgrund der gegenseitigen Akzeptanz entwickelte sich hier ein offenes und freundschaftliches Miteinander, aus dem ich für mich eine Menge neuer Erkenntnisse gewonnen habe.

Darüber hinaus aber lag gerade auch in der Polarität unserer Auffassungen ein Spannungspotenzial, das uns gereizt hat. Wie gehen zwei so unterschiedliche Persönlichkeiten wie wir beide mit gleichen Themen um? Wo zeigen sich die bis dato festgestellten Kontraste? Oder sind die Unterschiede doch gar nicht so groß, wie sich vermuten ließe?

Wie funktioniert eine enge gestalterische Zusammenarbeit – vor allem an gemeinsamen Werkstücken? Inwieweit muss man sein Ego zurückschrauben, um überhaupt zu Ergebnissen zu gelangen? Wie geht der einzelne mit der durchaus vorhandenen Konkurrenzsituation um?

Die Erfahrung aus diesem Projekt zeigt, dass solche ungewöhnlichen Konstellationen zu besonders nachhaltigem und begründetem Arbeiten anregen. So war es für mich noch einmal eine wichtige persönliche Auseinandersetzung mit meinen eigenen Gestaltungsprinzipien. Das gezielte „kontroverse Miteinander" hat sich meines Erachtens als ein hervorragendes Instrument zur Feinjustierung der eigenen Position herausgestellt.

Mehr denn je bin ich überzeugt davon, dass die Menschen eine intakte Floralkultur wollen als Ausgleich zu den oftmals sehr oberflächlichen Beziehungen in unserer heutigen Welt. Das Gestalten mit Blumen und Pflanzen gehört ganz wesentlich dazu. Daher liegt es mir am Herzen, bei Fachleuten wie Liebhabern Begeisterung zu wecken, vor allem aber dem Berufsnachwuchs Mut zu machen, ein zeitgemäßes Bild von Blume und Pflanze zu entwickeln. Denn eine lebendige Floralkultur braucht dauerhaft neue kreative Impulse. Wenn wir mit den Inspirationen in diesem Buch dazu beitragen können, haben wir viel erreicht.

Some people will certainly be surprised to see that two floral designers, who have so far pursued their ways rather individually and whose philosophies concerning floral designing differed quite clearly, came together to realize a common book project. This lifestyle, which is based on plants and supported by Klaus Wagner, didn't really seem to fit my own credo for an intensive relation between man and plant.

The fact that we have yet decided to realize this project, proves our enormous respect for the professional achievement of one another. In the course of our cooperation, this was exactly confirmed. Thanks to our mutual acceptance we could develop an open-minded and friendly cooperation, which provided me personally with a lot of new insights. Moreover, our opposite views created a potential full of tension, which tempted us both. How do two such different personalities, like us, deal with the same topics? Where do the contrasts, so far detected, get visible? Or, are the differences not that big as they might be suggested?

How does a tight designing cooperation – especially concerning common works function? To which extent do we have to give up our self-interests in order to achieve any results at all? And how does the individual deal with this undeniable competitive situation?

Our experiences with this project show, that such unusual constellations can lead to particularly sustainable and reasonable workings beyond all expectations. Thus, this was an important opportunity for me, to deal with my own designing principles. From my point of view, this targeted "controversial cooperation" has proved to be the perfect occasion to adjust one's own position.

More than ever, I am now convinced that people want to live in a world where they can take care adequately of their flowers in return to our world of today, which is characterized by superficial relations. Designing with flowers and plants is a real essential part of this. Therefore, it is extremely important for me, to evoke the enthusiasm of experts and fans, but above all to encourage the young professionals to develop a contemporary image of flowers and plants. A vivid cultural use of plants and flowers needs permanently new creative impulses. If we could contribute to this purpose with the help of this book's inspirations, we might already achieve a lot.

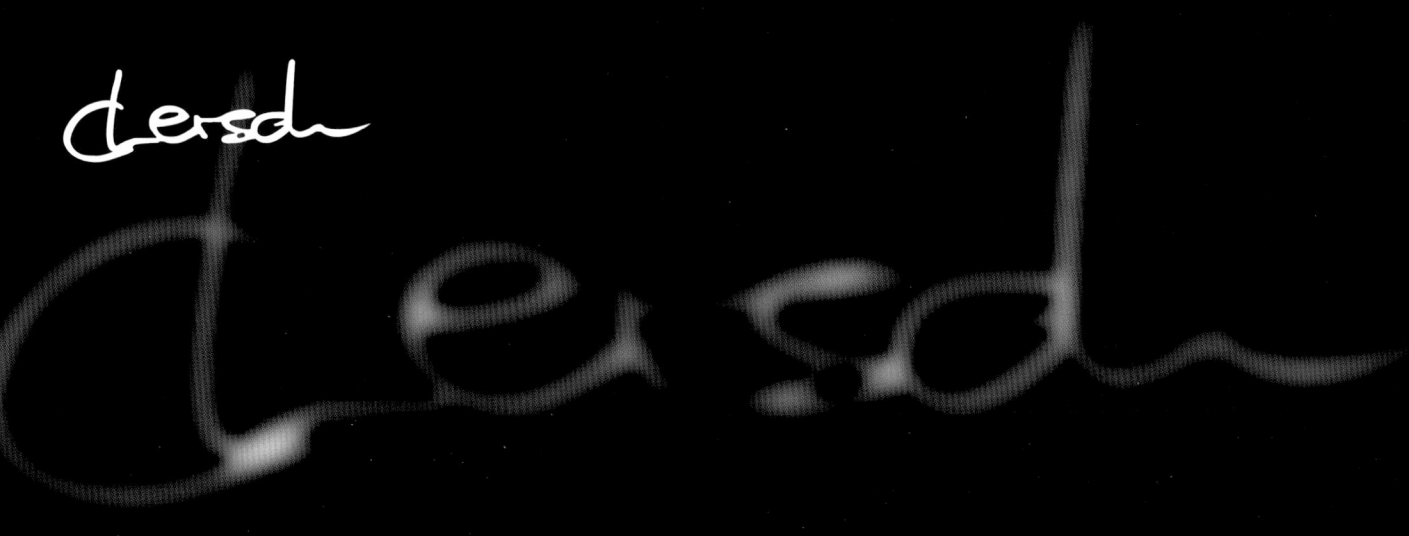

Gregor Lersch wurde am 20. Oktober 1949 in Bad Neuenahr geboren. Das Leben rund um die elterliche Gärtnerei prägte ihn sehr früh. Schon mit 6 Jahren stand sein Berufswunsch fest, Gärtner zu werden. Dementsprechend folgte eine Ausbildung in einem Blumen- und Zierpflanzenbetrieb, wo er gleichzeitig auch Einblick in Landschaftsbau, Gemüsebau und Friedhofsgärtnerei bekam. Danach folgten eine Florist-Ausbildung mit integriertem Gastjahr an der Meisterschule Bonn-Friesdorf bei dem von ihm verehrten Lehrmeister Albert Eurich und die anschließende Tätigkeit im elterlichen Betrieb. 1974 absolvierte er die Florist-Meisterprüfung an der FDF-Meisterschule in Köln-Auweiler. Die nächsten Stationen: Teilnahme an verschiedenen Berufswettkämpfen auf Landes- und Bundesebene. 1976 Gewinn der „Goldenen Rose". Teilnahmen am World-Cup 1977 in Nizza, 1979 in Melbourne und 1981 in Hamburg. 1978 wurde Gregor Lersch erster deutscher Europacupsieger in Rom. 1979 siegte er beim europaweiten Wettkampf „Goldene Tulpe" des holländischen Fernsehens. Ständige Beteiligungen auf Bundesgartenschauen an Floristik-Wettbewerben und gärtnerischen Schaustandgestaltungen wurden insgesamt mit 7 großen Goldmedaillen, über 30 Gold-, 22 Silber- und etlichen Bronzemedaillen ausgezeichnet. 1979 überreichte man ihm den Goldenen Staatspreis der Floristik für die Gesamtleistung auf der Bundesgartenschau in Bonn. Große nationale Beiträge auf ausländischen Gartenschauen für den Zentralverband Gartenbau erhielten höchste Auszeichnungen. In den 90er Jahren befruchtete er die Branche mit floralen, von FDF und CMA gemeinsam getragenen Trendpräsentationen. Gestützt auf Megatrends der Gesellschaft waren sie Inspiration für Floral Designer von Essen bis Tokio, von Europa bis Amerika. Ideale Plattform dafür war alljährlich die Internationale Pflanzenmesse IPM in Essen. Ständige Seminare, Vorträge, Workshops und Demonstrationen in Deutschland und mehr als 40 Ländern rund um den Erdball sowie Buchveröffentlichungen zu diversen floristischen Themenrunden das Arbeitsspektrum des vielsprachigen Floral Designers Lersch ab. Begleitet haben ihn dabei auf weiten Strecken kriener-potthoff communications und deren FloralDesign Edition, die seine Bücher verlegt.

Gregor Lersch was born on the 20th October in 1949 in Bad Neuenahr. The life around his parents' nursery influenced him from the very beginning. At the age of 6, he already knew what he wanted to become, namely a gardener. Accordingly he served an apprenticeship in a company producing flowers and decorative plants. At this occasion he gained insight into the landscape, the vegetable gardening and the cemetery nursery. Afterwards, he served a second apprenticeship to become a florist and spent a year as a guest student at the Master School in Bonn-Friesdorf. Here he met Albert Eurich, the taskmaster he admired a lot, before finally working in his parents company. In 1974, he passed the examination for master craftsman's diploma for florists at the FDF-Master School in Cologne (Köln-Auweiler). The next stages in his life: Participation at various professional competitions at regional and federal level. In 1976, he won the "Golden Rose". In 1977, he participated in the World Cup in Nice, in 1979 in Melbourne and in 1981 in Hamburg. In 1978, Gregor Lersch became the first German winner of the European Cup in Rome. In 1979, he won the European competition "Golden Tulip" of the Dutch television. Thanks to his several attendances at federal horticultural shows, floral competitions and horticultural trade shows, he was awarded 7 big gold medals, over 30 golden, 22 silver and a number of bronze medals. In 1979, he was handed out the golden State award of floristry for his overall achievement at the federal horticultural show in Bonn. Due to his important national achievement at foreign horticultural shows on behalf of the German association of horticulture, he received the highest awards. During the nineties, he provided the industry with floral trend presentations with the support of the companies, FDF and CMA. Being based on mega trends of the society they served as inspirations for floral designers from Essen to Tokyo and from Europe to USA. The annual International Plant Fair, IPM, in Essen offered the perfect stage for presentation. Regular workshops, lectures and demonstrations in Germany and more than 40 countries all over the world, as well as book pub-lications concerning various floral topics complete the field of activity of the multi-lingual floral designer, Gregor Lersch. During large episodes of his career he has been accompanied by kriener-potthoff communications and their book range, FloralDesign Edition, releasing his books.

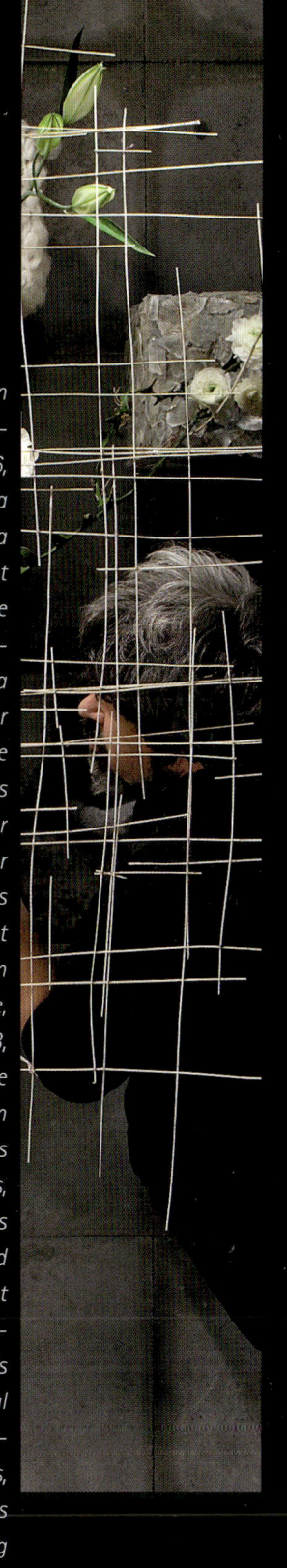

Lersch | Inhalt | Content

2 | 3 Vorwort / Preface	36 | 37 Asymmetrische Spannung / Asymmetric Tension	70 | 71 Erregend sinnlich / Sensual Excitements	104 | 105 Leben & Sterben / Life & Death
4 | 5 Inhalt | Impressum / Content | Imprint	38 | 39 Dekorative Ansichten / Decorative Views	72 | 73 Inspirierend sexy / Sexy Inspirations	106 | 107 Ordnung kontra Chaos / Order versus Chaos
6 | 7 **Professionelle Leidenschaft** / **Professional Passion**	40 | 41 Vegetative Erkenntnisse / Vegetative Insights	74 | 75 Maßlos opulent / Excessive Abundance	108 | 109 Mono kontra Masse / Mono versus Mass
8 | 9 Geheimnisvolle Wurzeln / Mysterious Roots	42 | 43 Formal-lineare Phantasien / Formally linear Fancies	76 | 77 Minimalistisch reduziert / Minimalist Reductions	110 | 111 Tempo in der Stadt / Speed in the City
10 | 11 Erstaunliche Triebe / Astonishing Shoots	44 | 45 Einsichtige Strukturen / Insightful Structures	78 | 79 Heimat: Wein und nochmals Wein / Homeland: Wine and Wine again	112 | 113 Beschaulichkeit auf dem Land / Rural Tranquility
12 | 13 Dynamische Stiele / Dynamic Stems	46 | 47 Gewagte Konstruktionen / Risky Constructions	80 | 81 Heimat: Efeu und Wein / Homeland: Ivy and Wine	114 | 115 Engagement bei der Arbeit / Commitment at Work
14 | 15 Aufregende Blätter / Exciting Leaves	48 | 49 Beeindruckende Texturen / Impressive Textures	82 | 83 Heimat: Weide und Wein / Homeland: Willow and Wine	116 | 117 Feiern mit Freunden / Celebrating with Friends
16 | 17 Faszinierende Blüten / Fascinating Blossoms	50 | 51 Innovative Objekte / Innovative Objects	84 | 85 Heimat: Gras und Moos und Wein / Homeland: Grass, Moss and Wine	118 | 119 Aufblühen im Rampenlicht / Flourishing in the Limelight
18 | 19 **Meisterliches Handwerk** / **Master Handcraft**	52 | 53 Monochrome Raffinesse / Monochromatic Finesse	86 | 87 **Individuelle Ansichten** / **Individual Views**	120 | 121 **Engagierte Synergien** / **Committed Synergies**
20 | 21 Gebündelt zu starken Kompetenzen / Bundled to strong Competences	54 | 55 Farbige Lust / Colourful Delight	88 | 89 Elementar wichtig / Basic Importance	122 | 123 Kopfstand der Kontraste / Contrasts upside down
22 | 23 Geknotet zu festen Verbindungen / Knotted to firm combinations	56 | 57 Bunte Leidenschaft / Coloured Passion	90 | 91 Heiß geliebt / Precious Treasures	122 Werkstück | Work Lersch 123 Werkstück | Work Wagener
24 | 25 Geflochten zu erfolgreichen Synergien / Braiding to successful Synergies	58 | 59 **Ganz persönliche Gefühle** / **Very private Emotions**	92 | 93 Neu entdeckt / New Discoveries	124 | 125 Erkennbare Parallelen / Visible Parallels
26 | 27 Gewoben zu effizienten Netzwerken / Woven into efficient Networks	60 | 61 Frühlingshaft heiter / Spring-like Serenity	94 | 95 Natürlich gewachsen / Natural Growth	124 Werkstück | Work Lersch 125 Werkstück | Work Wagener
28 | 29 Geschichtet zu neuen Dimensionen / Coated to new Dimensions	62 | 63 Sommerlich berauschend / Summer-like Exhileration	96 | 97 Architektonisch konstruiert / Architectural Constructions	126 | 127 Harmonie der Gegensätze / Harmony of the Contrasts
30 | 31 Gereiht zu überraschenden Aufstellungen / Ranked to amazing Settings of Rows	64 | 65 Herbstlich überschwinglich / Autumn-like Exuberance	98 | 99 Themen – Trends – Tendenzen / Topics – Trends – Tendencies	Werkstück | Work Lersch/Wagener 128 | 129 Verbindung von Kompetenzen / Combination of Competencies
32 | 33 **Gestalterische Bekenntnisse** / **Creative Confessions**	66 | 67 Winterlich zart / Winter-like Delicateness	100 | 101 Feuer – Wasser – Erde – Luft / Fire – Water – Earth – Air	Werkstück | Work Lersch/Wagener
34 | 35 Symmetrische Ruhe / Symmetric Silence	68 | 69 Heillos romantisch / Unlimited Romanticism	102 | 103 Natur & Technik / Nature & Technology	130 Zusammenspiel der zwei Gesichter / Interaction of the two Faces Werkstück | Work Lersch/Wagener

Sie können es drehen und wenden, wie Sie wollen,
aber dieses Buch ist einfach nicht normal. „two faces of Floral Design" präsentiert die Arbeiten von zwei Designern an gleichen Themen. Gleiche Seitenzahlen – gleiche Themen. Auf der einen Seite die Werke von Gregoer Lersch, auf der anderen Seite die von Klaus Wagener. In der Mitte des Buches treffen sich dann beide zu immer intensiveren gemeinsamen Arbeiten. Also ein Buch zum Drehen und Wenden, zum Blättern und Vergleichen, zum Vorwärts- wie Rückwärts- und Querlesen.

You can turn it the way you want,
but this book is simply not ausual one. In "two faces of Floral Design" two designers present their work concerning the same topics. Same number of pages – same topics. On the one hand, the works of Gregor Lersch, on the other hand those of Klaus Wagener. In the middle of the book, you can find their common work. Well, a book to turn, compare, browse, and to read as well as backwards and crossways.

Lersch | Impressum | *Imprint*

Herausgeber | *Publisher*
FloralDesign Edition
by kriener-potthoff communications
Münsterstraße 111
48155 Münster | Germany
Phone: +49 (0) 25 06 - 93 09 - 0
Fax: +49 (0) 25 06 - 93 09 - 50
info@floraldesign-edition.de
www.floraldesign-edition.de
und | *and*
Profil floral
by BLOOM's GmbH, Ratingen | Germany

Floristik | *Florist Work*
(Seiten | *Pages* Lersch)
Gregor Lersch

Mitarbeit am floristischen Konzept
collaboration for the floristic concept
Jennifer Haverkamp, St. Martin | Germany

Mitarbeit bei der floristischen Arbeit
collaboration for the floral arrangements
· Timo Bolte, Bad Neuenahr | Germany
· Corinne Geiger, Zürich | Switzerland
· Jürgen Herold, Maykammer | Germany
· Heike Klingler, Treis | Germany
· Andrea Lehmann, Bern | Switzerland
· Mi Na Yo, Seoul | Corea
· Lena Werner, Sindelfingen | Germany
· Anne Wolf, Wemmetsweiler | Germany

Fotografie | *Photography*
· Ralf-C. Stradtmann, Hamburg | Germany
 (Seiten | *Pages* Lersch 2 -119)
· Dominik Ketz, Bad Neuenahr | Germany
 (Seiten | *Pages* Lersch 62-63; 110 -111)
· Jörg Manegold
 c/o Patrick Pantze Werbefotografie, Lage | Germany
 (Seiten | *Pages* Lersch 120 -131 und | *and* Portraits)

Layout | *Layout*
(Seiten | *Pages* Lersch)
kriener-potthoff communications
Münster | Germany

Herzlichen Dank für die
freundliche Unterstützung an:
Special thanks *for kindly*
support go to:
· Landpartie zu Adendorf
· Baron und Baronin Loe
· Gregor Schober

© Copyright 2006
FloralDesign Edition
by kriener-potthoff communications
ISBN 10 3 - 938 521-17-1
ISBN 13 978 - 3 - 938 521-17- 5

und | *and*
Profil floral
by BLOOM's
ISBN 10 3-9810443-6-3
ISBN 13 978 - 3 - 9810443-6-2

Jede Verwertung außerhalb der engen Grenzen des Urheberrechts ist ohne Zustimmung des Herausgebers unzulässig und strafbar. Insbesondere gilt dies für Vervielfältigungen, Übersetzungen, Mikroverfilmungen sowie die Einspeicherung und Verarbeitung in elektronischen Systemen.

Any use outside the strict limits of copyright law without the editor´s permission is forbidden and may be prosecuted. This applies in particular to copying, translation, microfiche, copies and storage and processing in electronic systems.

Professionelle Leidenschaft

Wenn ich die ungeheure Vielfalt der Pflanzenwelt erlebe, frage ich mich immer wieder, wer sich bloß den Code ausgedacht hat, der für diese unglaublichen Differenzierungspotentiale verantwortlich ist. Ich gebe ja zu: Ich bewundere und liebe diesen grünen Kosmos über alles. Oftmals gehen dabei die Pferde mit mir durch, wenn ich vor Menschen öffentlich meiner Begeisterung freien Lauf lasse. Dann befürchte ich schon fast, dass mein Enthusiasmus lächerlich wirken könnte. Vielleicht auch gerade aufgrund meines kompromisslosen Eintretens für eine Floristik, die sich eindeutig zu pflanzlichen Werkstoffen bekennt. Denn nur so wird sie meines Erachtens als eigenständige Gestaltungsdisziplin wahr genommen und überleben können. Die Pflanze ist und bleibt das originäre Element der Floristik. Jeder Versuch, sie zum Hilfsinstrument für andere Lifestyle-Welten zu degradieren, wird diesen treuen Weggefährten des Menschen nicht gerecht. Blumen und Pflanzen sind ein nicht zu unterschätzender, eigenständiger Bestandteil unseres Lifestyles. Sie sind also nicht nur Inspirationselemente für die Gestaltungsarbeit, sondern sie selbst sind es, denen die Inszenierung gilt. Genau dies versuche ich mit meinen Arbeiten bewusst zu machen.

Professional Passion

Whenever I experience nature's impressive diversity of plants, I am stunned by this incredible potential of differentiation, which always keeps me wondering how this is possible. Indeed, I must admit that I love this green cosmos more than everything. Sometimes, I get completely thrilled when I let people share my enthusiasm almost fearing that I could appear ridiculous. Maybe it's also because of my uncompromising standing up for a floristry, which is clearly based on vegetable materials. In my eyes, this is the only way to realize its acceptance as a designing discipline in the long term.

Plants are and remain the originating elements in floristry. Any attempt of reducing them as auxiliary means for other lifestyle-worlds does not do justice to these faithful companions of men. Flowers and plants are an independent part of our lifestyle, which shouldn't be underestimated. Thus, they do not only serve as inspiring elements for the designing, but also as a presentation of themselves. This is exactly what I'm trying to make clear through my creations.

Geheimnisvolle Wurzeln

Das Wurzelwerk der Pflanzen unter der Erdoberfläche hat uns Menschen seit jeher zu mystischen Phantasien angeregt. Dass sie aber auch über Tage geheimnisvollen Reiz auszustrahlen vermögen, überrascht doch eher. Auch sind es nicht nur die Farben und Texturen, die uns an Wurzeln faszinieren, sondern individuelle Eigenschaften wie zum Beispiel die welligen Bewegungen dieser frei im Raum hängenden Vanda rothschildiana, die das Bild vertikal durchdringen. Auch der horizontal hochgestellte Zylinder ist durchwirkt mit diesem Werkstoff. Sein Körper ist aus 1,8 mm starkem Draht sowie aus dem Draht geformt, der schon in lange vergangenen Zeiten den Floristen half, Floralien zusammen zu halten. Seine bräunlich roten Füße bestehen aus Zuckerrohr, wie auch alles andere exotischen Ursprungs ist. Keine botanischen Kompromisse. Urwald pur. Der Ursprung unserer Flora und Fauna. Aus dem Wasser geboren. Ein Arrangement, in dem es eine Menge zu entdecken gibt.

Mysterious Roots

The root system of plants underneath the earth's surface has always incited mankind to mystical fancies. But the fact that the roots' mysterious charm can shine through reaching over ground is rather surprising. Besides, we are not only fascinated by the roots' colours and textures, but also by individual characteristics, for example wavy movements, which penetrate the image vertically, of this Vanda rothschildeana hanging loosely in the space. The horizontally placed cylinder has also been worked with this material. Its body is formed by a thick wire of a diameter of 1.8 millimetres and by a wire which already used to help florists combining flora long time ago. Its brown-like red feet consist of sugar beet, just like everything else has an exotic origin. No botanic compromises, a real jungle, the origin of our flora and fauna, born out of the water- all in all an arrangement with a lot of things to discover.

Erstaunliche Triebe

LERSCH | Professionelle Leidenschaft *Professional Passion*

10 | 11

Manchmal auch als die grüne Dynamik bezeichnet, geistert der Spargel als Synonym für Triebhaftigkeit durch unseren Sprachgebrauch. So „schießt" er auch hier dynamisch aus einem zum Teil mit geweißtem, getrocknetem Ton überzogenen Birkenholz und lässt in einen tiefgründigen grünen Krater blicken. Der grüne Speisespargel hat noch einen grünen Verwandten mitgebracht – den Asparagus scandens deflexus. Auch alles andere wie Ceropegia-sandersonii-Ranken und winzige Kürbisfrüchte bleiben monochrom in Grün. Eine alte Leidenschaft von mir, die ich auch immer wieder gern mit kühlem Stahl konfrontiere – statt wie hier mit Weiß und Grau. Ein Gegensatz, der mir als Inspirationsquelle unerschöpflich zu sein scheint. Überhaupt suche ich in meiner Arbeit häufig Kontraste, die ich im Leben persönlich eher zu vermeiden suche. Dann kann es manchmal gar nicht genug leblos gegen lebendig gehen. Allerdings diktiert mir ein für mich selbst erlassenes Gesetz, dass das Lebendige immer die Oberhand zu behalten hat.

Astonishing *Shoots*

Sometimes classified as the green dynamism, the asparagus is known as a synonym for sensuality in our language use. Thus, it "shoots" even here dynamically out of a birch wood being partly covered with whitened, dried clay revealing its profound green crater. The green consumer's asparagus has brought along another green relative – the Asparagus scandens deflexus. Everything else like the Ceropegia-sandersonii twines and the tiny pumpkins remain monochromatic in green. This is part of one of my old passions, which I prefer confronting with cool steel – in stead of white and grey as in this case. A contrast, which seems to be an inexhaustible source of inspiration to me. Actually, I'm often looking for contrasts at work, which I rather try to avoid in my personal life. In this case, contrasts like lifeless versus lively never seem to be sufficient enough. However, according to my own personal rules liveliness must always have the upper hand.

Dynamische Stiele

Die Dynamik – als die Kraft, die unaufhaltsam in eine Richtung drängt – ist ein unerschöpfliches Thema in der Floristik. Gerade Stiele, Stäbe, Gräser, Halme vermögen dabei Ruhe und Statik, aber auch Vitalität und Bewegung zu vermitteln und sind in jeglicher Form ein dominierendes Gestaltungsmittel in meiner Blumenarbeit. Hier ermöglichen einige wenige, fast unsichtbare Hilfsmittel ein spannungsreiches Geschehen. So ist der schwarze Steckdraht gerade stark genug, das Gewicht der Blüten und vor allem der wassergefüllten und hinter Rinde versteckten Röhrchen zu tragen. Die Dysia- und Vanda-Orchideen sowie die schwarzen Calla neigen die cool-schwarzen Cornus-Stäbe dynamisch nach vorn, während ein paar zarte Epidendrum so gerade noch aufgesprungen zu sein scheinen. Das Schuhhandwerk hat es uns vorgemacht: Nicht nur ein filigraner Absatz verschlankt ein jedes Damenbein, auch florale Stiele, auf dünne Stäbe gestellt, scheinen über der Basis zu schweben und ziehen den Blick auf sich und die von ihnen präsentierten Blüten.

Dynamic Stems

Dynamism – the ultimate power urging irresistibly in one direction – is an inexhaustible topic in floristry. It's especially the stems, sticks, grasses and halms that can convey an air of silence and static, but also vitality and movements. Thereby, they are in any case a predominant designing instrument for my flower arrangements regardless of their forms. Here, a few almost invisible aids permit eventful actions full of tension. Thus, the black floral wire is just strong enough to bear the weight of the blossoms, but especially that of the tubes filled with water, being hidden behind the bark. The Dysia and Vanda orchids as well as the black Calla dynamically bend the black cool Cornus sticks forward, while a few delicate Epidendrum orchids seem to have just sprout. The footwear industry showed us how to do it: Not only filigree high heels slenderise a woman's leg but also floral stems, put on thin sticks seem to float over the ground drawing all attention on them and on the blossoms they present.

Aufregende Blätter

Blätter verschiedener Welten und in diversen Formen präsentieren sich in einer tonigen Struktur mit natürlicher Steckmasse darunter. Sie alle kommen, bis auf die kleine Blattspitze der Anthurie auf ihrem Wurzelhaufen, aus den Reihen der Xerophyten. Blätter waren häufig in meinem Blumenleben wichtige Begleiter. Vor allem dann, wenn es um etwas ging, wenn etwas Einschneidendes geschah: bei Wettbewerben, bei der Wiederbelebung unseres alten Gartens, bei der nicht ganz unwichtigen zweiten Chance der persönlichen Gesundheit. Blätter waren tausendfach wichtig für mich und sind es immer noch. Denn an ihnen vermag ich immer wieder aufregend Neues zu entdecken.

Exciting Leaves

Different forms of leaves from all over the world are presenting themselves in a clayey structure with natural floral foam products put underneath it. All of them belong to the Xerophytes species, except the small leaf apex of the Anthurium emanating from its bunch of roots. Leaves have always accompanied me throughout my florally based life, especially in dramatic moments, like at competitions, during the process of revitalization of our own old garden to which I owe a quite remarkable second chance I was given after having suffered from health problems. Leaves have always been extremely important to me providing me with inspiration to discover new exciting things.

Faszinierende Blüten

Wie interessant und wichtig die verschiedenen Teile der Pflanze für die florale Gestaltung auch immer sein mögen, so sind es doch letztendlich immer wieder die Blüten, die alle anderen Lebewesen – vornehmlich natürlich die Menschen – in ihren Bann schlagen. Ihre spektakulären Formen und Farben faszinieren und begeistern. Ihnen erweisen wir als Gestalter unsere Referenz, indem wir ihnen den besonderen, eher ungewöhnlichen Auftritt verschaffen. Doch ist es heute für mich nicht die botanische Raffinesse, mit der ich sie früher sicherlich versucht hätte zu präsentieren, sondern gerade die Reduktion auf ganz Einfaches: das „Wenigerlei", das der Schönheit dieser zarten „Toscana"-Amaryllis und Nerinen Wirkung verleiht. So halten dicke Bündel aus Birkenreisig als Steckhilfe die kräftigen Stengel und die Knöterichröhren und bilden einmal eine etwas andere Füllung für die riesigen Glasaquarien. Fast schon ein Grenzfall zwischen Floristik und Dekoration. Doch ohne diskrete floristische Technik geht es auch hier nicht. So halten zum Beispiel horizontal eingesetzte Hölzchen die Bündel in der Waage.

Fascinating Blossoms

How interesting and important the different parts of a plant may be for a floral design, it's always the blossoms that keep fascinating all other creatures in nature, of course mainly us humans. Their spectacular forms and colours are inspiring and enthusiastic. We, as designers dignify them by giving them a particular, rather unusual appearance. Today however, it's not the botanic finesse, which I would have surely used to present them in former times, but precisely the affiliation to the very simple things which reveal the beauty of this delicate "Toscana"-Amaryllis. In this way, thick bunches of brushwood, used for fixation, carry the healthy stems and the knotgrass tubes representing once a somewhat different type of filling for the huge glass aquaria. This is almost a borderline case of floristry and decoration. However, even here a discrete floristic technology seems absolutely necessary. Horizontally placed small pieces of wood help for example keeping the wooden bunches balanced.

Meisterliches Handwerk

Im Floral Design hat das Handwerk in den letzten Jahren gewaltig an Bedeutung gewonnen. Denn neben den botanischen Kenntnissen stellen florale Techniken die berufliche Grundlage und Identität her. Viele andere Berufe sind schließlich auch in der Lage, Formen zu schaffen, gestalterisch und kulturell Interessantes mit Pflanzen zu leisten und Emotionen zu bedienen. Doch Systematik, Habitat, Morphologie und Geschichte der Pflanzen sind eigenständige Komponenten des Floral Design, die Werkstoff bezogene, individuelle handwerkliche Techniken erfordern. Das bedeutet: Hände trainieren, ausprobieren, studieren, vergleichen, suchen und sich ständig verbessern. Neues mit Floralem entwickeln, woran auch andere Gestaltungsdisziplinen partizipieren können. Florale handwerkliche Techniken als Inspirationsquelle für gestalterische Ideen.

Master Handcraft

In floral design handcraft has tremendously gained in importance during the last years. Besides the botanic know-how, floral techniques constitute the professional basis and identity of a designer. After all, in many other professions techniques like shaping and creating culturally interesting designs with the help of plants while evoking certain emotions are also possible. However, the plants' systematic, habitat, morphology and history are independent components of a floral design requiring individual techniques related to the materials. This means: training hands, testing, studying, comparing, searching and improving oneself steadily. To develop new things combined with floral elements makes other designing principles participate. Floral techniques serve as an inspiring source of creative ideas.

Durch Bündeln und zu Einheiten Zusammenfassen entstehen Ruhe, Ordnung und Gliederung innerhalb einer Arbeit, um so das pflanzliche Individuum erkennbar werden zu lassen. Doch auch hierbei ist es mir äußerst wichtig, Blumen durch Leichtigkeit unübersehbar zu machen, sie zu erheben und schweben zu lassen. Starke Drähte verschaffen den edlen Orchideen auf dem lichten Glastisch alle Transparenz der Welt. Mehr Aufmerksamkeit für die mächtigen Blüten der Vanda und die feingliedrigen Epidendrum mit ihren Blättchen, Ästchen und Minihaftwurzeln ist für mich kaum vorstellbar. Fließend breiten sich darunter die langen Vandawurzeln, in denen sich Glasröhrchen verstecken, über das Glas hinaus aus und verschwinden praktisch im Nichts.

Bundled to strong Competences

Bundling and combining units create silence, order and structure within an arrangement in order to make the individual plant discernbible. But even here, it is extremely important for me to let the plants appear extremely clear through lightness, to rise them and let them float. Strong wires offer all the transparency of the world to the noble orchids put on the light glass table. I can't imagine more attention for the mighty blossoms of the Vanda and the delicate Epidendrum with its leaflets, branchlets and miniaturized roots. Underneath it, the long Vanda roots in which small glass tubes are hidden are spread fluently out of the glass disappearing almost in the emptiness

Gebündelt
zu starken Kompetenzen

Ich liebe verwittertes Holz. Inzwischen leicht angegammelt, schmuddelig hat es seine ganz eigene Geschichte. Vielleicht hat es Schweres auszuhalten gehabt, hat etwas getragen, verdeckt, abgedichtet, unterlegt, beschützt, getrennt, verbunden... Die unterschiedlichsten Gedanken ranken sich sofort um ein solch charaktervolles Holz. Für mich der Anlass, es mit Floralem zu verbinden. Löcher bohren, Weide durchstecken und an beiden Enden mit Knoten versehen, die schließlich knallhart werden. Eine Harfe entstehen lassen, die so gar nichts mit himmlischen Tönen zu tun hat. Dieses Werkstück will nicht lieb sein. Es ist rau und lebensnah. Selbst die elegante Calla strahlt eine fast freiheitskämpferische Härte aus. Meinetwegen kann man diese Arbeit auch als typisch männlich bezeichnen. Jedenfalls gibt es nicht viele Arbeiten in all meinen Floristenjahren, die ich so stark empfunden habe wie diese.

Knotted to firm Combinations

I love weathered wood. Meanwhile slightly mouldered and filthy it can tell its own story. Maybe it must have borne something heavy or carried, covered, sealed, put underneath, protected, separated or combined something... The most different thoughts are ranking around such a wood full of character. This is my occasion to combine it with floral elements: to drill holes, insert the willow while arranging knots at both ends, which become finally really hard. In a way it is like creating a harp, which has nothing in common with heaven's tones. This work piece is not supposed to display a gentle air; it is more harsh and naturalistic. Even the elegant Calla is radiating an almost freedom-fighting strength. I don't mind if this work is considered as typically male. Anyways, there are not many arrangements I have created during all the years as a florist that had such a strong emotional impact on me than these.

notet zu festen Verbindungen

Das Ganze ist mehr als die Summe seiner Teile. Das gilt für gedankliche Verflechtungen sicherlich ebenso wie für handwerkliche Flechtarbeiten. Die Strategie ist einfach: Die vielfachen gegenseitigen welligen Durchdringungen der Birkenwickel mit ihrem leblosen winterlichen Braun lassen in ihrer Gesamtheit genau die Düsternis entstehen, die als Kontrast das heitere Formen- und Farbenspiel der Orchideen erst richtig zur Geltung kommen lässt. Dass alles schwungvoll wogt, ist den leuchtend grünen Stielen der schwarzen Calla zu verdanken. Wie die an der Wand lehnenden Bücherregale aus den Wohnzeitschriften sind die Flechtwerke aufgestellt und lassen in ihrer Vervielfältigung neue Gedankenverflechtungen entstehen. Man sucht nach Gemeinsamkeiten und Unterschieden und kommt zu neuen Erkenntnissen.

Braided to successful Synergies

The whole is more than the sum of its parts. This is surely valid for thoughtful interweaving as well as handmade braiding. The strategy is simple: The multiple, mutual, rolling penetrations of the birch sleeves with their lifeless, wintry brown reveal as a whole the darkness, whose contrast especially emphasises the orchids' cheerful play of forms and colours. Thanks to the bright green stems of the black Calla an overall lively atmosphere is created. Just like the bookshelves leaning on the walls, illustrated in the housing magazines, these braiding arrangements are placed and make create new interweaving forms of thoughts through their duplication. While looking for similarities and differences we encounter new insights.

Geflochten
zu erfolgreichen Synergien

Gewoben
zu effizienten Netzwerken

Statik ist die enorme Konzentration auf eine Stabilität, die mit einem Minimum an verbauter Masse auskommt. Auf der Suche nach einer guten Balance zwischen Emotion und Rationalität stoße ich häufig auf diese mathematische Logik in der Floristik. Netzwerke mit ihren oft unzähligen Kreuzverbindungen sind eine dieser filigran daher kommenden Stabilisatoren. Selbst sehr fragilen Pflanzenteilen vermögen sie eine faszinierende Kraft zu verleihen. Es macht mir unendlichen Spaß, eigentlich ungeeignete Pflanzenteile mit Hilfe von handwerklichen Tricks und langjähriger Erfahrung zu überlisten. Insofern sind Netzkonstrukte nicht nur sehr bedeutsam für meine Arbeit, sondern auch ein wichtiger Bestandteil der präsenten floralen Trends.

Woven into efficent Networks

Static is the enormous concentration on a stability, which only needs a minimum of worked mass. When looking for a good balance between emotions and rationality I often come across this mathematic logic in floristry. Networks with their often endless cross combinations represent one of these filigree upcoming stabilizers. They even give very delicate parts of plants a fascinating energy. It is an indescribable pleasure for me to outsmart the parts of a plant, usually being supposed to be improper, with the help of technical tricks and many years of experience. In this respect network constructions are not only very important for my work, but also an essential part in current floral trends.

Durch Schichtungen Formen und Strukturen zu bilden, die aus unterschiedlichen Blickwinkeln neue Dimensionen entstehen lassen, war der Grundgedanke. Das Lichtelement deutet es an: Je nachdem aus welcher Perspektive man dieses gebogene schaukel- oder hängebrückenartige Konstrukt betrachtet, entstehen tatsächlich komplett andere Eindrücke. Seine gesamte bzw. ursprüngliche Form wird nicht mehr als solche wahrgenommen. Durch die Bogenform entstehen Verkürzungen. Ausschnitte fokussieren den Blick. Neue Dimensionen treten zutage und neue Assoziationen werden geweckt, was die Vielschichtigkeit unserer Wahrnehmung verdeutlicht.

Coated to new Dimensions

The basic idea was to create - with the help of superpositions - forms and structures which offer new dimensions out of different views. The element light indicates it in the following way: depending on the perspective from where you look at this swing- or rope bridge-like construction, actually completely different impressions emerge. Its entire or originating shape is no more recognized as such. With the help of the arch form foreshortenings are created. Our view is focused on extracts. New dimensions arise and new associations are revealed which stress the complexity of our percipience.

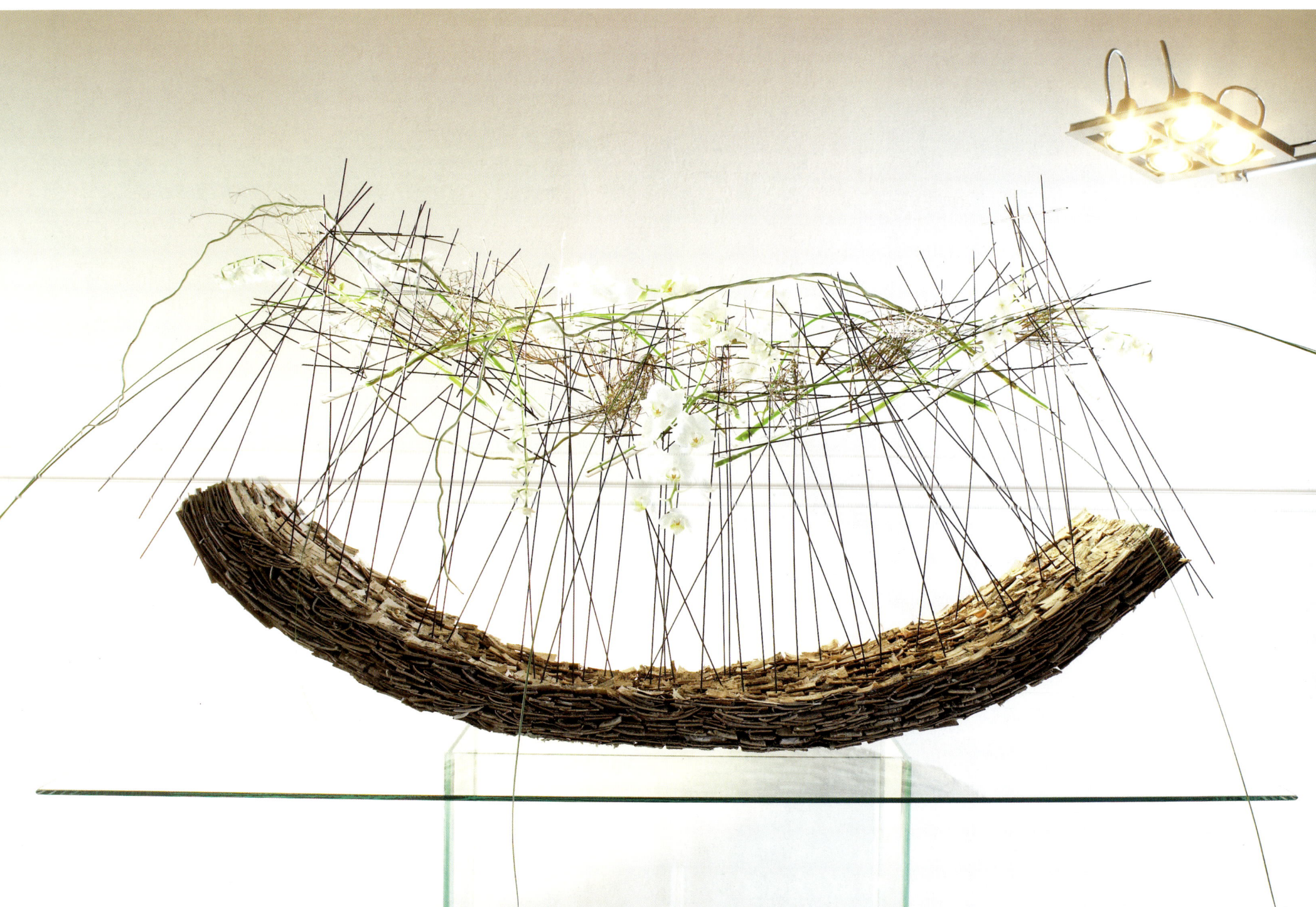

Geschichtet
zu neuen Dimensionen

Gereiht
zu überraschenden

Reihungen entstehen zu lassen, ist die eine Sache, mit ihnen zu überraschen, eine andere. Einen Auftritt von Floralien zu inszenieren, ohne sie zu verändern ist eine weitere Herausforderung. Oft werden sie auseinandergenommen und mit Klebstoff oder ähnlichem neu und anders zusammengesetzt. Ich wollte es anders. Angeregt dazu haben mich die Amarylliszwiebeln, die im Gewächshaus auf dem Tisch lagen und so schön gebogen austrieben. Ist es Zufall? Oder ist es gerade das kreative Auge, das, in vielen Jahren geschult, Formen und gestalterische Chancen erkennt? Wer die Pflanzen liebt, der sieht auch genau hin und entdeckt an ihnen immer wieder, wie einzigartig jedes einzelne dieser Geschöpfe ist. Der Auftritt dieser Schar von „Urweltvögeln" in vorgeschichtlicher Nacht verdeutlicht, welch unglaubliche Vielfalt an Formen, Farben, Strukturen und Texturen die Natur für jedes lebende Individuum bereit hält.

Ranked to amazing Settings of Rows

Rows provide all sorts of challenges: at first the process of the making-of itself, then the creation of surprises with the help of rows and at last, the production of a floral performance without modifying the flora itself. They are often cut up and put together with glue or the like to become something new and different. I preferred another approach. I was inspired by the amaryllis onions, which were lying on the table in the greenhouse sprouting so beautifully in a bended form. Is this an accident? Or is it just the creative eye that, trained during many years, recognizes forms and designing opportunities? Someone who loves flowers looks very precisely while he always discovers how unique every single part of these creatures is. The appearance of this flock of "primeval world birds" in prehistoric night emphasises the unbelievable variety of forms, colours, structures and textures nature is offering to any living individual.

Gestalterische Bekenntnisse

So wie die Hochphasen vergangener Jahre wird auch die heutige Zeit noch von den gestalterischen Errungenschaften eines Albert Eurich und eines Moritz Evers geprägt. Wir Nachfolgenden haben sie verändert, zeitgemäß angepasst oder einfach nach eigenen Vorstellungen modifiziert. Doch für mich bleiben ihre Grundzüge erhalten und jeder erste Gedanke in der Arbeit gilt ihnen. Häufig wird mit der gestalterischen Lehre viel zu viel kokettiert. Meines Erachtens müssen sich floristische Arbeiten an allgemein gültigen Gestaltungsregeln messen lassen können. Dann und nur dann sind wir in der Lage, uns gemeinsam über ihre Bedeutung zu unterhalten, um letztendlich das Floral Design als eigenständige Gestaltungsdisziplin auch für die Zukunft zu erhalten.

Creative Confessions

Just like during peak phases of the last years our time today is also determined by creative achievements of a certain Albert Eurich and Moritz Evers. We, the successors have changed them, adapted them to the time or just modified them according to our own ideas. However, their main features remain valid for me and my very first thoughts at work are dedicated to them. Designing know-how is often used with too much flirtation. In my eyes, it should be possible to compare floral arrangements with generally valid designing rules. Only in this case, we will be able to discuss their meaning together in order to preserve the floral design as an independent designing discipline also for the future.

Die Epoche des Jugendstil hat mich mein ganzes Leben über begleitet. Angefangen mit dem Jugendstilhaus, das mein Großvater in Bad Neuenahr erbaute und in dem wir heute noch wohnen und unser Blumengeschäft betreiben, über die Inspirationen der Werke Gaudis, die ich in den 80er Jahren in Barcelona erfahren habe, bis hin zu den Sammlerstücken, die ich immer wieder mit Begeisterung aufstöbere. Wie zum Beispiel diese schön geschwungene Schale des Art Nouveau aus Kopenhagen. Hier arrangiert mit Helleborus niger, Pinusnadeln und Aspidistra, die den Steckschaum bedecken, ist sie für mich der Inbegriff für Ruhe und Symmetrie – ohne dass jemals Langeweile aufkommt. Blütenblattlose Nelken in den Vasen begleiten die Schale stilgerecht.

Symmetric Silence

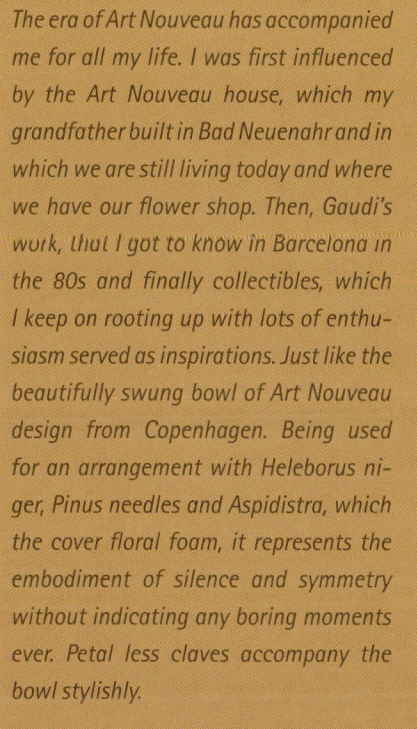

The era of Art Nouveau has accompanied me for all my life. I was first influenced by the Art Nouveau house, which my grandfather built in Bad Neuenahr and in which we are still living today and where we have our flower shop. Then, Gaudi's work, that I got to know in Barcelona in the 80s and finally collectibles, which I keep on rooting up with lots of enthusiasm served as inspirations. Just like the beautifully swung bowl of Art Nouveau design from Copenhagen. Being used for an arrangement with Heleborus niger, Pinus needles and Aspidistra, which the cover floral foam, it represents the embodiment of silence and symmetry without indicating any boring moments ever. Petal less claves accompany the bowl stylishly.

Symmetrische Ruhe

Wenn das Werkstück fertig ist, sieht alles immer so logisch und einfach aus. Einfach logisch. Doch die konsequente Umsetzung von Asymmetrie ist eine intellektuelle Herausforderung – voll von angewandter Mathematik und tiefsinniger Logik. Denn auch Zufälle und spontane Entscheidungen haben ihre rationalen Begründungen. Eine zweite Herausforderung besteht in der visuellen Balance, die Wiederholungen in gleicher Menge und gleicher Position vermeidet. Selbst die Position des formalen oder farblichen Blickpunkts wird hier eminent wichtig. Um so mehr, wenn beide in einem Punkt zusammenfallen. Geht es dann auch noch um eine statische Herausforderung – wie hier im frei stehenden Werkstück – wird es besonders spannend. Da werden oft viele Kilos an floralem Gewicht ohne faule Tricks, wie in der Luft schwebend, in ihrer diagonalen Position gehalten.

Asymmetric Tension

After an arrangement has been completed everything seems to be so logical and easy, simply logical. However, the consequential realization of asymmetry is an intellectual challenge – full of applied mathematics and profound logic. Even accidents and spontaneous decisions have their rational explanations. The visual balance avoiding the same repetitions according to quantity and position is a second challenge. Even the position of the formal or coloured focal point is becoming extremely important here and especially there where both get together in one point. If the arrangement provides then also a static challenge – as in this loose arrangement – it is getting particularly exciting. Heavy floral arrangements without any monkey business are hold like floating in the air in their diagonal position.

Asymmetrische Spannung

Dekorative Ansichten

LERSCH | Gestalterische Bekenntnisse Creative confessions

Auf diesem riesigen Teller ist gestalterisch ganz dick aufgetragen. Üppig und vital. Viel von allem. Die ganze Arbeit steht auf einem mit dünnen Zweigen umwickelten Metallring. Ein zartes Gitter aus feinen Aststückchen rankt sich von dort nach oben. Blüten in vielerlei Form – von klein und bescheiden bis extrovertiert und dominant – teilen sich den großzügig zugeordneten Raum. Gruppierungen verschmelzen eher spontan miteinander, während sich die soziale Rangordnung in der Höhe durch Blütenformen und Stiellängen ergibt. Wie im richtigen Leben. Ich gestalte nicht oft mit so viel Farbe. Aber wenn, dann immer sehr verschwenderisch und ein wenig übertreibend. Wie ein Ausbruch, der Balancen schafft. Eigentlich liebe ich Grau, aber manchmal eben auch knalliges, komplementäres Rot.

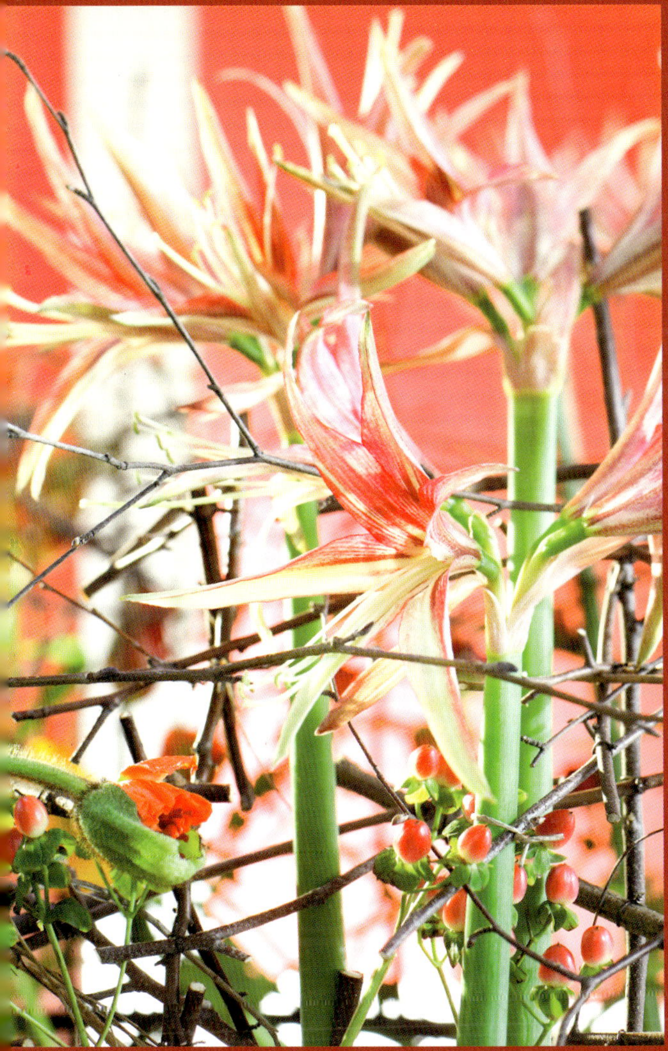
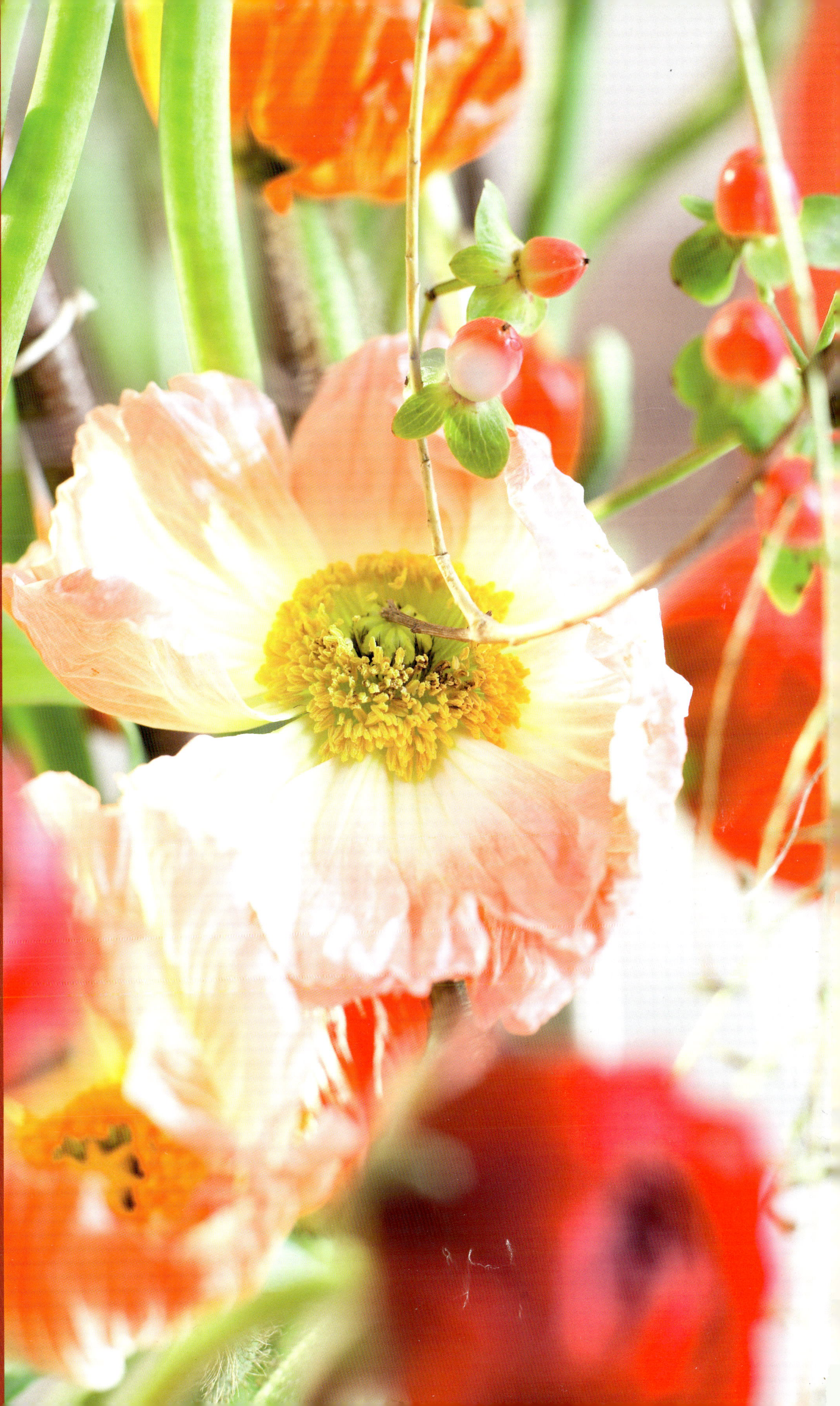

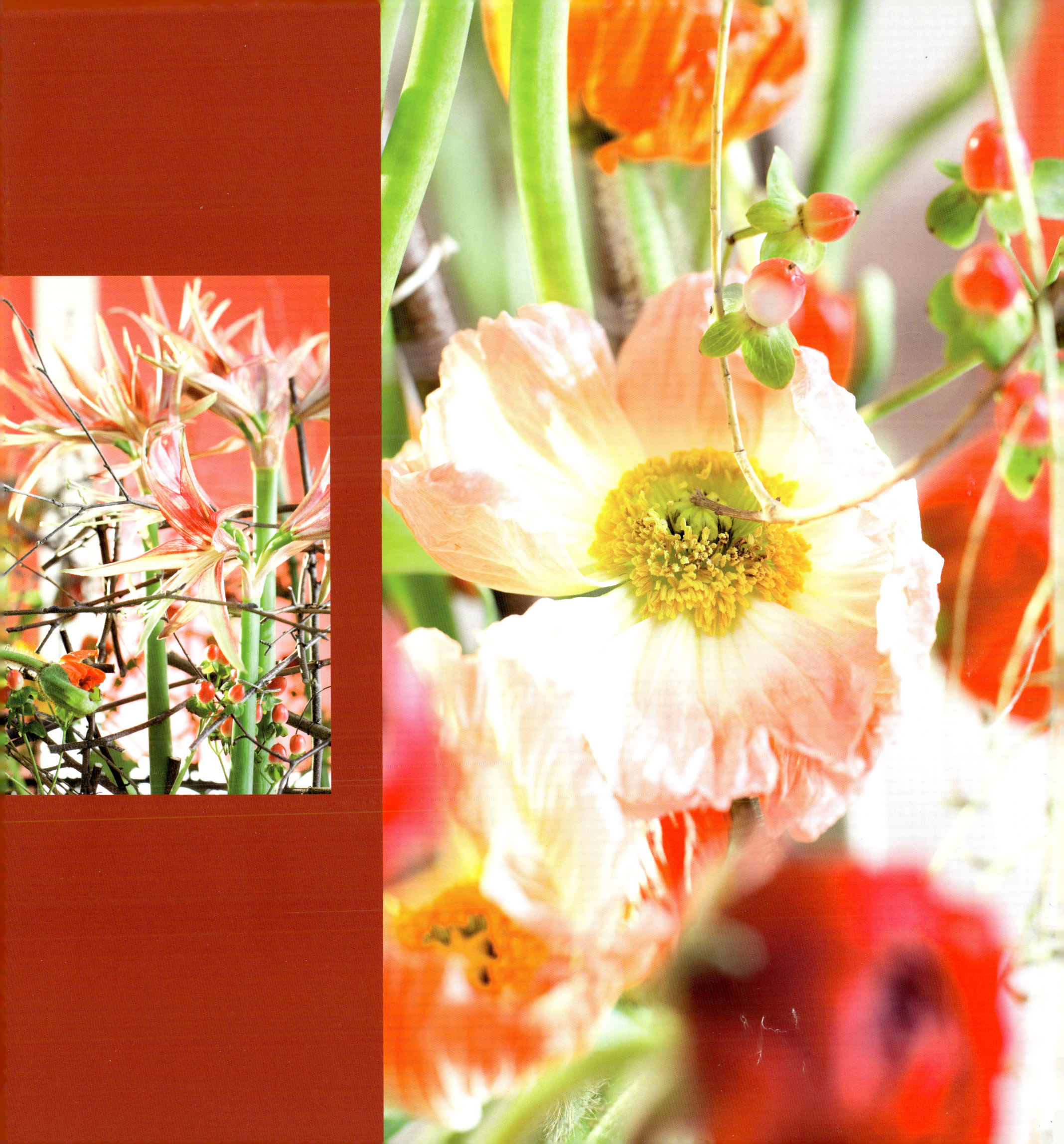

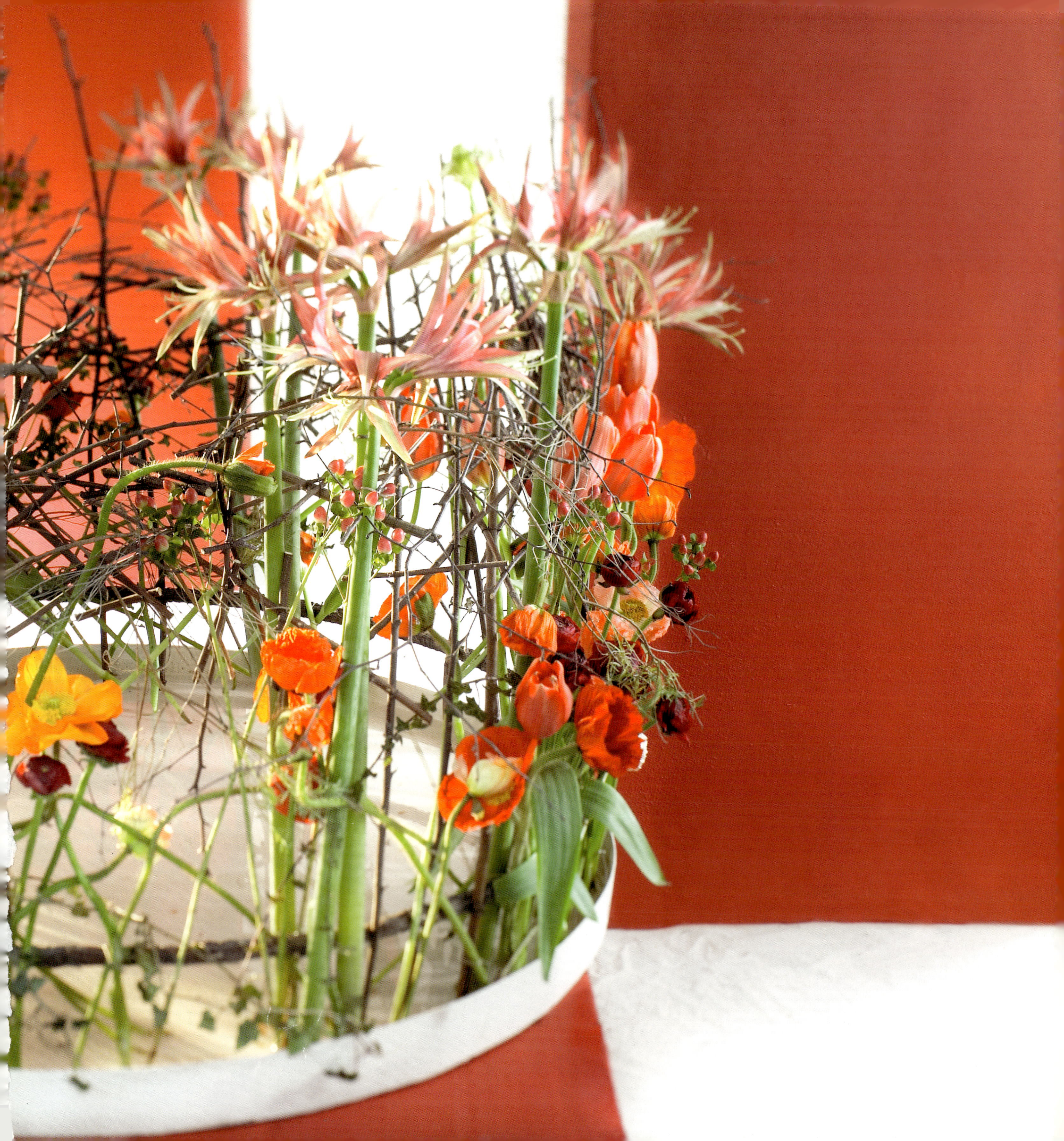

Decorative Views

This huge plate has been creatively really piled on with exuberance and vitality: Lots of all sorts of things. The whole arrangement is placed on a metal ring enwind with thin branches. A delicate grid of fine branchlets is growing from there on to the top. Blossoms of various forms – from small and modest to extroverted and dominating ones – are sharing the generously assigned space. Arrangements are melting rather spontaneously with each other, while the social hierarchy in the height is represented by forms of blossoms and lengths of stems. Just like in real life. I don't often use so many colours in my designs. But the moment I utilize colours, I am always very wasteful and a bit exaggerating. Like an outbreak creating balances. Actually, I like grey but sometimes even loud, complimentary red.

Vegetative Erkenntnisse

Floral Design hat viel damit zu tun, die Pflanze den eigenen gestalterischen Vorstellungen entsprechend zu präsentieren, ihre Darstellung aber auch den Vorlieben derer anzupassen, die man damit beglücken will. Doch für jeden Floral Designer sollte es eine schöne Last sein, sich mit den ursprünglichen Prozessen in der Natur zu befassen und ihre Abläufe zu studieren. Die Vegetative Gestaltungsart wirkt dann wie ein strenger Lehrer, der viel verbietet und nur wenig gestattet. Sie fungiert wie ein Anwalt der Blumen und Pflanzen, der seinen Schüler ständig ermahnt, diese zu achten und nicht durch gestalterischen Egoismus ihrer Würde zu berauben. Hier will man sich in die Floralien und ihre angestammte Umgebung hineinversetzen und sie allenfalls in ungewöhnlichen Kombinationen zu Dialogen miteinander animieren, um selbst nur als bescheidener Zuschauer dabei zu stehen.

Vegetative Insights

Floral design is a lot about presenting the plant in accordance with one's own ideas, but also corresponding to the preferences of those we want to make happy. However, it should be a pleasant burden for every floral designer to study nature's original process and its development. The vegetative type of design appears similar to a severe teacher who forbids a lot and allows only few. It functions as an attorney of flowers and plants who always reminds his students to respect these and to avoid stealing their dignity by creative egoism. Here, we just want to put ourselves in the position of the flora and their environment and animate them at best to unusual combinations in order to enjoy the construction just as a modest spectator.

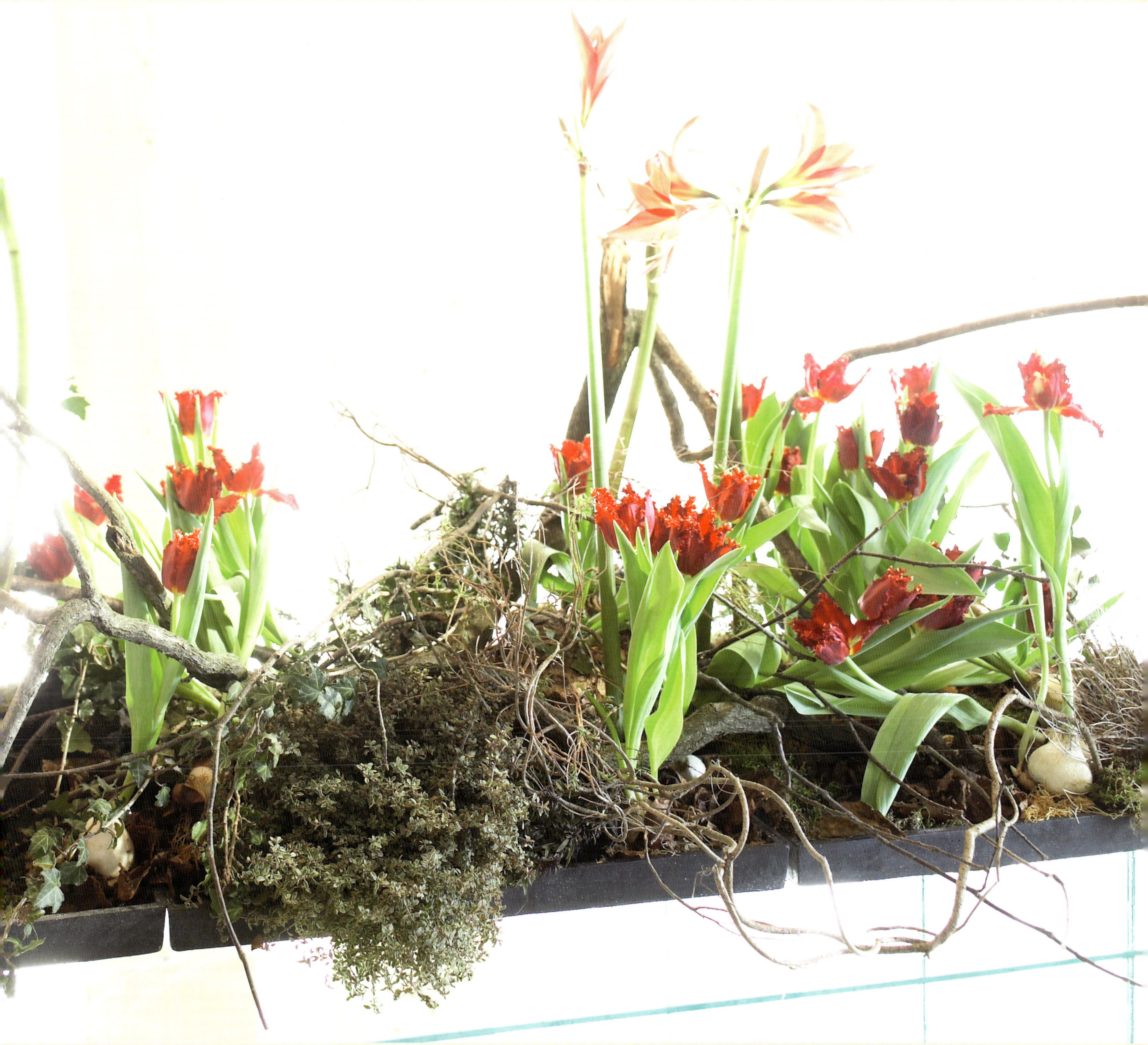

Formal-lineare Phantasien

Steigende, fallende und schwingende Linien. Dominante und sich stark unterordnende Formen. Starre und bewegte. Überall Kontraste, wenigstens in formaler Hinsicht. Dagegen halten sich die Farben eher zurück, wenn die allerschönsten Persönlichkeiten aus dem tropischen Pflanzenreich mit ihrer vollkommenen Figur reizen. Nicolaia, Heliconia und Alocasia fühlen sich allesamt wächsern glatt an. Schließlich entstammen sie alle ähnlichen Bedingungen des Regenwaldes. Ihre Formen ähneln denen seltener Land- und Wassertiere. Im Formal-Linearen herrscht das Individuum, nicht der Chor, die Gruppe, die Fülle. Jede Form hat ihren eigenen Platz. Jeglicher Anklang an Symmetrie würde das Wesentliche dieser Gestaltungsart einengen.

Formally linear Fancies

Rising, falling and swinging lines; dominating and strongly subordinating forms, rigid and flexible ones. Everywhere there are contrasts, at least concerning forms whereas the colours are rather restrained when the most beautiful personalities of the tropical plant kingdom seduce us with their perfect figures. Nicolaia, Heliconia and Alocasia altogether they have a smooth plant surface. Indeed, they all originate from similar conditions of the rain forest. Their shapes are comparable to those of rare land and water animals. In the context of formally linear structures, the individual is dominant, not the choir, group or abundance. Each form has its own place. Any echo of symmetry would narrow the essential part of this type of design.

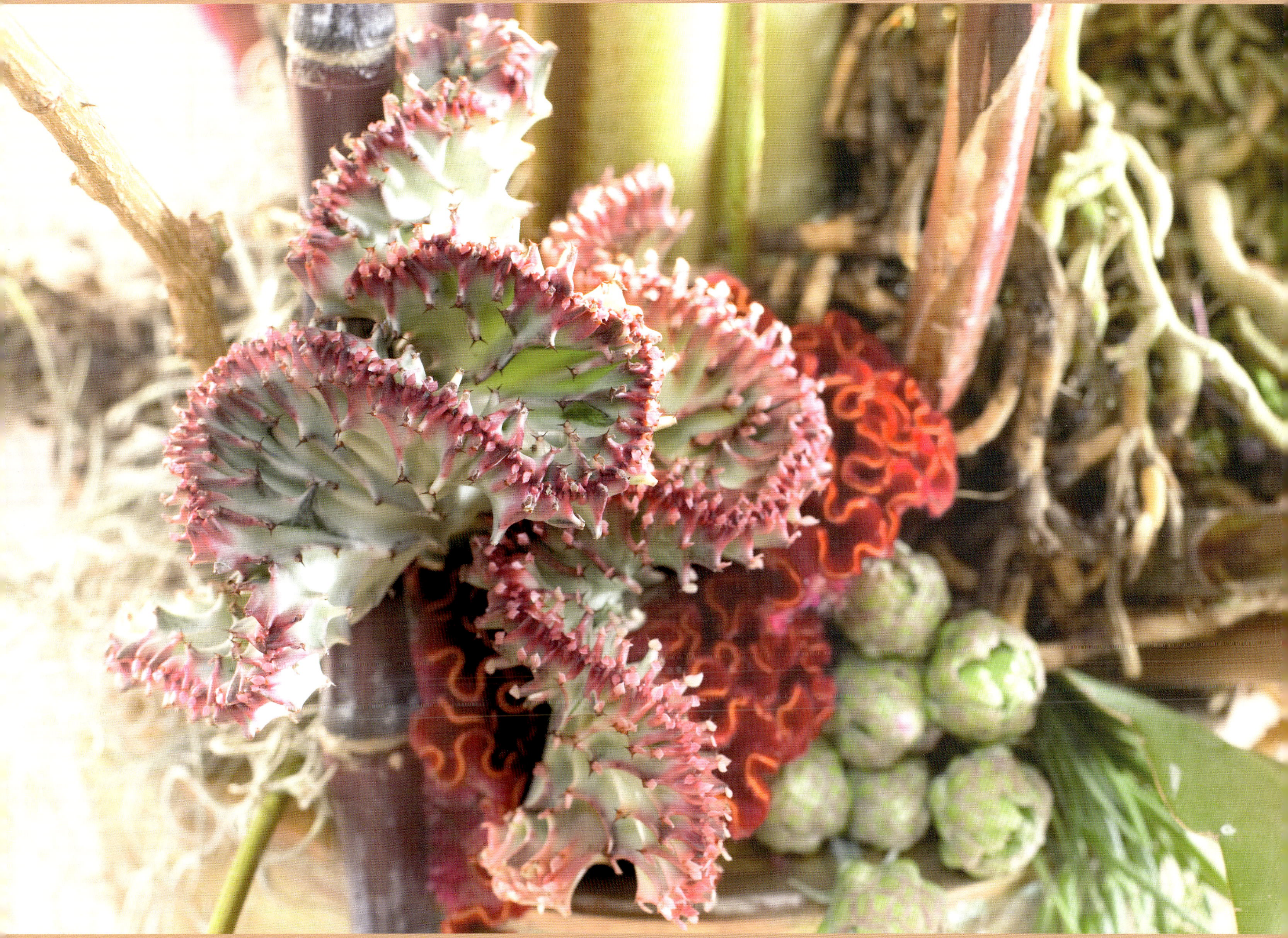

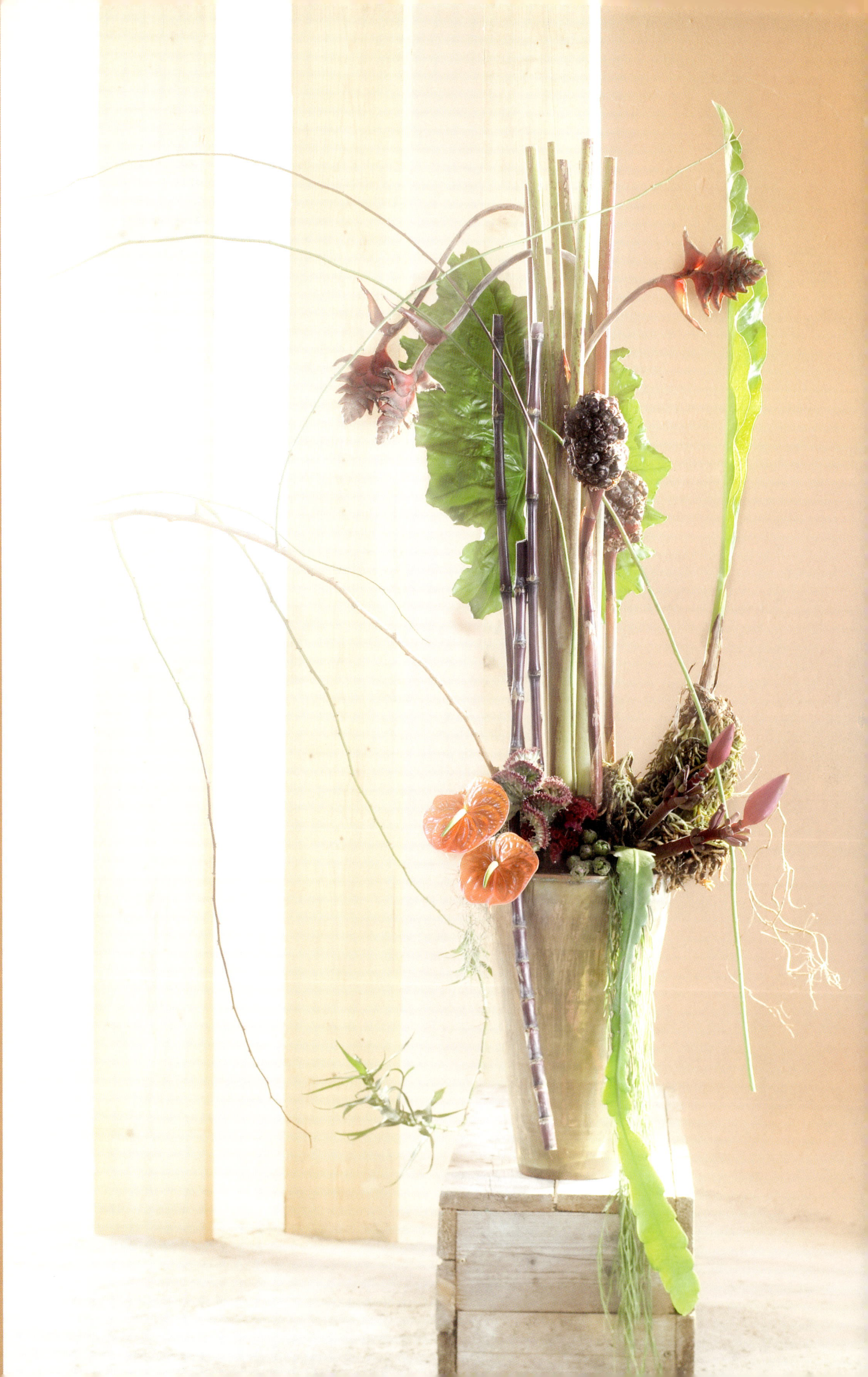

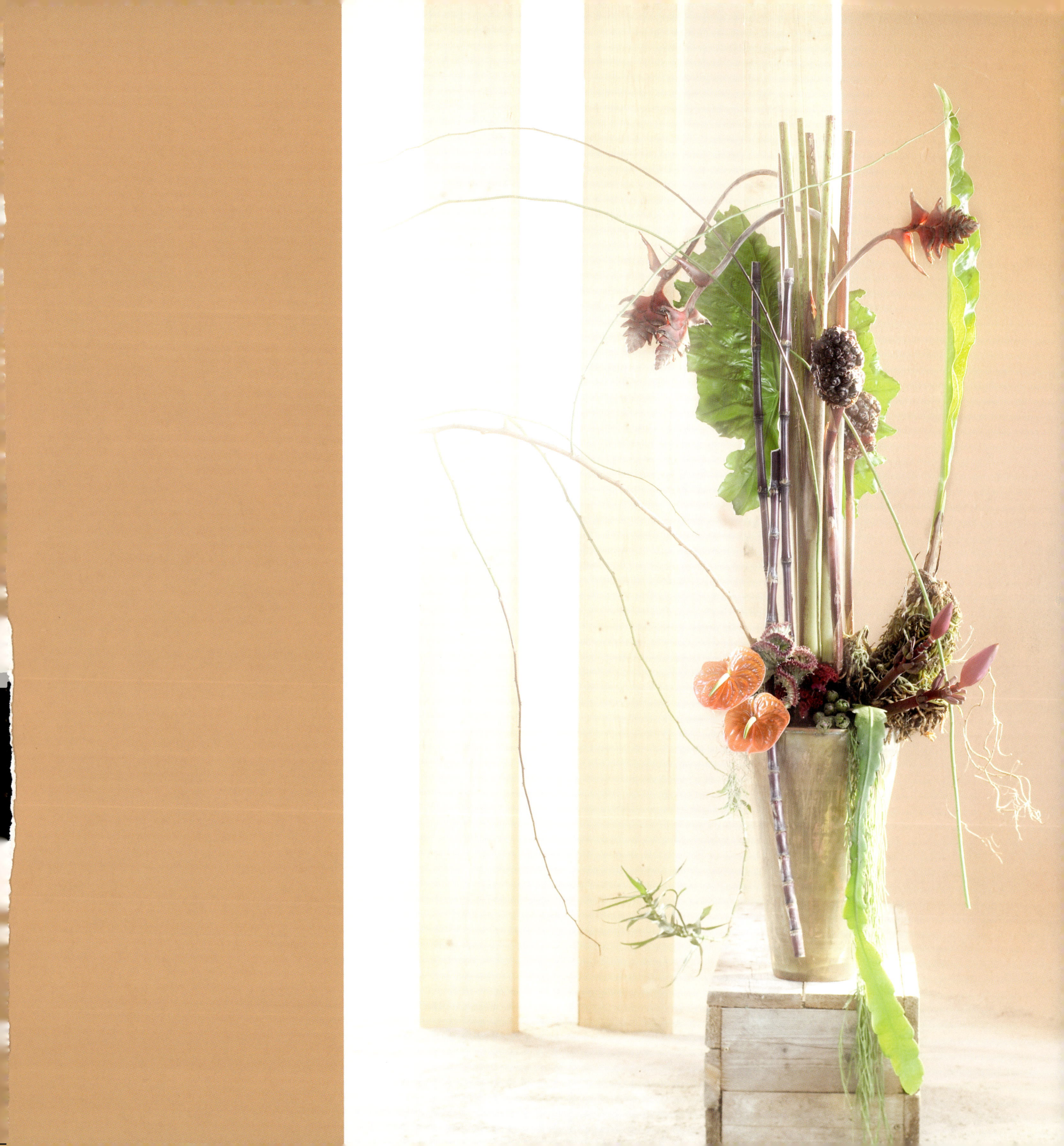

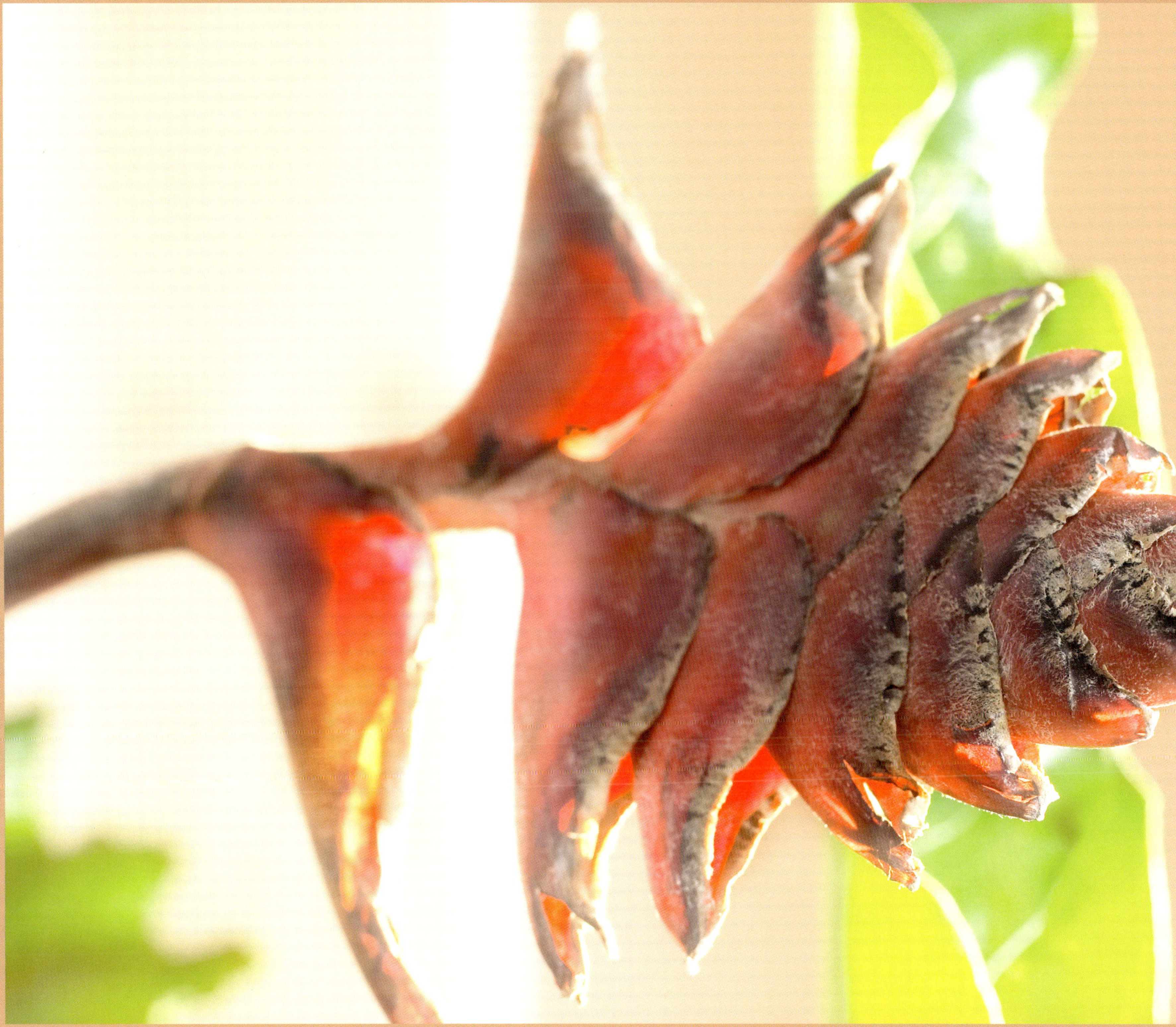

Will man für sich Neues entdecken, muss man hin und wieder ungewöhnliche Wege gehen. Wie zum Beispiel sich ein Wörterbuch zur Hand nehmen und Tätigkeitswörter heraussuchen. In vielen von diesen Verben stecken Anregungen und Anweisungen auch für floristisches Arbeiten. In diesem Falle war es der Begriff „durchstecken", der mich zu einer neuen Form des Strukturierens animiert hat. Dann braucht es noch die richtigen Werkstoffe, um die langsam sich entwickelnde Idee in Form und Farbe umzusetzen und ihr die entsprechende Anmutung zu verleihen und einen Sinn einzuhauchen.

Entscheidungen über eine extro- oder introvertierte Form des Werkstücks, über Dominanzen und Unterordnungen spielt man vorher gedanklich durch. So sorgen die kleinen, ja winzigen Oncidienpflänzchen hier für ein Minimum an vitaler Pflanze gegenüber den massiert auftretenden und eine relativ geschlossene Form bildenden, trockenen floralen Formen. Sie sind handelsübliche Neuheiten und in Gläser gepflanzt, die mit ganz feinem Sand überzogen sind.

Einsichtige Strukturen

Insightful Structures

If you want to discover something new for yourself, you will have to try unusual ways every now and again: to take a dictionary and look for verbs is just one example. Many of these verbs contain tips and instructions for the floral working. In this case, it was the term "inserting" that inspired me to create a new type of structuring. Then the right materials are needed in order to realize this gradually developed idea with the help of forms and colours giving it an appropriate beauty and sense. Decisions over extroverted or introverted types of arrangements, over dominance and subordinations are run through in advance. The small, almost tiny Oncidia plantlets serve here as a minimum of vital plants in contrast to the dry floral forms, which appear more compact forming relatively closed shapes. They are commercially available novelties and planted in glasses, which are coated with very fine sand.

Kon

Gewagte strukturen

Risky Constructions

Häufig stehe ich staunend vor der oft unglaublichen Statikleistung eines Gebäudes. Diese Ingenieurskunst auf das Floral Design zu übertragen, fasziniert mich immer wieder aufs Neue. Schweres weglassen, Leichtigkeit überhöhen und steigern bis an die statische Schmerzgrenze, um so aus alten bewährten Techniken heraus mit gewagten Verknüpfungen und Verflechtungen neue Bilder zu schaffen. Bis dahin, wo man sagt: Ich kann kaum glauben, dass so etwas noch steht und hält. Es reizt mich einfach, Florales so fein, transparent und durchsichtig zu zeigen, dass es zu schweben scheint, gleichzeitig aber auch eine absolute Stabilität zu erreichen. Ich liebe es, Pflanze und Co in gewagten Konstruktionen überraschend anders zu präsentieren.

I often stand astonished in front of the incredible static performance of a building. Using these engineering skills in a floral design has always had a fascination on me once again. This includes leaving out heavy elements, extending lightness up to the static limits in order to create new images out of old proven techniques through combinations and interweaving. All this to the point where you can't but say: I can scarcely believe that this is still firmly standing. I am just tempted by presenting the flora in such a delicate, transparent way that it seems to be floating, but also by reaching at the same time an absolute stability. I love to present plants and all of its accessories surprisingly different in risky constructions.

Beeindruckende Texturen

Beinahe schon ein wenig übertrieben kommt diese Textur daher. Dennoch sorgt selbst ein sonst so leblos wirkender Werkstoff wie die gebleichten Reedstäbchen auf dem leicht gewellten Steckschaum-Untergrund für Bewegung. Denn keine Position eines Stäbchens gleicht der eines anderen. So entsteht in dem mit Sand beklebten Rahmen ein lebendiges Eigenleben auf kleinstem Raum. Damit das Auge aber auch ein wenig Halt finden kann, unterbrechen ein paar „hungrige" Ceropegia-Ranken scheu die horizontale Struktur, während drei seltene, edle Masdevallia-Blüten den Blickpunkt bilden. Sie werden durch kleine Röhrchen, die im Schaum versteckt sind, mit Wasser versorgt. Und überall drum herum und dazwischen verspielt sich der feine, helle Sand.

Impressive Textures

Almost a bit exaggerating does this texture come along. However, even such a lifeless seeming material like this bleached reed sticks offers movement on the slightly wavy foaming underground since every stem has its unique position. As a result, an independent life of its own is created in the tiniest space in this frame glued with sand. As eye catchers a few "hungry" Ceropegia-ranks interrupt in a shy way the horizontal structure while three rare, noble Masdevallia-blossoms are forming the focal point, which gives our eyes orientation. Through small tubes, which are hidden within the foam, they are provided with water. And everywhere around it and in between, the fine, bright sand is being played.

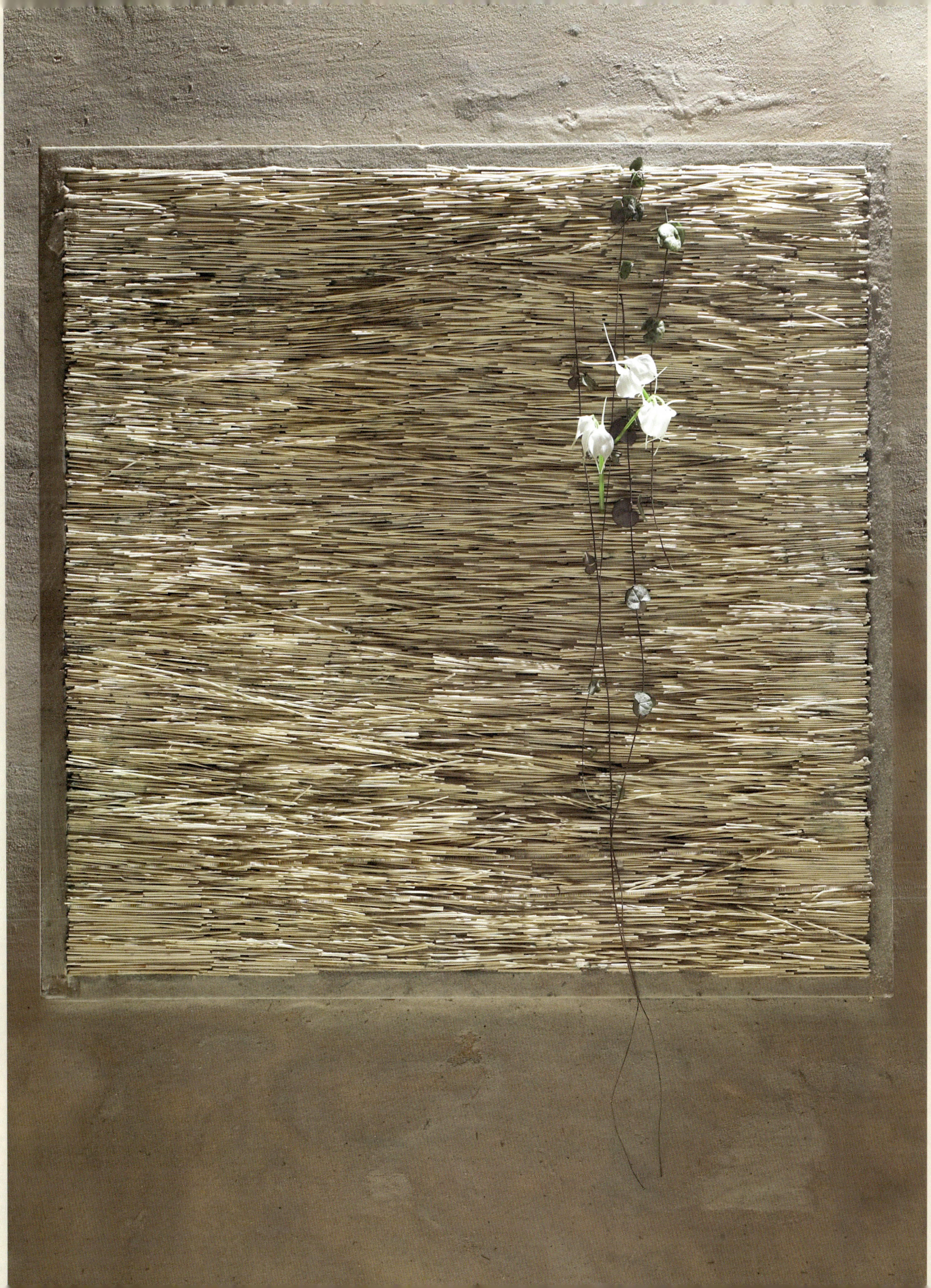

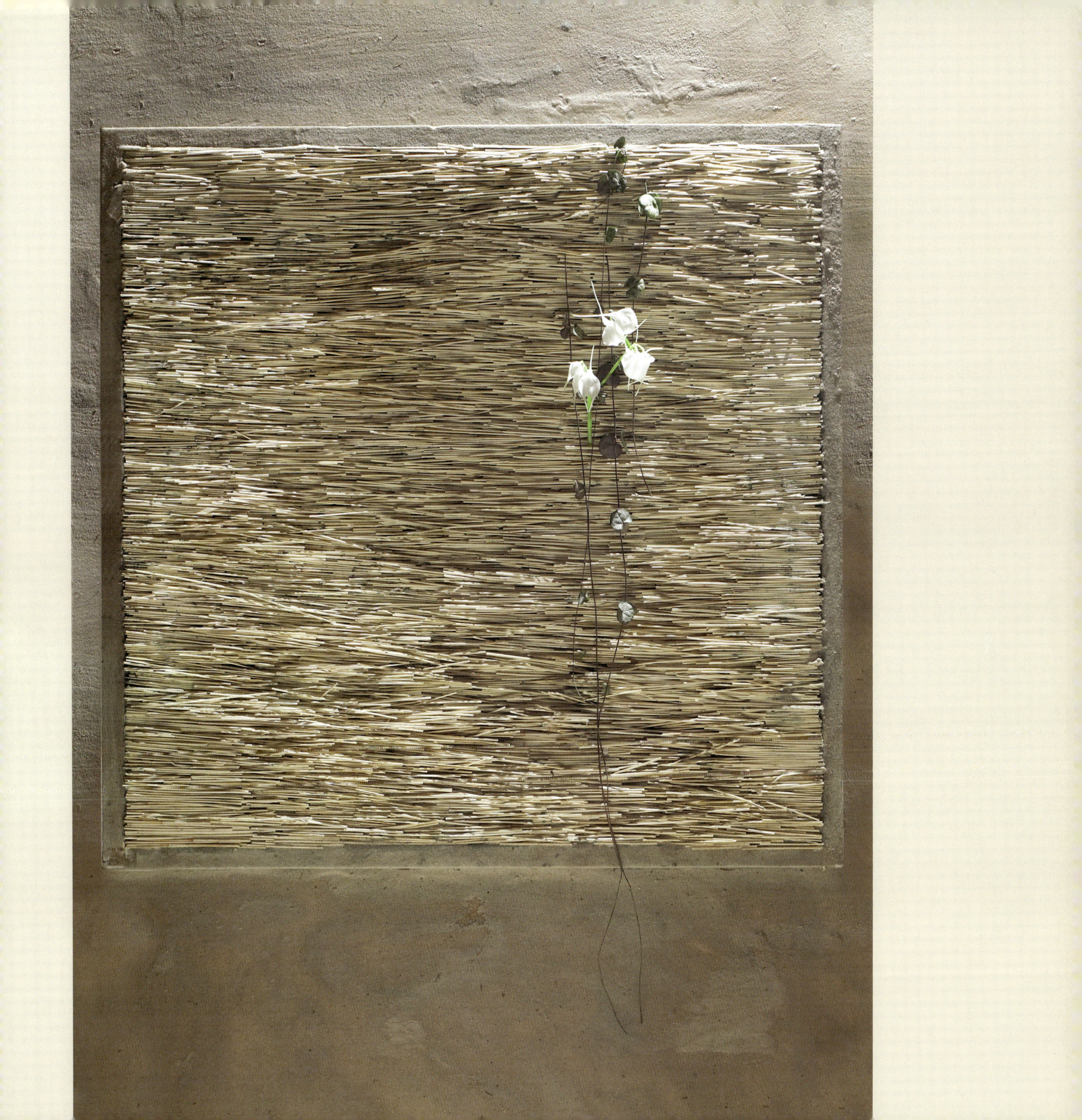

LERSCH | Gestalterische Bekenntnisse *Creative Confessions*

50 | 51

Innovative
Objekte

Aus Palmenfruchtstand-Sprossen entstehen durch Aneinanderreihen auf feinem Kupferdraht zarteste Schleier. Dysia-Orchideen aus Australien schweben wie exotische Schmetterlinge mitten durch das Gewebe hindurch. Raumgliederung mit Blumen und Pflanzenteilen ist ein altes Thema, das zu den ansonsten üblichen Interieurmaterialien eine interessante Bereicherung darstellt. Und das sogar auch ohne das Blühende. Solche innovativen Objekte stellen sich außerhalb des traditionellen Kontextes zwischen Blume und Gefäß. Florale Träume in neuen Formen, Texturen und Strukturen lassen sich erahnen. Neue Techniken mit neuen Hilfsmitteln schaffen ein Berufsbild mit veränderten Tätigkeiten. Denn der Mensch liebt die Pflanze in seinem Umfeld, wenn sie praktischen, emotionalen oder physischen Nutzen bietet. Das eröffnet Chancen für den Floralgestalter.

Innovative Objects

The most delicate veils are created by stringing together scions from palm's infructescence on a fine copper wire. Australian Dysia orchids are floating like exotic butterflies across the texture. Room structuring with flowers and parts of plants is an old topic, which is an interesting enrichment to the usual interior materials in other respects. And this even without blossoming. Such innovative objects are placed between the flower and the container outside the traditional context. Floral dreams of new shapes, textures and structures can be anticipated. New techniques with new aids create a profession with modified activities. Man loves the plant in his environment because of its practical, emotional or physical benefits. This creates opportunities for a floral designer.

Ich mag die skurrilen Motive eines Antonio Gaudi, die von Tieren, Insekten und hin und wieder von bizarren Pflanzen abgeleitet sind. Bewundernswert seine Fähigkeit, selbst Beängstigendes, Finsteres in heitere Objekte zu verwandeln, die wieder leben und etwas zu erzählen haben. Hier sind es die schwarzen Calla, die den kandelaberähnlichen Objekten neues Leben einzuhauchen scheinen. Die Szenerie vor dem schmuddeligen Fenster – vielleicht in einem Loft in Manhattan? – regt die Phantasie unweigerlich an. Ich höre schon das Gemurmel der Partygäste und sogar das Klavier im Hintergrund, auf dem Ragtime gespielt wird. Auf diese Weise möchte ich mit Floristischem Bilder in Szenen tauchen und zum Leben erwecken.

Monochromatic Finesse

I like the odd motives of Antonio Gaudi, which are derived from animals, insects and now and then from strange plants. His ability to transform even something frightening and of the night in gay objects, which have regained life again and have something to tell, is really impressive. In this case, it is the black Calla which seems to revive Candelabra-like objects. The scenery in front of the dirty window – which reminds us maybe of the atmosphere in a loft in Manhattan - inevitably animates our imagination. I can already hear the muttering of the party guests and even the piano in the background on which ragtime is being played. This is how I want to plunge into a scenery with the help of floral images creating life.

Raffinesse Monochrome

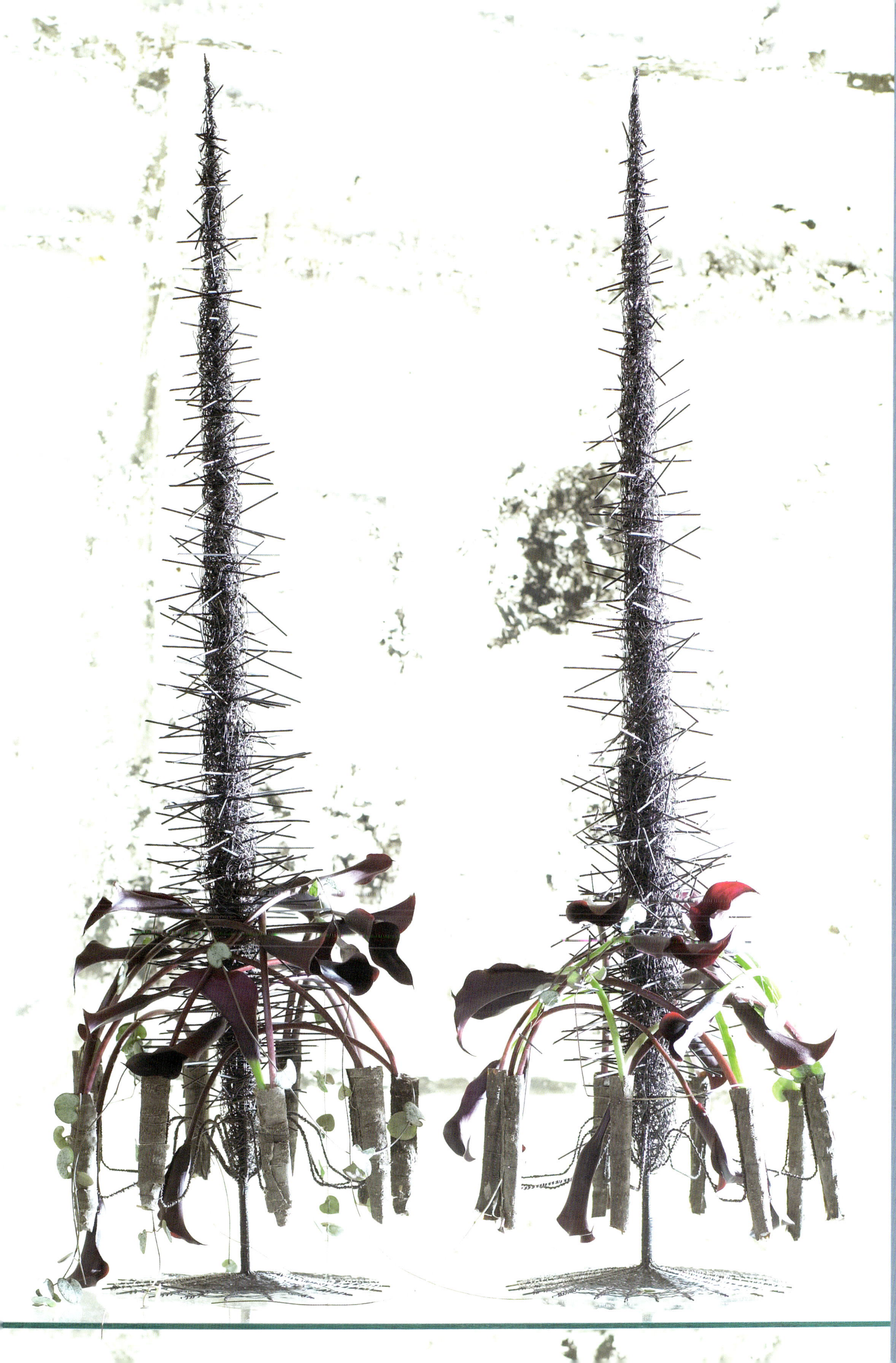

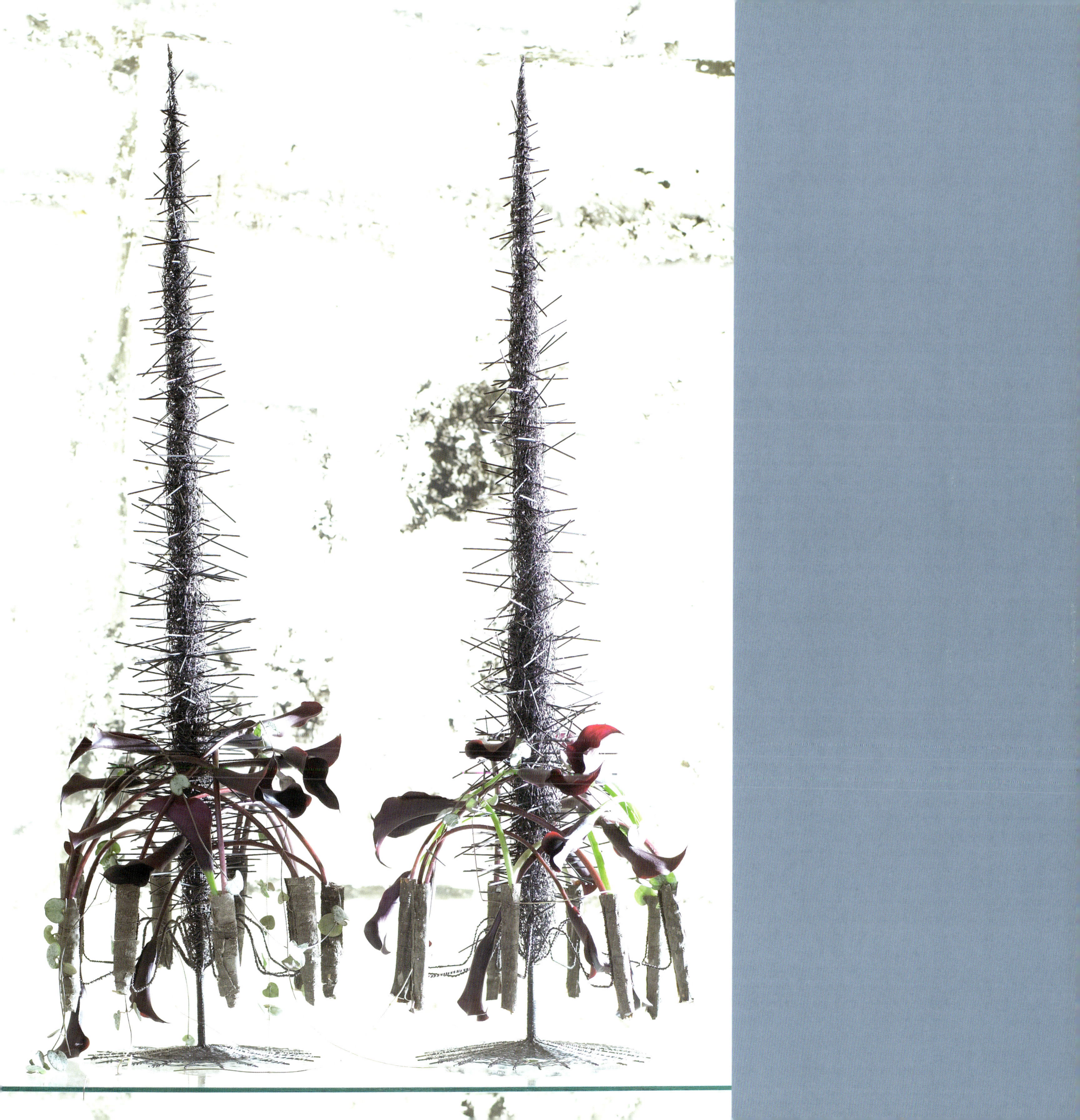

Lust auf Farbe? Ja. Aber wie schnell gleitet Farbigkeit in Buntheit ab und wird zu Kitsch. Um das zu vermeiden, muss Struktur her und die klare Entscheidung für bestimmte Werkstoffe, dann mag auch ich vielfarbig arbeiten. Doch eigentlich gestalte ich viel lieber mit gedeckten Tönen in monochromen Farbräumen, um dann einzelne farbige Highlights setzen zu können. Manchmal allerdings packt mich tatsächlich die Lust, aus der überschäumenden Vielfalt des Marktangebots aus dem Vollen zu schöpfen. Dann entstehen blühende Phantasien in verschwenderischen Farben. Allerdings nur ab und zu. Und sehr strukturiert.

Colourful Delight

Feel like colours? Yes. But how fast does colourful turn into varicoloured becoming trashy in the end. In order to avoid this, structures and a clear decision for certain materials are required. In this case, I also enjoy working with various colours. However, I prefer to utilize muted colours in monochromatic colour spaces, in order to set single colourful highlights. But sometimes I feel in fact like using the overwhelming variety of colours the market is offering in order to manufacture from solid materials. Then blooming fancies in abundant colours start emerging. However, only now and then and very structured.

Farbige
Lust

Bunte Leid

Buntheit mag ich nicht. Sie hat mir zu viel mit Unordnung, Unstrukturiertsein zu tun. Es sei denn, Buntheit bezieht sich nicht auf Farbe sondern auf die vielfältigen Möglichkeiten der Gestaltung. Einer solchen Provokation – denn so klingt der Begriff für mich – stelle ich mich selbstverständlich gern. Einen „bunten Strauß" an floralen Gestaltungselementen zu entwickeln und sich dabei dennoch innerhalb der selbst definierten Gestaltungsregeln zu bewegen, ist eine hochinteressante Aufgabenstellung. Wenn dennoch Vielfarbigkeit angesagt ist, kann sie für mich allenfalls in Trübungen bestehen.

Coloured Passion

I don't like the variegation. In my eyes it is too much related to disorder and lacks structure. The only exception is if it does not refer to colours but to the various possibilities of designing. As a matter of course, I enjoy facing this kind of provocation – as the term itself appears to me. It is an extremely interesting task to create a "variegated bouquet" of floral designing elements while observing anyhow the individually determined designing rules. Yet, if variegation is hot, tarnishing is the best case for me.

enschaft

Ganz persönliche Gefühle

In der Floristik mit Emotionen umzugehen, ist nicht so ganz einfach. Wer zu dick aufträgt, macht Kitsch. Wer gekonnt übertreibt, gilt wiederum als raffinierter Ästhet. Ein wenig Understatement tut da manchmal recht gut. Doch es ist ein durchaus schmaler Grat zwischen Unterkühlung und Überhitzung. Auch hat sich der Umgang mit Gefühl in den letzten Jahren stark verändert. Aus den Romantikklischees der Jahrhundertwende ist inzwischen ein sehr reduziertes Ausleben von Emotionen entstanden. Leisere Töne auch in der Gestaltung mit Blumen.

Very private Emotions

It is not easy to handle emotions in floristry. Someone who piles on with his design creates trash. On the other hand, someone who combines exaggerations with cleverness is considered to be a sophisticated aesthete. A bit of understatement can sometimes be quite helpful. However, it is a narrow ridge between super-cooling and super-heating. Besides, the way people deal with emotions has remarkably changed over the last years. The former clichés of romanticism at the turn of the century have meanwhile become a reduced let out of emotions. Gentle hues to be found even in floral designs.

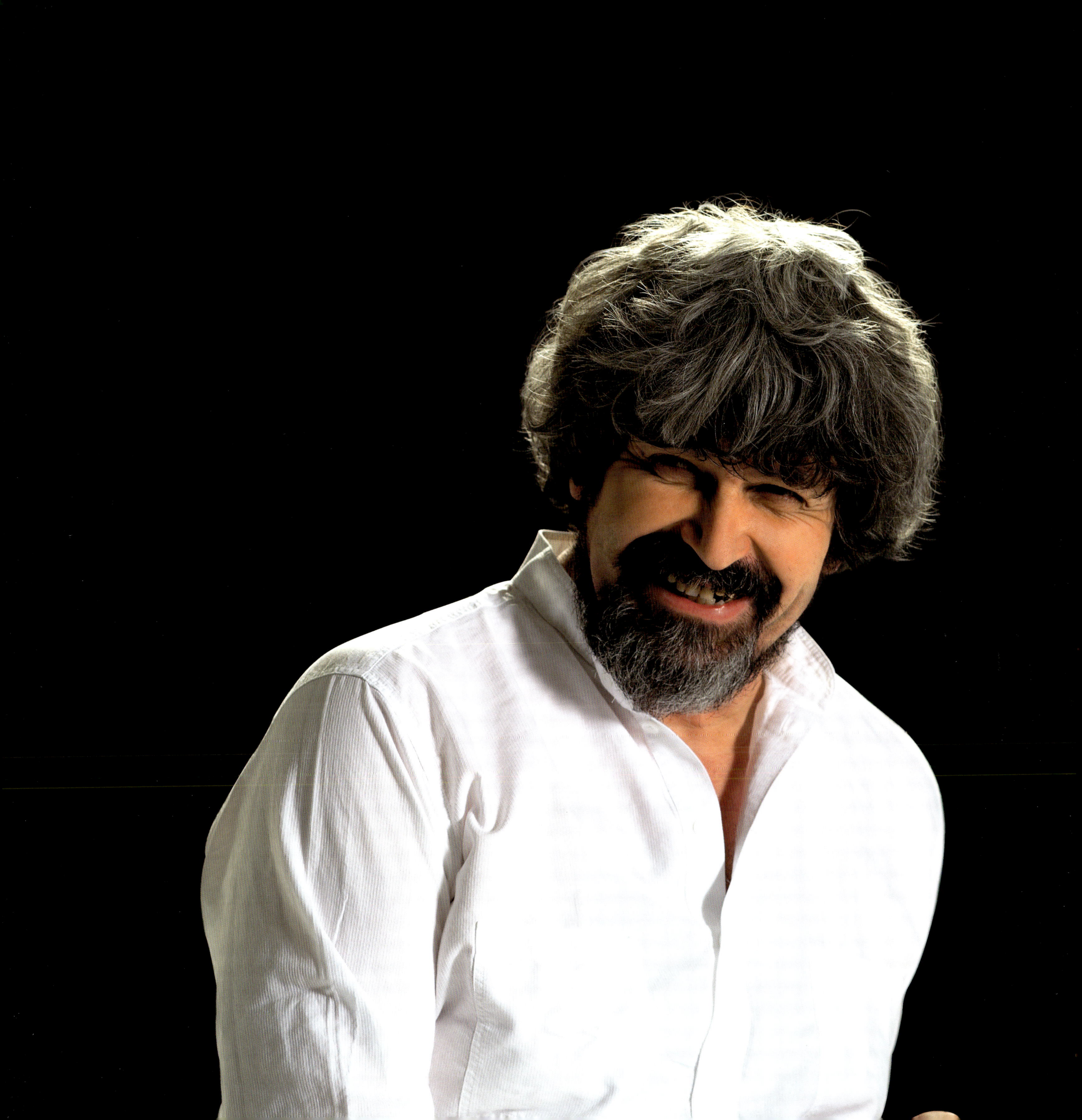

LERSCH | Ganz persönliche Gefühle *Very private Emotions*

Frühlingshaft

Olive, Kamelie, Zitrone, Mohn sind Botschafter mediterranen Frühlings, der dort ein wenig früher beginnt als bei uns und von daher umso strahlender und heiterer auf uns Nordlichter wirkt. Der umgedrehte Teller kehrt gleichzeitig die gewohnte Sehweise um, indem die Floralien aus der Mitte des Werkstücks eruptiv hervorquellen und jede Menge Vitalität ausstrahlen. Die Formgebung ergibt sich fast zwangsläufig aus dem puren Gewachsenen.

Spring-like Serenity

Olives, Camellia, lemons and poppy seed are the ambassadors of Mediterranean spring, which begins a bit earlier in this kind of regions than in ours. This is why it has a more radiating and cheerful impact on us people from Northern countries. The reversed plate turns back at the same time our usual view while the flora protrudes from the middle of the arrangement radiating lots of vitality. The process of shaping almost inevitably results from the purely grown.

Sommerlich berau

Der phantastische Blick in einen Tunnel aus Hunderten von Paeonien lässt uns in die orgiastische Fülle des Sommers fallen. Zusammen mit den vollreifen, köstlichen Erdbeeren entsteht Schlaraffenland pur. Wie im Traum erscheint in der Ferne ein Juwel des weißgrünen Junisommers: eine Kugel aus Cornusblüten. Eine floristische Arbeit, die nicht nach Sinn oder Nutzen fragt, sondern einzig und allein rauschhafte Freude am Sommer vermitteln möchte.

Summer-like Exhileration

The fantastic view into the tunnel of hundreds of Paeonia lets us sink into the breathtaking abundance of summer. Together with the ripe, delicious strawberries a complete cockaigne arises. Like in a dream a jewellery of June's white-green summer emerges in the distance: a bowl of Cornus blossoms. As a result we have a floristic arrangement, which ignores sense and benefit, but wants solely to transfer an exhilarating joy of summer.

Herbstlich

LERSCH | Ganz persönliche Gefühle Very private Emotions

64 | 65

schwänglich

Füllhörner gab es schon immer im Herbst. Ich wollte es allerdings ein wenig dezenter und zeitgemäßer, nicht so opulent, sondern ohne viel Masse und ohne quälend quellende Fülle. So entstand aus dem feinen Drahtgeflecht sehr schnell eine zart fallende tropfige Form mit edlen floralen Details und Früchten in teilweise kräftigen herbstlichen Farbtönen. Die prächtige und doch filigrane Cattleya avanciert zum unumstrittenen Blickpunkt. Die hohe, schmalhalsige Vase ermöglicht der Arbeit den nötigen, statisch gut ausbalancierten Schwung.

Autumn-like Exuberance

There have always been Cornucopias in autumn. However, I preferred it more decently and contemporary, not that abundant, but without too much mass and without agonising, dwelling abundance. In this manner the delicate network of wires turned very fast into a delicately falling, dropping shape with noble floral details and fruits in partly strong autumn hues. The glorious but filigree Cattleya advances to an undisputable focal point. The tall, narrow-necked vase offers the required, statically well balanced swung for this arrangement.

Winterlich zart

LERSCH | Ganz persönliche Gefühle Very private Emotions

Winter-like Delicateness

Mit Pflanzlichem ist hier Kühle und Distanz, ja klirrende Kälte entstanden. Dennoch erhält der Winter durch die zarten Blumen einen sympathischen Anstrich, denn Blumen sind gerade in dieser Jahreszeit Hoffnungsträger für mehr Sonne und Wärme. Ein feines Konstrukt aus 1,8 mm Draht hält das natürliche, feine Netzwerk der Calocephalus-brownii-Triebe zusammen und kontrolliert so die Form. Der Auftritt im Doppelpack macht die Wirkung umso eindrucksvoller.

Coolness and distance, almost a clashing cold has been created here by the flora. However, winter is provided with a friendly coating through delicate flowers, since flowers are especially in this season a symbol of hope for more sun and warmth. A delicate construction of a wire with a diameter of 1.8 mm sustains the natural, fine network of the Calocephalus-brownii-shoots controlling thus its form. This double presentation intesifies its impressiv impact.

LERSCH | Ganz persönliche Gefühle *Very private Emotions*

Wie schwebend windet sich eine sehr transparente Girlande um die beiden Etageren. Fast wie im Wind wehend verspielen sich Ranken blattloser Euphorbia spinosa aus Südeuropa darum herum. Ich mag Etageren. Sie geben Blumen so etwas Urbanes. Hier wohnen Floralien in Stockwerken, nehmen Rangordnungen ein und leben dabei – in ihren jeweiligen Etagen elegant eingebettet – in trauter Harmonie miteinander. Die Ranunkeln dagegen wirken eher wieder verspielt und kindlich.

Unlimited *Romanticism*

A very transparent garland enwinds both terraces with a floating air. Twines of leafless Euphorbia spinosa from South Europe are waving playfully around it almost like in the wind. I like terracing. This technique gives flowers something urban. In this arrangement, the flowers are living on floors in certain hierarchal positions in close harmony, embedded on their respective floors. The butter cops, in contrast, seem to be more playful and childish.

Heillos romantisch

LERSCH | Ganz persönliche Gefühle Very private Emotions

Erregend sinnlich

Wenn wir von Sinnlichkeit in der Natur und Kultur reden, meinen wir letztendlich wohl doch immer das erotische Spiel zwischen den Geschlechtern. Sinnlichkeit ist das, was sich, oft versteckt hinter einer spanischen Wand oder einem lasziven Fächer, erahnen lässt. Sinnlichkeit ist das, was hier die medusenhauptartige Wildheit der sich überschneidenden Linien andeutet: die Verwirrung der Gedanken und Gefühle, die kaum jemand rational erklären kann, den sie überfällt. Dazu die wie zufällig daliegenden Trauben als Zeichen angedeuteter Lust. Die Begegnung an Tisch oder Tafel, häufig der Auftakt für den Austausch der Sinne. Die winzigen „Isa"-Röschen erinnern schnell noch daran, dass Zärtlichkeit dem Ausleben der Sinnlichkeit die Oberflächlichkeit nimmt und die betörende Wirkung der Triebe vermindert.

Sensual Excitements

When we talk about the sensuality in nature and culture, we always mean the erotic game between the genders in the end. Sensuality is everything which can often be anticipated behind a Spanish wall or a luscivious fan. It is indicated by the Methuselah-like wildness of these crossing lines: confusion of thoughts and feelings which no one who becomes its victim can explain rationally. In addition, the grapes are lying accidentally like a symbolic allusion of joy. Meetings at table often serve as the initiation for an exchange of senses. Then, the tiny "Isa-flowerets remind us that tenderness takes away the superficiality of outliving sensuality and that it reduces the shoots' infatuating impact.

LERSCH | Ganz persönliche Gefühle *Very private Emotions*

Inspirierend sexy

Können Blumen sexy sein? Was wäre dann ihr Sexappeal? Ist Sex nicht eigentlich ein menschliches Attribut? Oder wie war das noch mal mit den Bienen? Fragen, die den Floral Designer nicht jeden Tag beschäftigen, jedenfalls nicht beruflich. Dennoch regt eine solche Aufgabenstellung die Phantasie an. Und siehe da: Es geht. Den Anfang macht die Heleconie mit Namen „Sexy Pink". Andere Assoziationen zu pflanzlichen Strukturen und Formen kommen hinzu. Der Fotograf mit seinen Verfremdungen über den Computer leistet ebenfalls seinen Beitrag. So entstehen Phantasien, die inspirieren und durch Anklänge an spärliche Verhüllungen des allzu Offensichtlichen ein leises Knistern entstehen lassen.

Sexy Inspirations

Can flowers be sexy? If yes, what would their sex appeal be? Isn't sex rather a human characteristic? And what was the story about the bees? Such questions do not occupy a floral designer every day; at least not professional-wise. However, such a task incites our imagination. Lo and behold: it works. The Heleconia, called „sexy pink", is the initiator. Other combinations of plant structures and forms are added. The photographer with his alienations on the computer contributes to the whole likewise. In this way, inspiring imaginations are created which provoke a quiet crackling through echoes of scarce disguises of the well evident.

Maßlos opulent

LERSCH | Ganz persönliche Gefühle *Very private Emotions*

Die maßlose Fülle des Sommers und Herbstes ergießt sich in den überquellenden Kelch. Florale Sinnenfreuden in Form von Farben, Formen, Blüten, Früchten, Edlem und Einfachem. Das Übermaß der Jahreszeiten, wie ich es empfinde, braucht seine adäquate Darstellung. Um aber die heiter-warme florale Überdosis nicht in eine Soap Opera abgleiten zu lassen, verhelfen die leblos-grauen Bleigefäße zu einer wohltuenden Erfrischung. Für mich ist ein solcher Kontrast wichtig, um drohendem Kitsch entsprechende kühlende Kräfte als Ausgleich entgegenzusetzen.

Excessive *Abundance*

The excessive abundance of summer and autumn is gushed in the overflowing calyx: floral, sensual pleasures in terms of colours, shapes, blossoms, fruits, nobilities and simplicities. The excess of the seasons, the way I feel it, requires an adequate presentation. But in order to prevent the bright-warm floral overdoses from drifting to a soap opera, the lifeless grey lead containers provide comforting refreshment. Personally, I think that such a contrast is important in order to oppose appropriate cooling energies to threatening kitsch as a way of compensation.

Minimalistisch reduziert

Minimalist Reductions

Reduktion ist das Zusammenschmelzen von Gestaltungselementen bis kurz vor dem Nullpunkt, wobei dennoch Balance, Blickpunkt, Handwerk und all die anderen Komponenten floraler Gestaltung gewährleistet werden müssen – praktisch mit nichts in der Hand. So besteht eine der großen Herausforderungen der Reduktion darin, die Spannungsmomente bzw. die Gründe zum Hinschauen nicht aus Menge und Vielfalt zu beziehen, sondern aus anderen Gestaltungsmitteln. Hier sind es zum Beispiel eine aufregende Statik – mit Metallbügeln im unteren Teil – und verschiedene, sich ergänzende Bewegungsabläufe. Werkstoffvielfalt spielt hier keine Rolle. Auch Farbe tritt zurück. So bleibt nur Form. Die florale Ikone minimalistischen Interieurs, die Phalaenopsis thront hoch über dem gesamten Auftritt: Alleinherrschaft über eine stark ornamentale Form.

In reductions, designing elements are combined just up to the verge of the zero point, while however balance, focal point, techniques and all other components of floral designing must be ensured – practically without any helping devices in our hands. Thus, one of the biggest challenges of reduction is to provide exciting, eye-catching moments not with the help of quantity and variety, but with other designing instruments. Here, it is for example an exciting static – with metal holders in the lower part – and different, complimentary motion sequences. A variety of materials doesn't play a role here. Colours are also neglected. By doing so only the form remains. The Phalaenopsis is enthroned high above the whole arrangement representing the floral idol of a minimalist interior: sovereignty rules the strongly ornamental form.

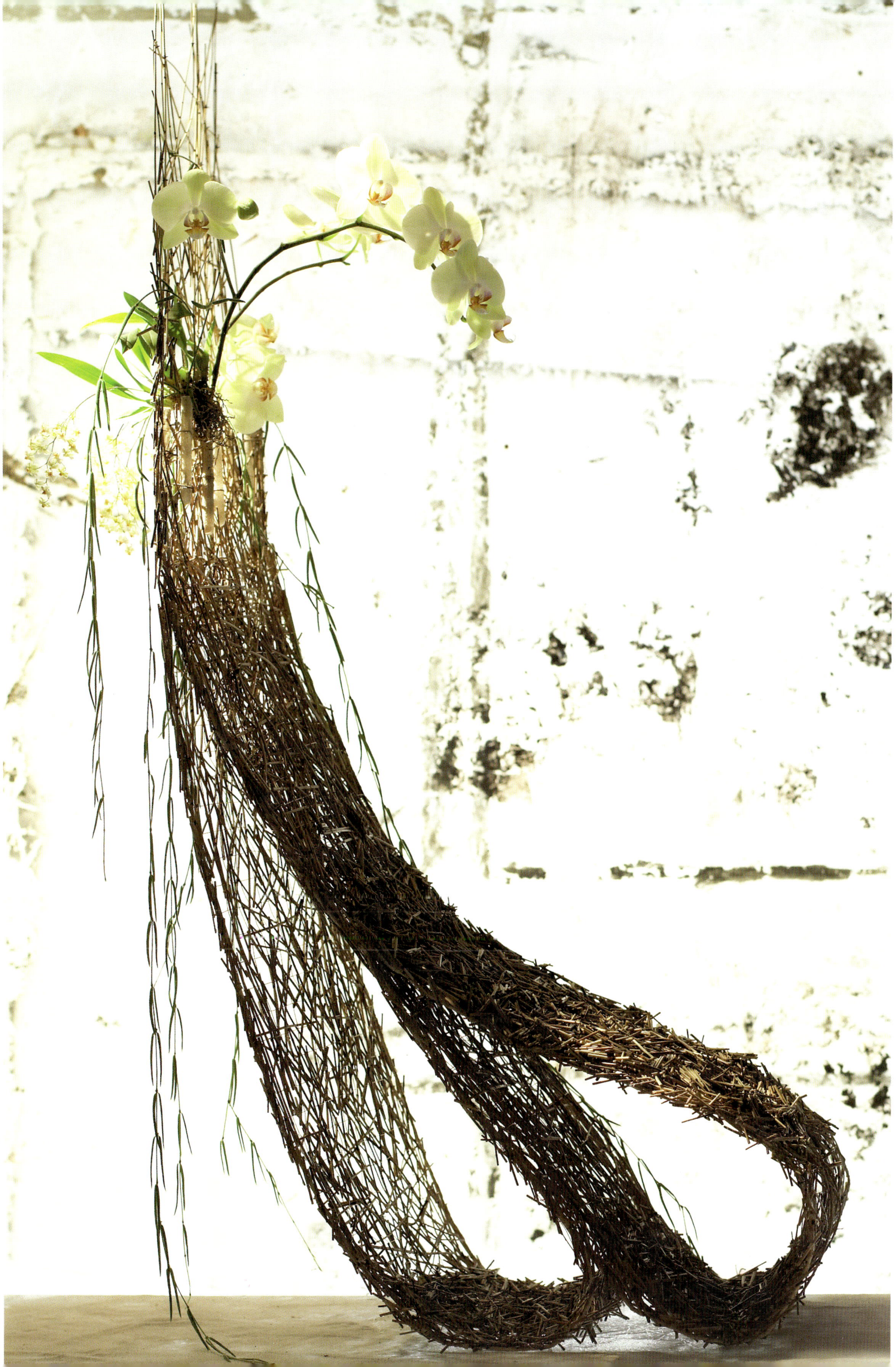

Heimat
Wein und nochmals Wein

Ein Element prägt meine engere Heimat in ganz besonderem Maße: der Wein. Vor allem reizt mich daran das Unprätentiöse, Bescheidene. Also weniger die vollreifen Trauben oder die malerisch gefärbten Blätter im Herbst – sie üben schon für sich allein eine starke Wirkung auf den Betrachter aus. Doch was können die Abfallprodukte der Kulturpflanze „Rebe" leisten, wenn man ihnen eine Chance gibt? Wenn etwa kleine und kleinste Rebenstückchen mit „unsichtbarem" Leim auf einem Baumetallgitter zu einem drei Meter langen Teppich zusammengeklebt werden, auf dem winzige Heuchera-Jungpflanzen einen farblichen Blickpunkt erzeugen und einige lange Reben ein modernes Muster bilden? Mir geht es bei solchen Darstellungen immer wieder darum, die Weinpflanze in ihrer Ganzheit zu thematisieren, um der tradierten Idylle der Weinfeste und Probierstuben zu entgehen und ihnen entgegenzuwirken. Zeitgerechte Floristik mit Wein – ohne den Muff des Altbackenen und Weinseligen.

Homeland: Wine and Wine again

An element, which characterizes my homeland in a particular way, is the wine. Above all, I am tempted by its unpretentious and modest character. Thus, not by the ripe grapes or the picturesque coloured leaves in autumn, which on their own already have a strong impact on the spectator. But what's the use of the waste products of the cultivated plant "vine" if they are given the opportunity to be implemented? For instance, when small and smallest vine parts are bonded with "transparent" glue on a metal grill to become a carpet with a length of three metres onto which tiny Heuchera seedlings provide a colourful focal point and when some long bines form a modern pattern? Such presentations always inspire me to broach the issue of the wine plant as a whole in order to avoid the traditional idyll of wine feasts and tasting rooms and counteract them. This displays contemporary floristry with wine – without the muff of the dowdy and maudlin.

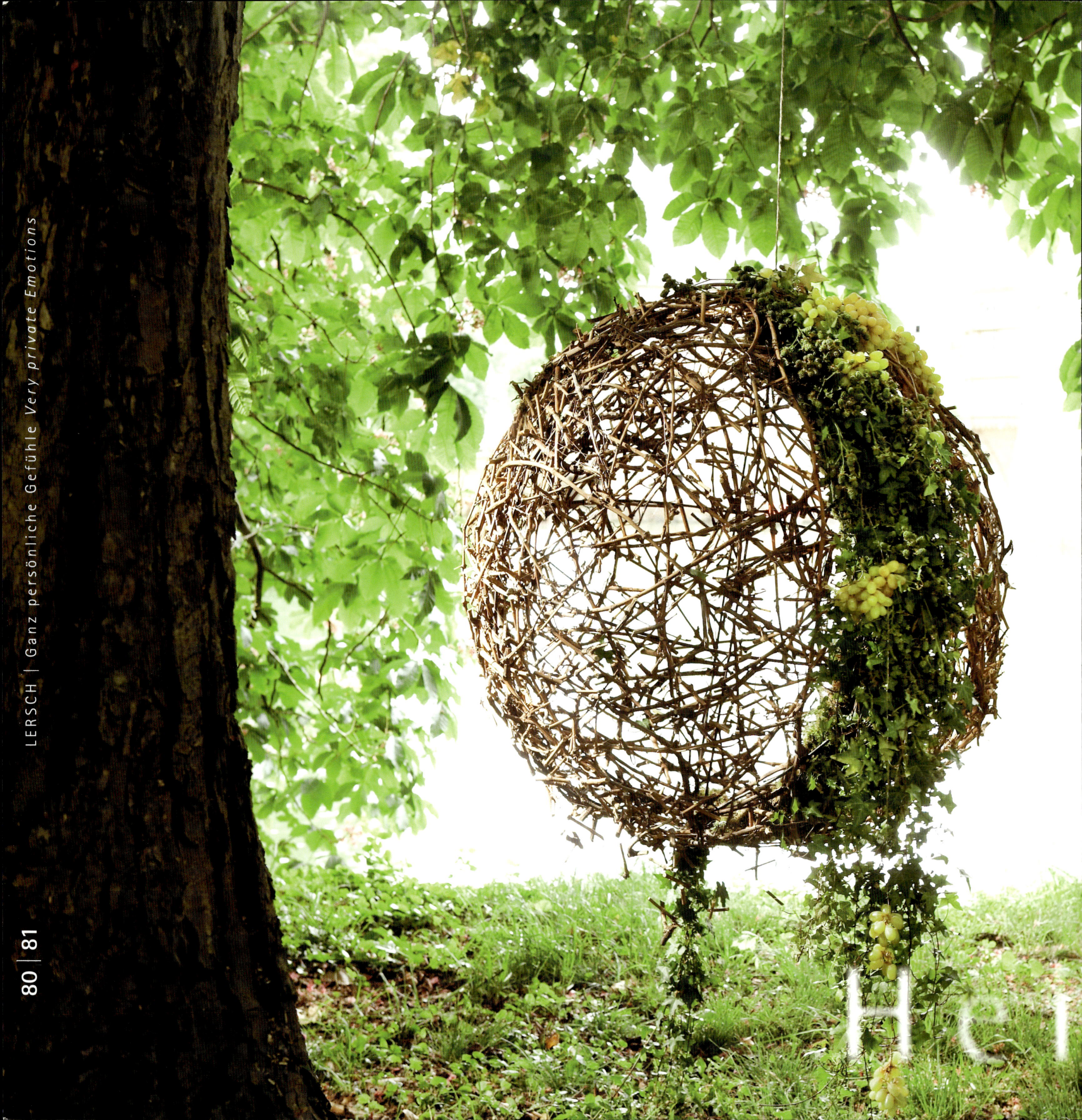
Her

Dem Stillen und Unscheinbaren eine Plattform zu verleihen, ist mir seit je her ein ganz besonderes Anliegen. Efeu ist eine solche gestalterisch stille Pflanze, die auf den Jahrhunderte alten Weinterrassen des Ahrtals mit dem Wein in Symbiose lebt. Hier verschafft man der ansonsten im Verborgenen existierenden Gemeinschaft einen öffentlichen Auftritt. Die frei im Raum schwebende Kugel ist aus Weinreben gefertigt, auf die wiederum winzige Weinhölzchen mit oxydierten dünnen Drähten aufgefädelt sind. Von ihr fließt ein Efeu-Fries ab, besetzt mit Trauben und noch grünen Brombeeren.

Homeland: Ivy and Wine

Creating a platform for the silent and the inconspicuous has always been a quite particular request to me. Ivy is such a silent plant from a designing point of view living on ancient wine terraces of the Ahr valley in complete harmony with the wine. Here, the community usually living in secrecy is provided with a public presentation. The bowl floating loosely within the space is made of grape-wine onto which tiny wooden sticks with oxidised thin wires are thread together. Ivy-frieze covered with grapes and still green blackberries is running off from it.

Efeu und Wein

Im Gegensatz zu vielen anderen lieblich daherkommenden oder gar mit üppiger Vegetation ausgestatten Regionen bietet die Eifel zwar ein vielgesichtiges, aber alles in allem doch recht karges Landschaftsbild. Will man hier etwas Außergewöhnliches entstehen lassen, muss man es selbst in die Hand nehmen. So wie etwa Baronin und Baron Loe, die jedes Jahr zur Landpartie ins Wasserschloss zu Adendorf laden. Dann entsteht Lebensart pur. Die riesigen, 4 m hohen Pokale vereinen diesmal Reben und Weide zu transparenten Formen. Die Blüten versprühen Frische und Vitalität vor den alten Gemäuern. Auch Efeu taucht wieder auf. Es verbindet und umschlingt, wie schon damals im Weinberg, wo auch die Weide eine entscheidende Rolle spielte. In den Nebentälern der Ahr nämlich pflanzte man Weide, mit deren biegsamen Ästen man die Reben auf den Stock band. Manchem Winzer sagt dieses Trio noch heute etwas.

Homeland: Willow and Wine

In contrast to many other lovely upcoming regions or regions with excessive vegetation, the Eifel offers a multifaceted but all in all a rather sparse landscape. If you want to create something extraordinary here, you have to do it on your own. Just like the baron and baroness Loe who invite their guests to an outing at the water castle in Adendorf. At this occasion, a pure savoir-vivre is created. The huge cups with a height of 4 metres combine this time vines and willows to transparent forms. The blossoms spray freshness and vitality in front of the ancient ruins. And also Ivy is emerging again. It combines and enwinds, like in former times when the willow used to play a decisive role in the vineyard. In the side valleys to the Ahr willow was planted and its flexible branches served to bind the grapes onto the vine. Some winemakers still know this trio even today.

Heimat
Weide und Wein

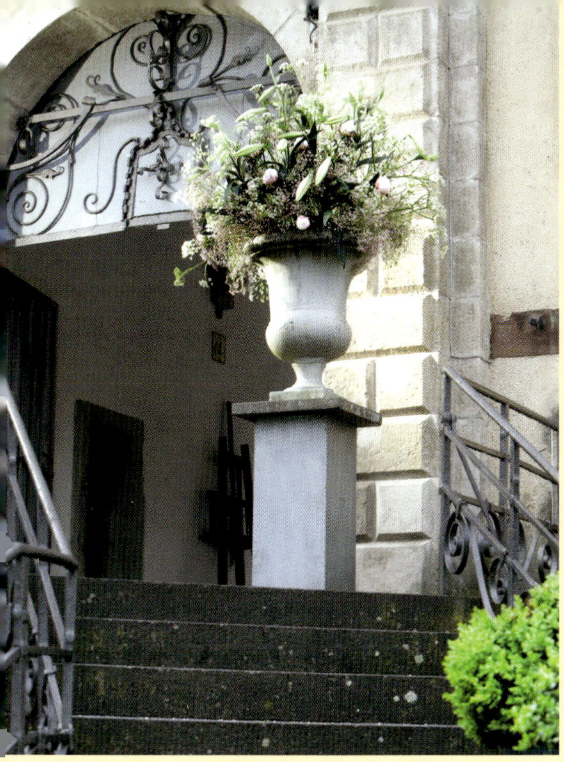

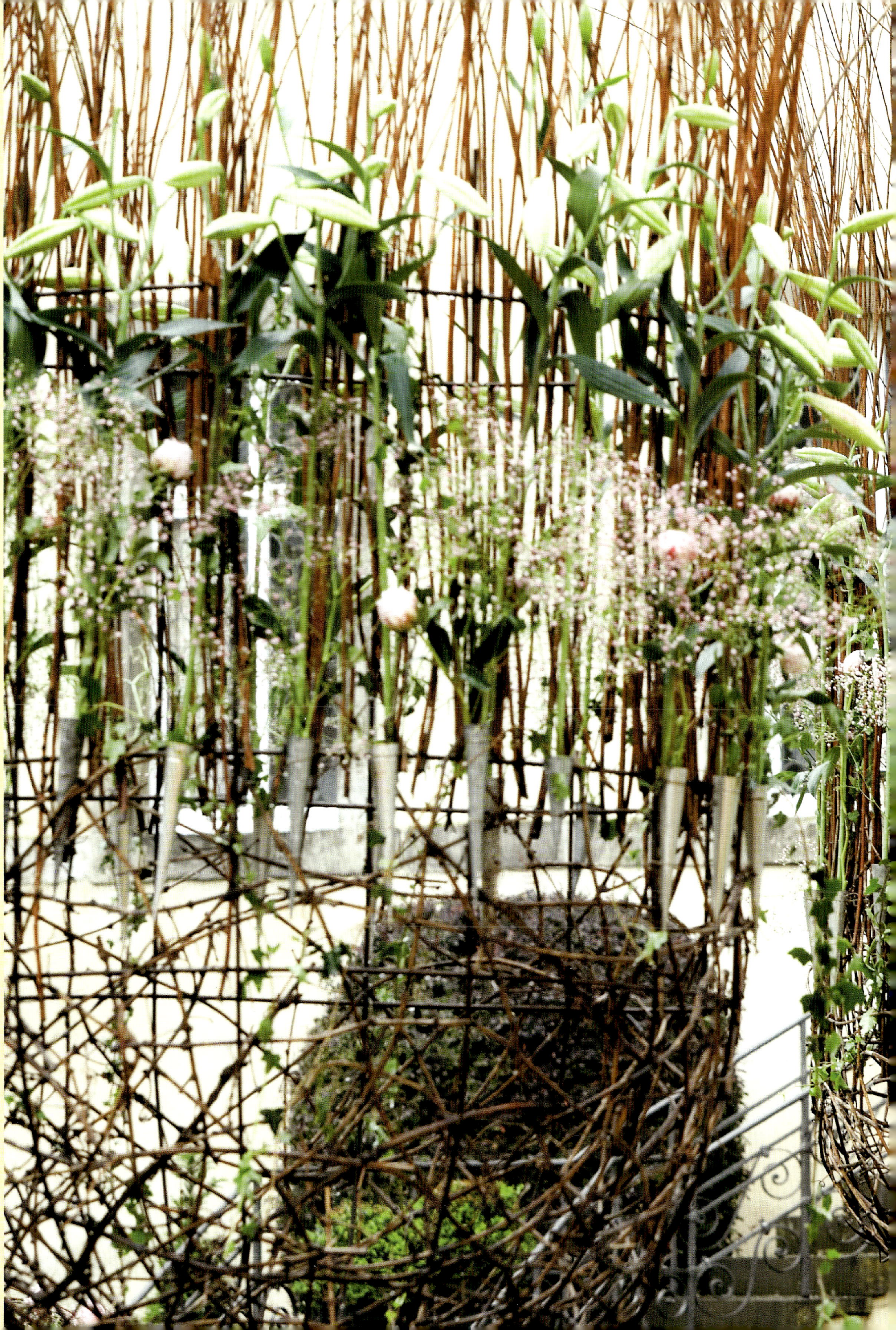

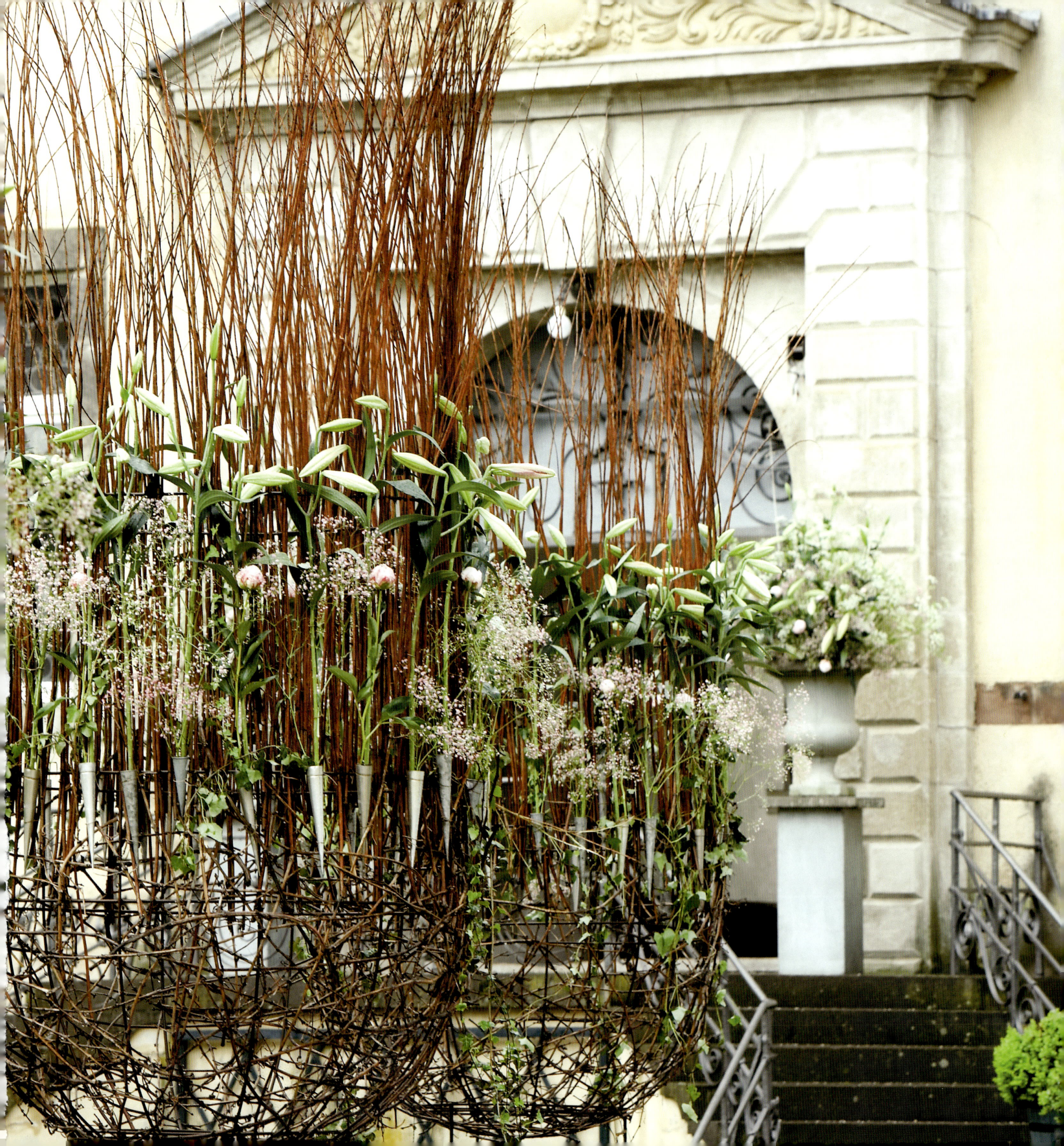

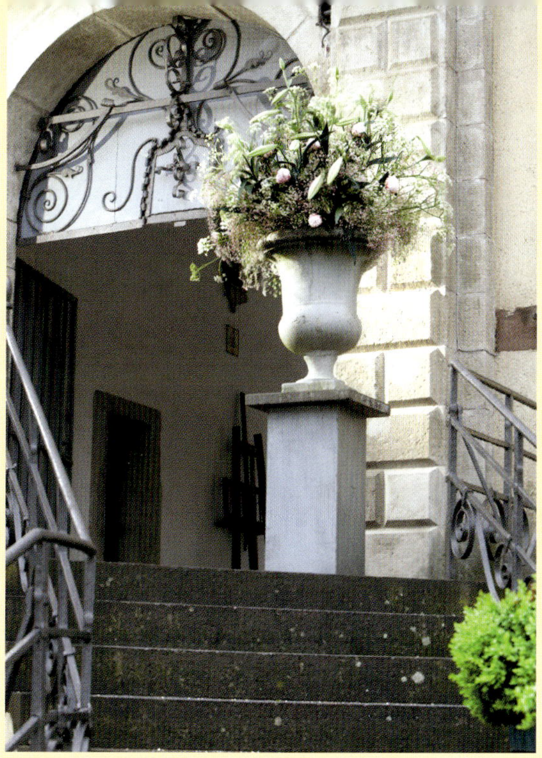

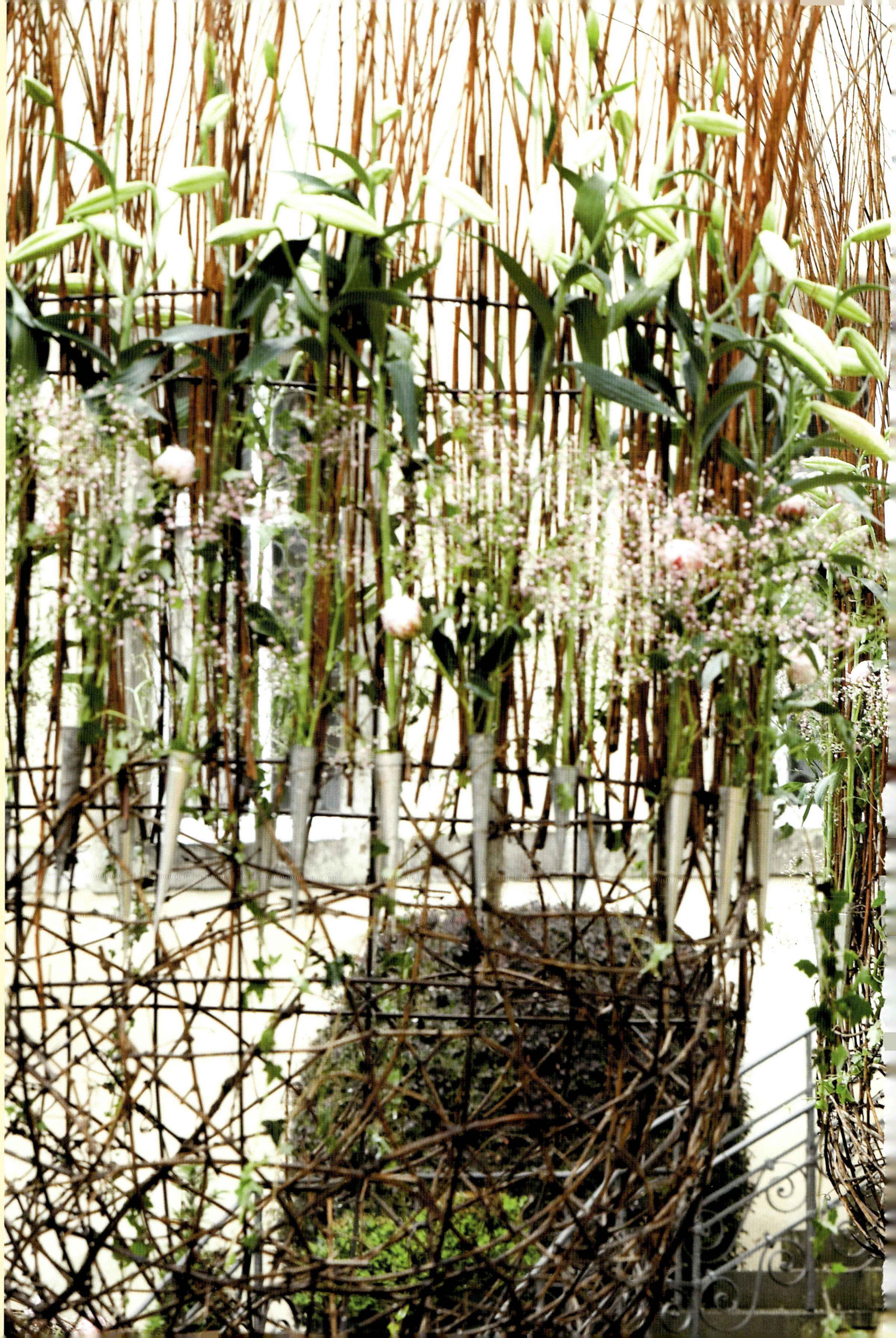

Heimat
Gras und Moos und Wein

LERSCH | Ganz persönliche Gefühle Very private Emotions

Nicht nur Wein, Efeu und Weide stehen als Floralien stellvertretend für meine heimatlichen Gefilde. Als Beispiele sollen neben anderen Schönheiten die Ginsterblüte im Mai oder die Golddistel im Herbst erwähnt sein. Auch Gras und Moos aus den feuchten Ecken unserer Gegend gehören dazu. Sie spielen in diesem Falle neben Trauben und Weidenstäben sowie Clematis aus den gestrüppartigen Hecken der Gegend eine Hauptrolle. Handarbeit formt diese Schlichtheiten zu einer symmetrischen, eher tradiert wirkenden Skulptur, die die Formen des Schlosses aufgreift. Grün in Grün – Friedlichkeit verbreitend.

Homeland: Grass, Moss and Wine

Not only wine, Ivy and willow represent my home fields as floral materials. Other examples, which have to be mentioned, are among other beauties, May's Genista blossom or autumn's Carolina thistle. Grass and moss originating from moist corners of our region also belong to this category. In this case they play a major part besides grapes and willow as well as Clematis from the brushy hedges of the region. Manual work forms this simplicity to a symmetrical, rather conventional appearing sculpture, which reflects the castle's forms in a purely green spreading peacefulness.

Individuelle Ansichten

Neben der Emotion sind es vor allem die individuellen Ansichten und Absichten, die ein Gestalter zur Standortbestimmung im Beruf wie auch in seinem gesamten sozialen Umfeld benötigt. Oft auch als Abgrenzung zum üblichen Einerlei oder zu den von anderen artikulierten Gedanken. Nur so entsteht Persönlichkeit. Nur so entwickelt man als Gestalter ein einzigartiges, unverwechselbares Profil. Dazu gehört eben auch, dass man sich auf Konfrontationen wie auch auf ein enges Miteinander einlässt, um die Unterschiede und Gemeinsamkeiten herauszufinden. So wie in der Arbeit an diesem Buch, in der ich eine ganze Menge für mich und meine Standortbestimmung erfahren habe. Einiges Neue und viel Bestätigung für meine Prinzipien. Neu ist vor allem die Erkenntnis, wie Einfluss nehmend die direkte Auseinandersetzung mit anderen Gestaltern und ihren Auffassungen für mich als Floral Designer sein kann. Denn solche Situationen fordern zu noch weit präziserem Gestalten heraus, als wenn man nur für sich formuliert – und sei es noch so engagiert und gewissenhaft. Ehrgeiz in der Konkurrenzsituation und Euphorie in der Zusammenarbeit sind äußerst wichtige Antriebsmittel.

Individual Views

Besides his emotions, a designer needs above all his individual ideas and intentions for his choice of location professional-wise but also concerning his entire social environment. They also serve quite often as a way of distinguishing oneself from the usual monotony or from thoughts expressed by others. This is the only way to develop personality and the only way for a designer to create a unique, distinct profile. But this includes also accepting confrontations as well as a tight cooperation in order to find out the differences and similarities. Just like the making of this book during which I have learned a lot about myself and my choice of location; many new things, but also the confirmation of my own principles. It was mainly new for me to recognize that the direct confrontation with other designers and their views can have a strong influence on me. Indeed, such situations require a far more precise way of designing than working individually, even if it's done with the fullest engagement and consciousness. Ambition in a competitive situation and euphoria in cooperation are extremely important incentives.

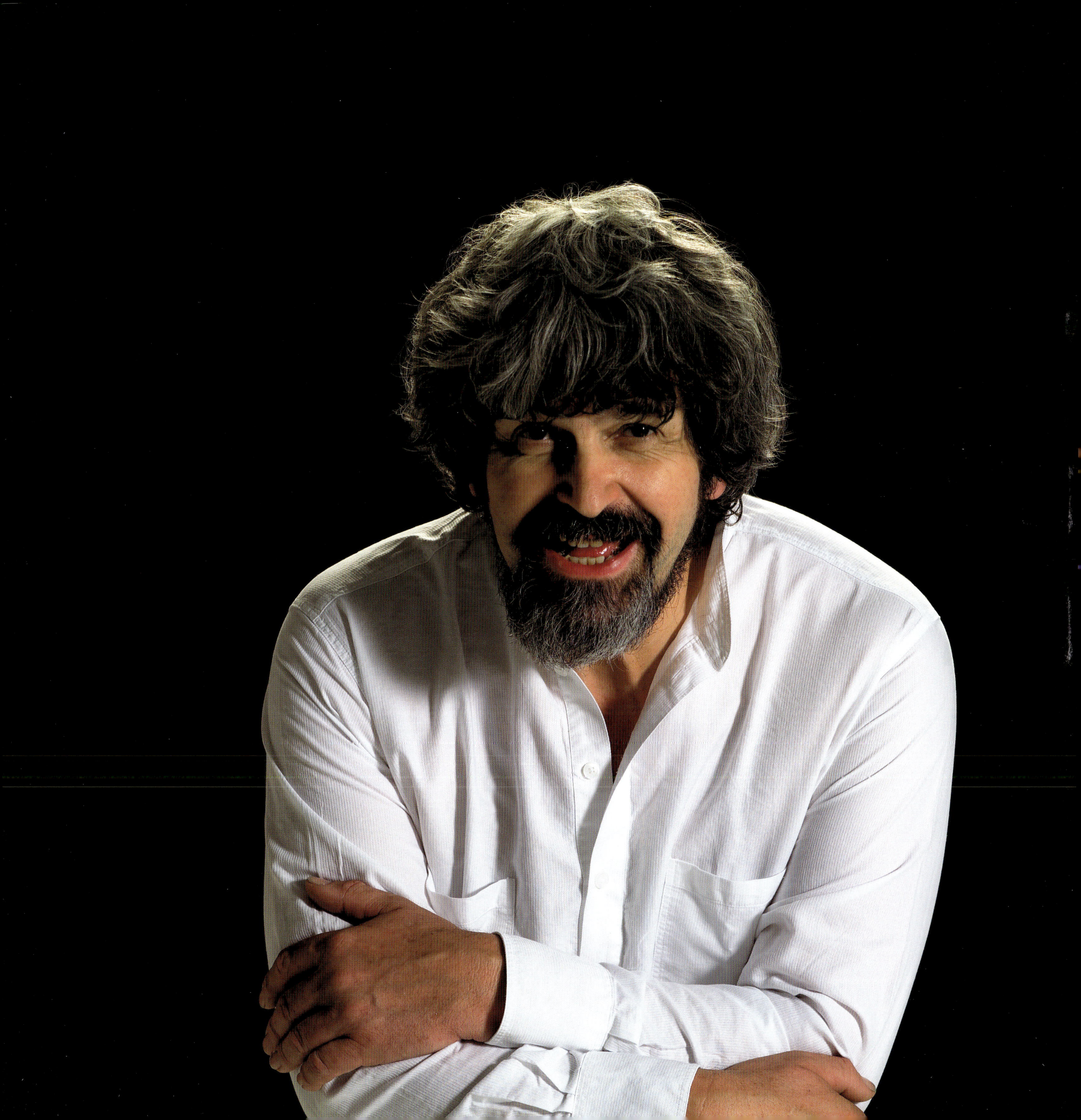

Elementar

In dieser konzentrierten Form macht sich die eher unspektakuläre Birke wirklich wichtig. Tausende von winzigen, dünnen Birkenästchen sind auf eine Kugel gesteckt und zwar ohne einen sogenannten Füllstoff als weitere Abdeckung für die Basis, die zudem mit viel Heißkleber zusammengehalten wird. Oben drin stehen die Frühlingsblumen in einem Extragefäß in Steckschaum. Die Kerzen sind 1,60 m hoch und wahre Giganten. Die dickeren Birkenäste scheinen die Kugel wie einen Lampion in der Luft zu halten. Das betont die handwerklich allein schon spektakuläre Birkenkugel noch zusätzlich und lässt Form und Material noch wichtiger erscheinen. Die Arbeit möchte ein Zeichen setzen auf der Suche nach neuen Ausdrucksformen von Floralkultur – als ausdrücklichen Gegensatz zu Vervielfältigung und Simplifizierung.

Basic *Importance*

The rather unspectacular birch appears really important in this concentrated form. Thousands of tiny, thin branchlets of a birch are stuck on a bowl, namely without a so-called filling as an additional coating of the foundation, which is hold together with a lot of hot glue. At the top spring flowers are placed in a special container in floral foam. With a height of 1.60 metres the candles look like real giants. The thicker branches seem to hold the bowl in the air like a lampion. This puts even more emphasis on the birch bowl, which as such is technically already impressive, and makes forms and materials appear even more important. This arrangement wants to impress while looking for new forms of expression of floral culture – as an explicit contrast to duplication and simplification.

LERSCH | Individuelle Ansichten *Individual Views*

Heiß geliebt

Licht und schwebende Kerzen, viel Weiß und klirrende Reinheit, Kühle und Transparenz erzeugen eine beeindruckende Schlichtheit. Auch die weißen Orchideen und die Wurzeln der Vanda wirken an der eisigen Geschichte mit und frieren das wenige kräftige Grün ein. Ich mag den jungen eiskalten Februarmorgen, an dem beim ersten Sonnenstrahl die gefrorenen Flechten, das mit Reif überzogene Grün langsam aus ihrer Starre erwachen und beginnen zu leben. Vitalität auf ihrer schwächsten Stufe. Ich liebe auch diese Umkehrungen des Denkens, die aus heiß kalt und aus kalt heiß machen. So spottet mein spanischer Freund Kike zum Beispiel freundschaftlich: „Gregorio sagt: Gris es vida – Grau ist Leben." Was aber ist Grün, ohne Grau zu kennen? Eine solche Erkenntnis ist mir ungeheuer wichtig und verhilft mir im Gestaltungsprozess zu neuen Inspirationen. Früher hätte ich hier auch viel mehr Grün als Füllung gebraucht. Die Sucht nach Formen hat das Beiwerk inzwischen aber deutlich zurückgedrängt. Es herrscht viel mehr der kühle freie Raum zwischen den Pflanzenteilen.

Precious Treasures

Light and floating candles, a lot of white and pureness, coolness and transparency create an impressive chasteness. The white orchids and the Vanda roots contribute to this frosty history by freezing the few strong green. I like the young ice-cold February morning with its first sunrays slowly waking up the frozen lichens and the green covered with frost and inciting them to revive. This displays vitality at its lowest level. I also like this converse of thinking, like from hot to cold and vice versa. Thus my Spanish friend Kike is flouting amicably: "Gregorio says: Gris es vida – grey is life". But what is green then without knowing grey? Such a realization is extremely important for me and helps me finding new inspirations in the course of designing. Earlier I would have needed even here more green for the filling. The addiction for forms has in the meanwhile explicitly pushed back the accessories. Moreover, the cool, free space between the parts of the plants is dominating.

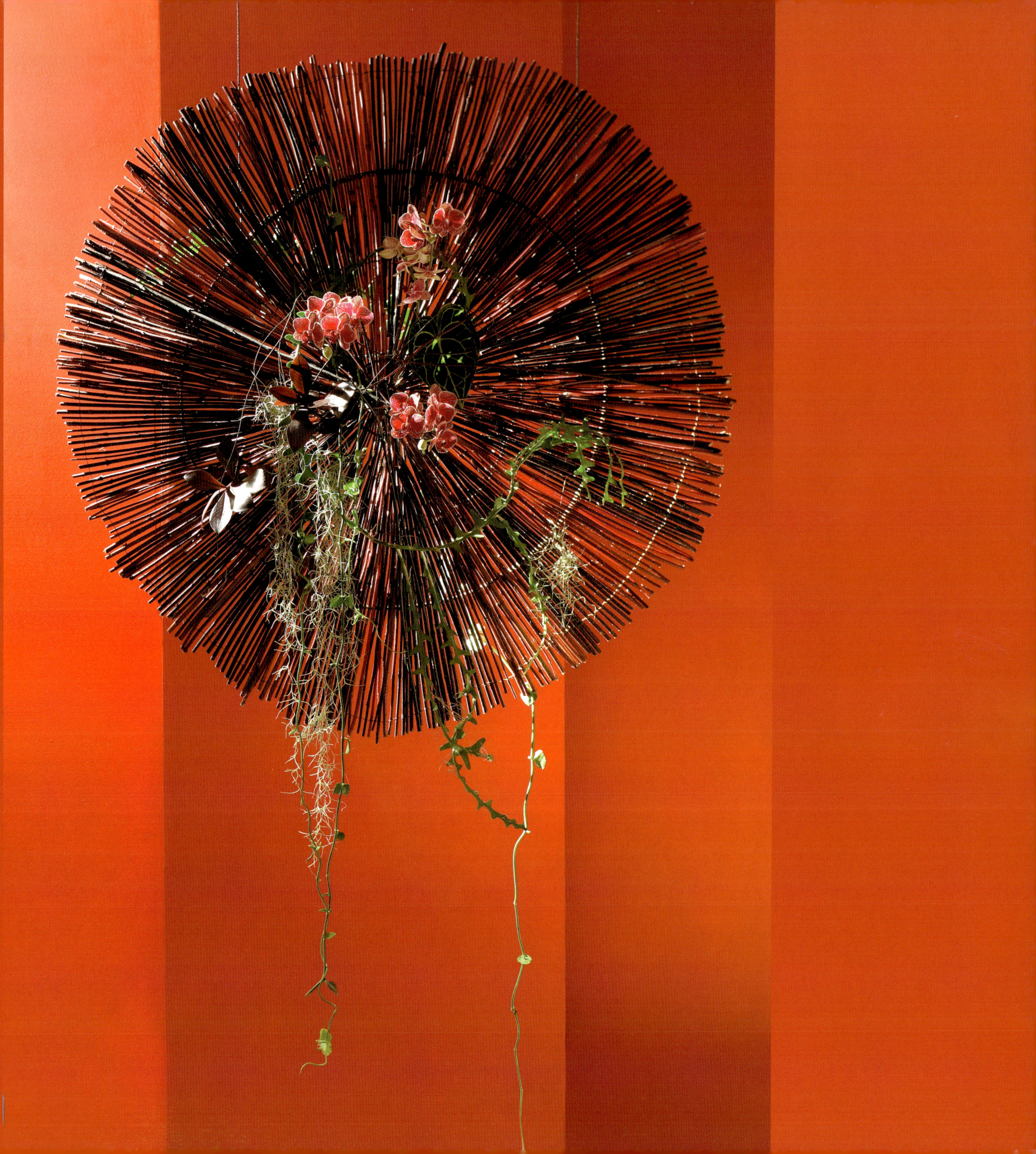

Neu entdeckt

Hier wird die radiale Gestaltung extrem überhöht, indem sich Cornus alba sibirica in zwei verschiedenen Farben zu einer Scheibe formt, während edle andere Formen überschneidend dagegen halten. So ergänzen sich der geometrische Blickpunkt, in dem sich die Linien zusammenfinden, und der ästhetische Blickpunkt, in dem sich die Farben und Formen der Blüten konzentrieren. Überraschend konnte ich dabei an mir eine völlig neue Begeisterung für das radiale Gestalten feststellen, nachdem ich in den letzten Jahren das offensichtliche Stecken auf einen Punkt so weit wie möglich vermieden hatte. Aber Übertreibung schafft Aufmerksamkeit und erreicht somit eine deutliche Trennung von Gewohntem. Eine neue Erfahrung für mich und Inspiration zu weiteren Versuchen mit einfachen und zunächst einmal allzu banalen Formen.

New Discoveries

The radial design is extremely heightened up here: The Cornus alba sibirica in two different colours is formed to a single disc while other crossed noble forms reveal the contrast. In this manner the geometric focal point – where the lines are combined – supplements the aesthetic focal point in which the blossoms' colours and forms are concentrated. To my own surprise, I could discover my completely new enthusiasm for radial designs after having avoided as far as possible obvious arrangements focused on one point during the last years. But exaggeration creates attention and thus a precise separation from the usual. This is a new experience and inspiration for me to try simple and firstly the most trivial forms.

War es früher hauptsächlich Keramik mit ihrer häufig doch sehr dominanten individuellen Ausstrahlung, in denen ich solche vegetativ anmutenden Arbeiten präsentiert habe, so gefällt es mir heute weit eher, sie sehr transparent zu zeigen. Zur Pflanze gehört die Wurzel. Sie repräsentiert Lebendigkeit. Und das darf und sollte man auch vermitteln. So avanciert der Glaskasten zur Vitrine, die Step by Step den graduellen Übergang von der Replik der Natur bis hin zu freieren Interpretationen dokumentiert. Die sich im Laufe der Zeit verändernden Sehweisen des Gestalters finden so in sich wandelnden Bildern ihren Niederschlag: verschiedene, für den Gestalter unerlässliche Studien in einem meterlangen gläsernen Dokument.

Natural Growth

Whereas earlier I used to present such vegetative appearing arrangements mainly with the help of ceramics with its dominating individual appearance, today I rather prefer to present it more transparently. Roots belong to a plant. They represent vitality. And this may and should be shown. Thus, the glass case advances to the showcase, which proves step by step the gradual transformation from replica to nature up to more flexible interpretations. The various sights of the designer changing in the course of time find their echo through changing images: different studies, irreplaceable for a designer, in a glassy document with a length of one metre.

Natürlich gewachsen

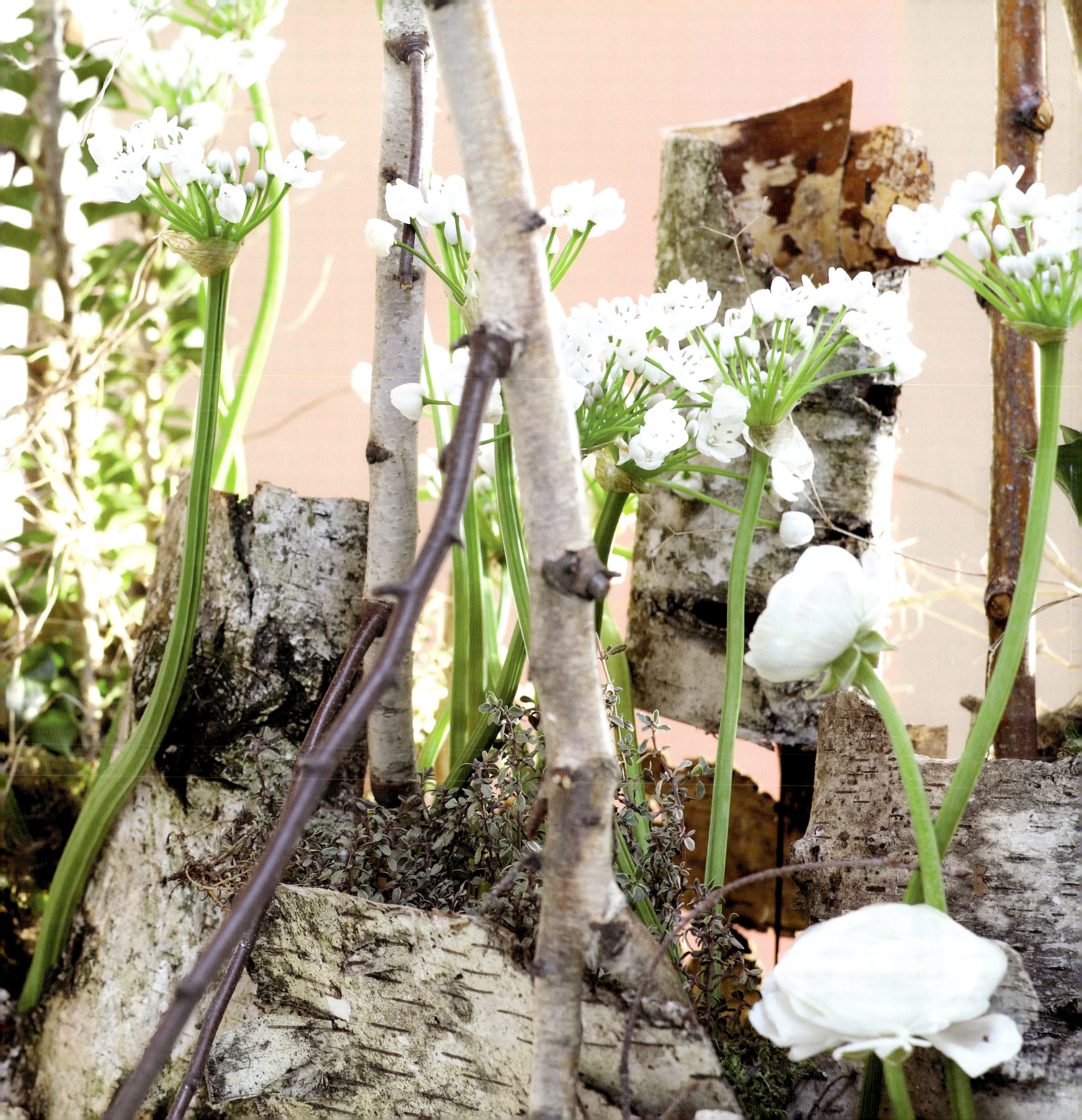

LERSCH | Individuelle Ansichten *Individual Views*

96 | 97

Architektonisch konstruiert

Man könnte es als ein „starkes Stück" bezeichnen. Allein von seiner Größe her – nämlich 2,40 m hoch. Wie viele interessante Gebäude auf der Welt lebt dieses dramatische Werkstück von einer gut durchdachten Statik. Während das starke Metallgefäß mit Steinen beschwert ist, trägt im Inneren der dynamischen Form ein Eisenstabgerippe das federleichte, gebleichte Mitsumata-Holz. Sandbedeckte Röhrchen ducken sich diskret in die Kanülen der Struktur, um Callablüten und Alocasienblätter zu halten und zu erhalten. Wie in der Architektur gilt es auch für den Floral Designer die Schwere und Kompliziertheit der inneren Konstruktion völlig vergessen zu machen, um pure Eleganz und Leichtigkeit zu erzielen.

Architectural Constructions

With a height of namely 2.40 metres, it could be considered as a "huge construction". How many interesting buildings in the world does this dramatic arrangement of a profound static live in? While the strong metal container is burdened with stones, a framework of rods carries the feathery, bleached Mitsumata-wood in the interior part of the dynamic form. Tubes covered with sand are discretely hidden inside the needles of the structure in order to hold and conserve Calla blossoms and Alocasia leaves. Similar to an architect, a floral designer must ensure that all weight and complicatedness of the interior construction disappear completely in order to achieve pure elegance and lightness.

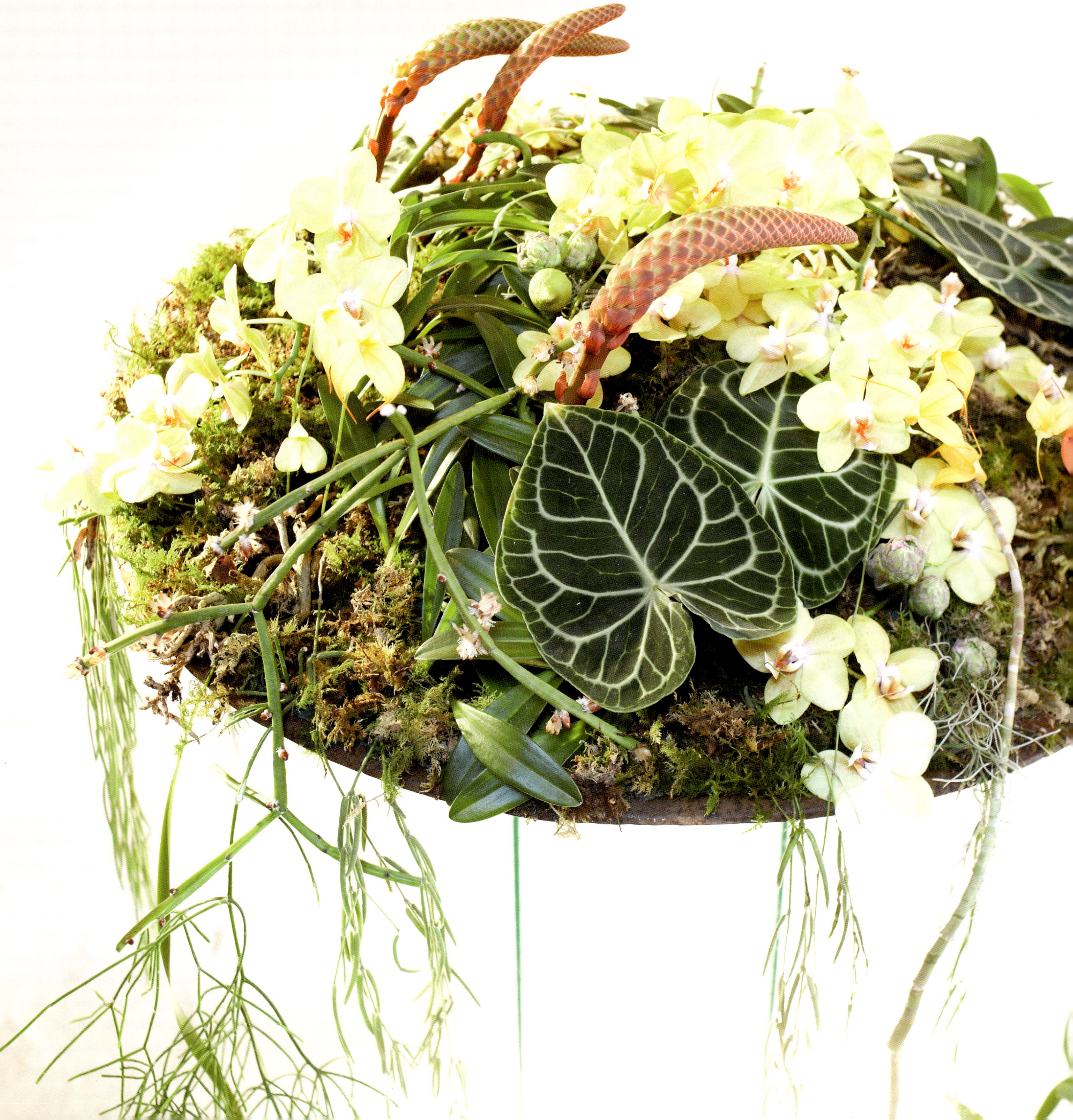

Themen · Trends · Tendenzen

Diese drei Worte haben mit ihren Folgen und Folgerungen die Kommunikation und Arbeit von Floristen mehr als eine Dekade lang beherrscht. Mit dem Ziel, die bestmögliche Vorhersage für eine Wunschökonomie zu tätigen. Heute sind viele Märkte gesättigt. An die Stelle von Produkten treten Kennen und Wissen, Erfahren und Erleben. Nach den letzten Zuckungen des goldenen Konsumrausches wird sich auf der Suche nach neuen Inhalten ein Nährboden für mehr Kultur ergeben. Denn künftig wird es zu wenig ökonomische Substanz geben, um die immer mehr zur Verfügung stehende Zeit wie bisher mit Kauftiraden füllen zu können. Blumen und Pflanzen Kennen, Sammeln, Hegen, Pflegen, Erleben wird zu einem wichtigen Freizeitfaktor der Zukunft. Konkreter Mainstream – nicht Trend.

Topics · Trends · Tendencies

These three words have been dominating the communication and work of florists over more than a decade with their consequences and conclusions. The target was to make the best possible prognosis for a dream economy. Today, many markets are saturated. Products replace know-how and experiences. After the last phase of golden consumerism a medium for more culture will be created while searching for new contents. In the future there will be less economic options in order to fill the time – which is becoming more and more available – with extensive shopping tours. Knowing, collecting, nourishing, cultivating and experiencing flowers and plants is becoming an important factor of leisure for the future. This is concrete mainstream – not a trend.

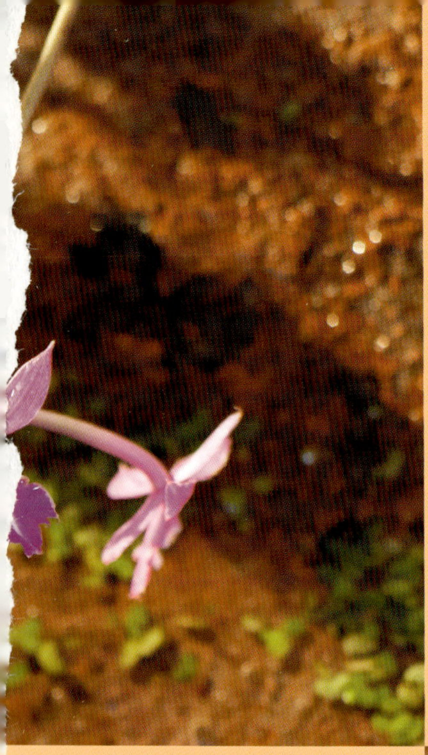
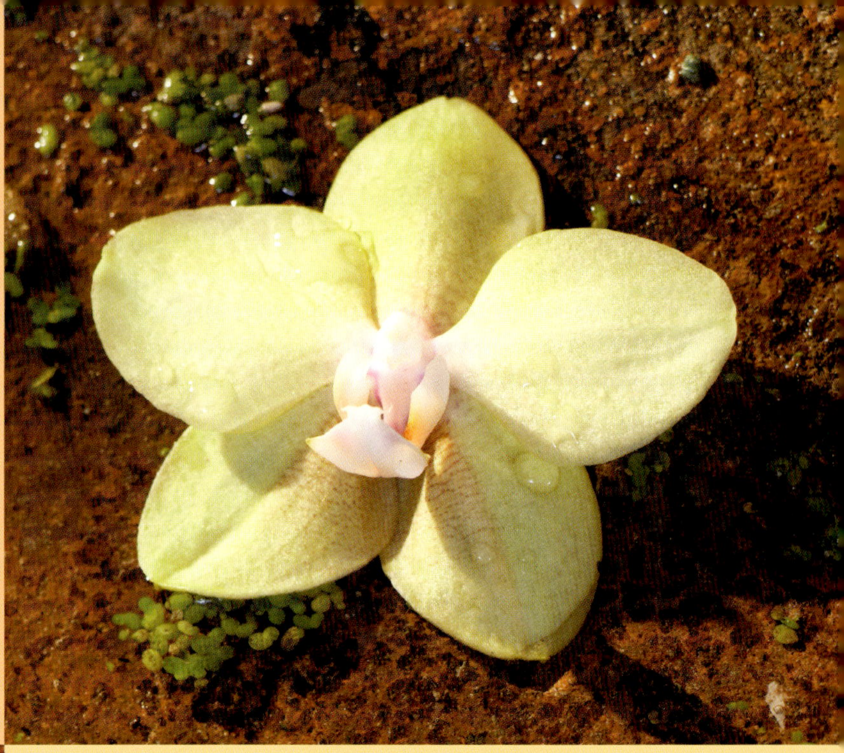
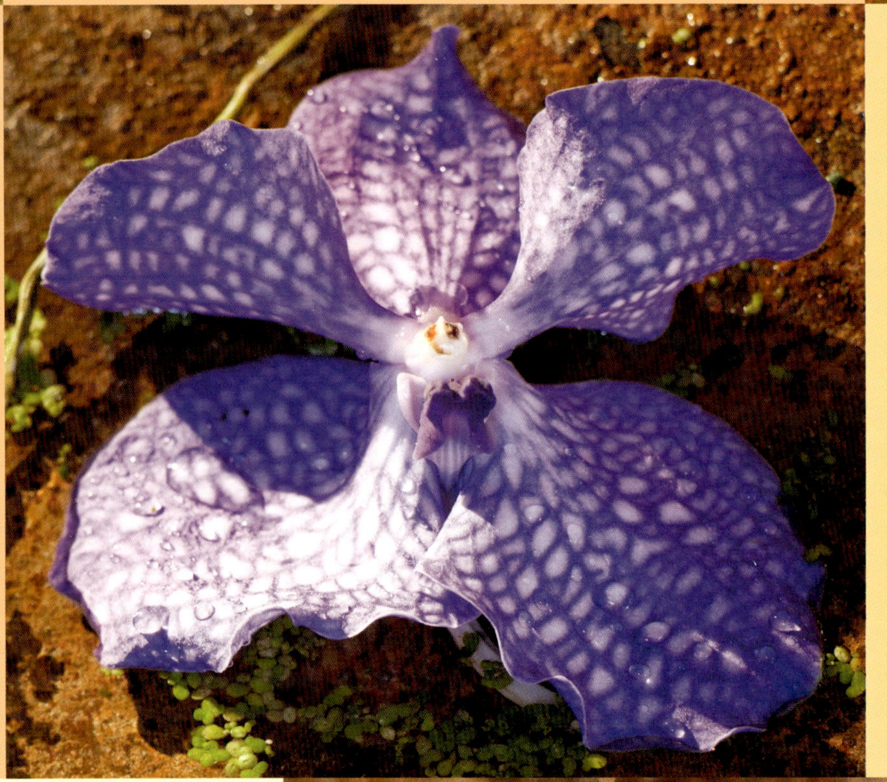
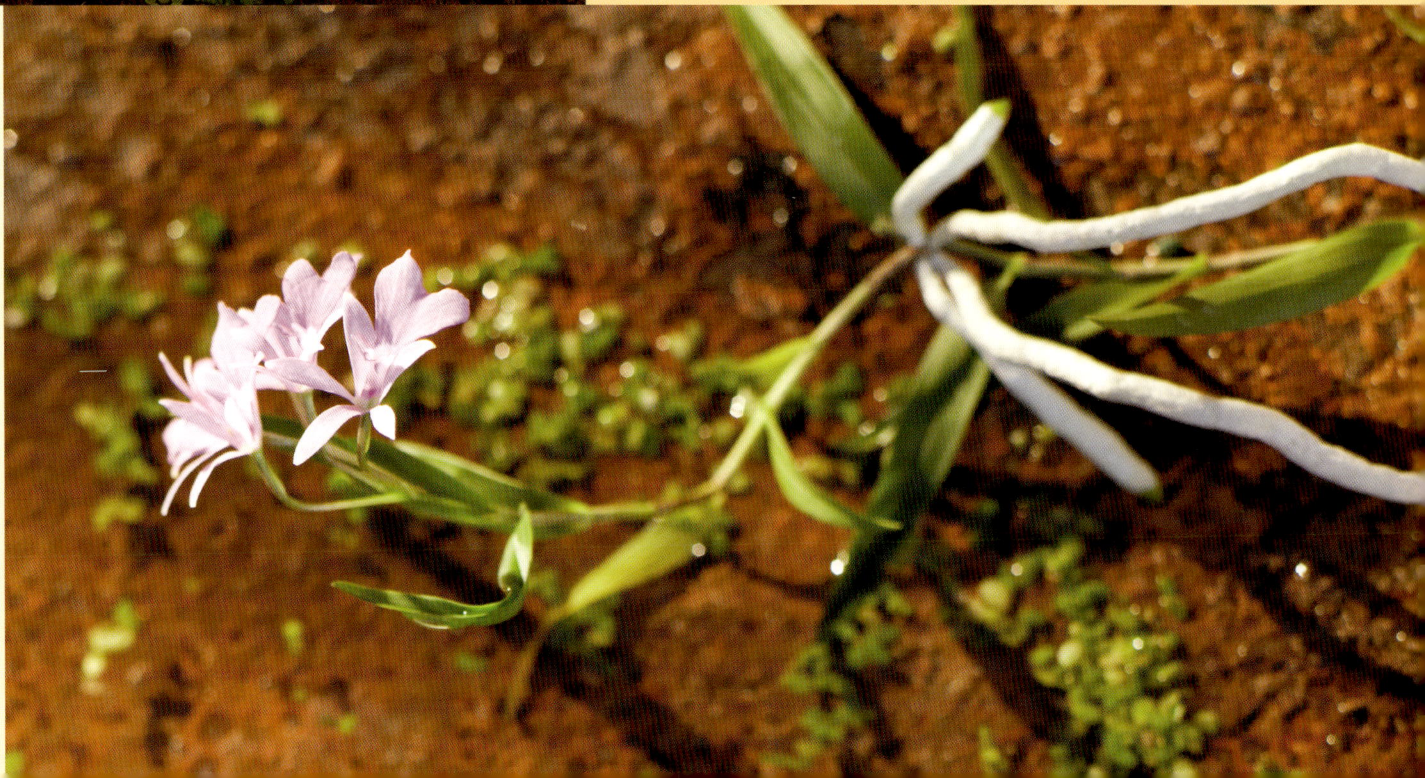

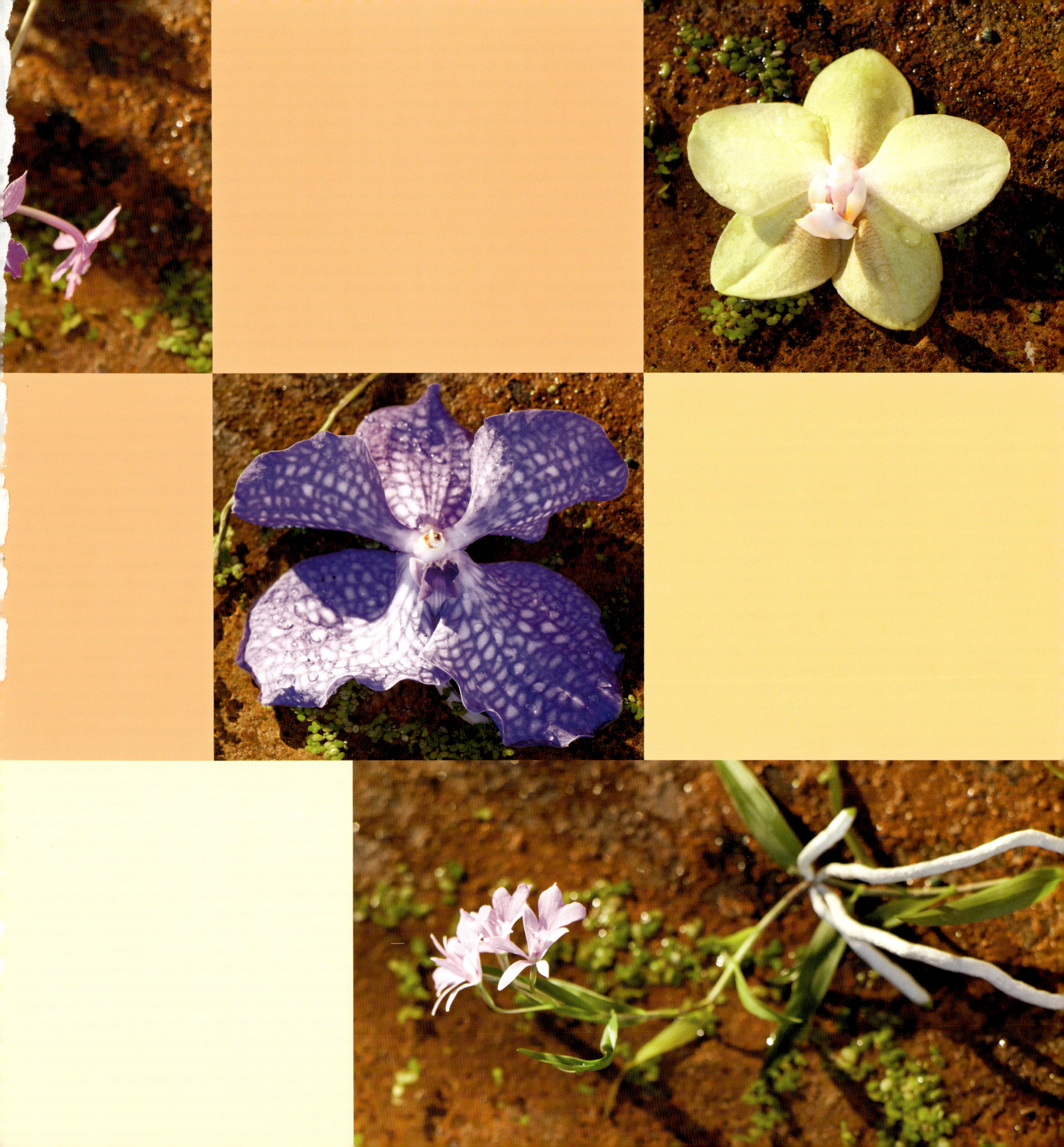

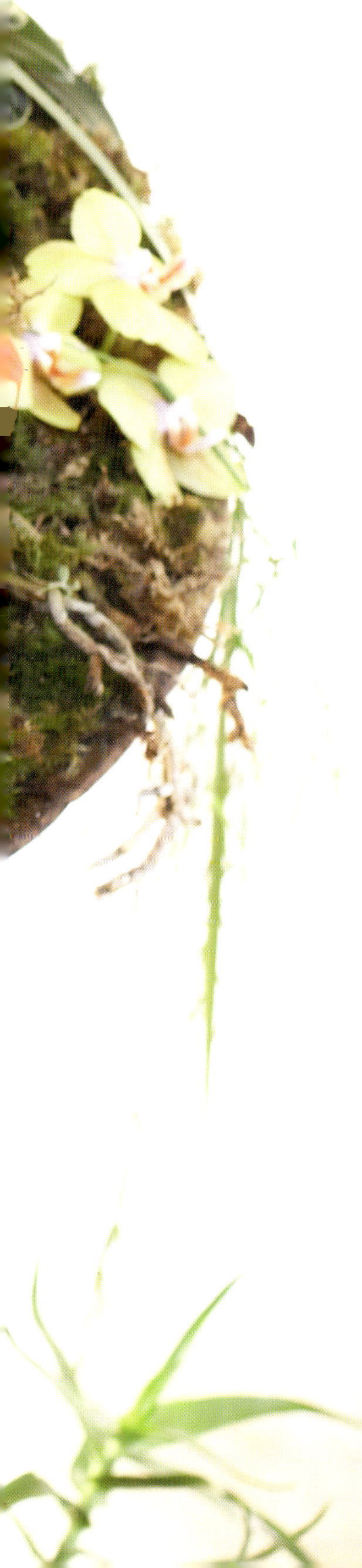

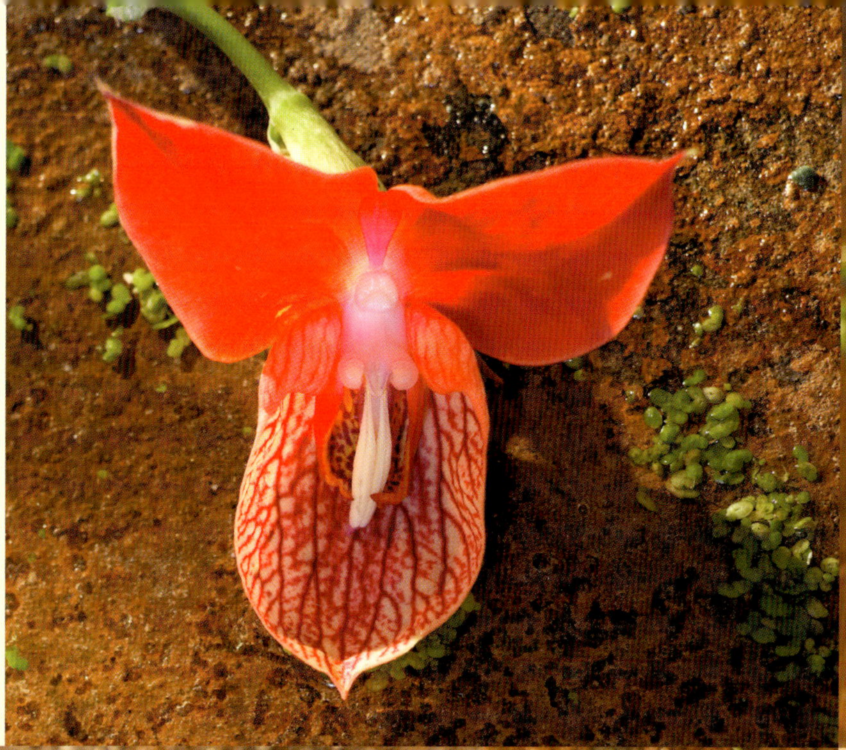

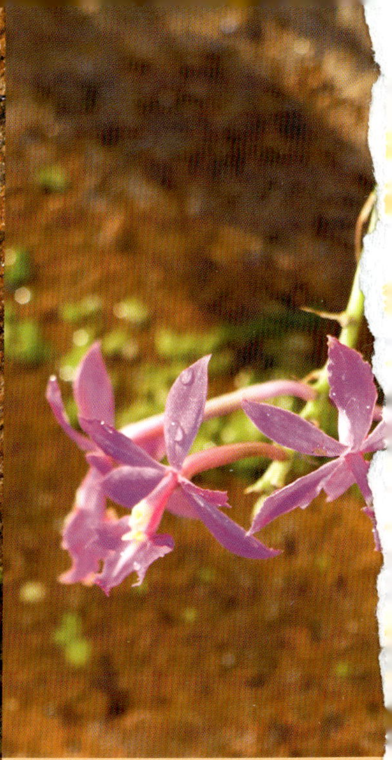

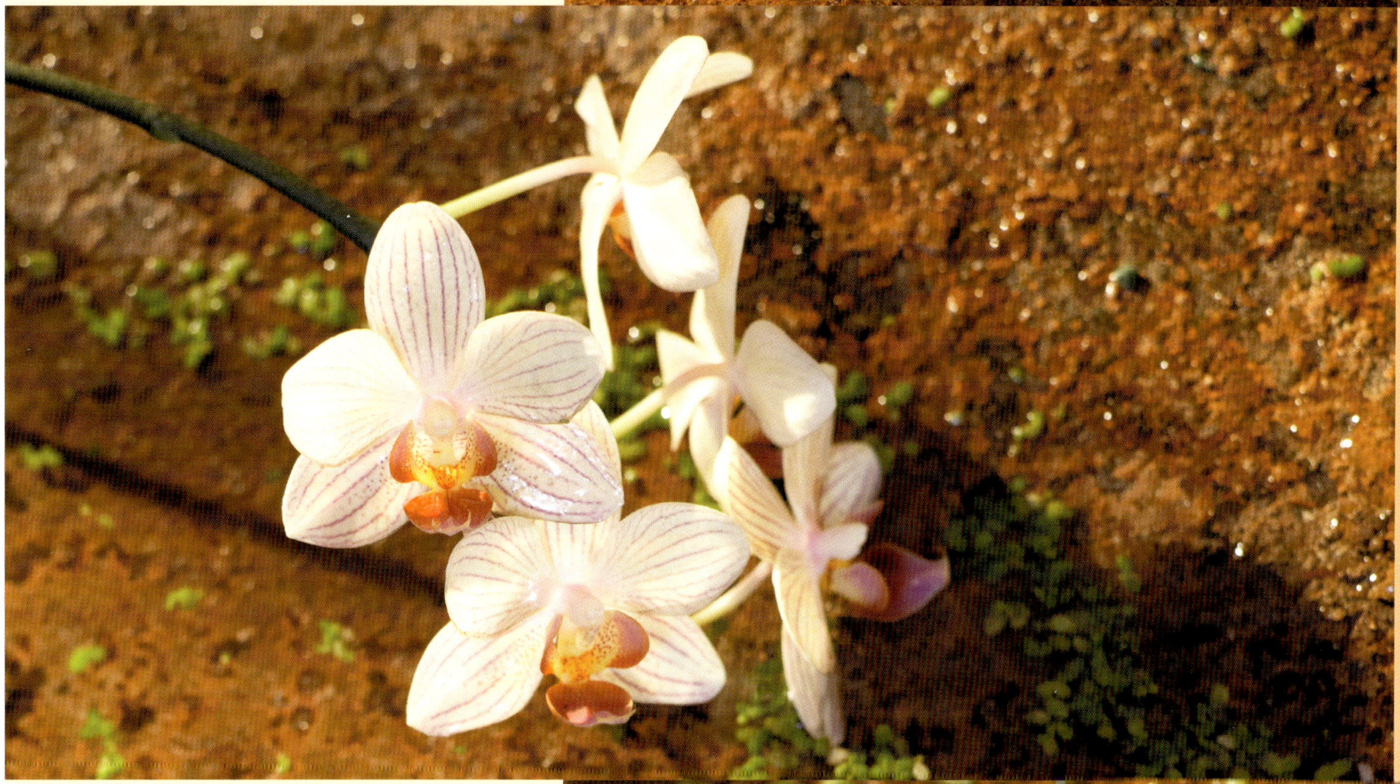

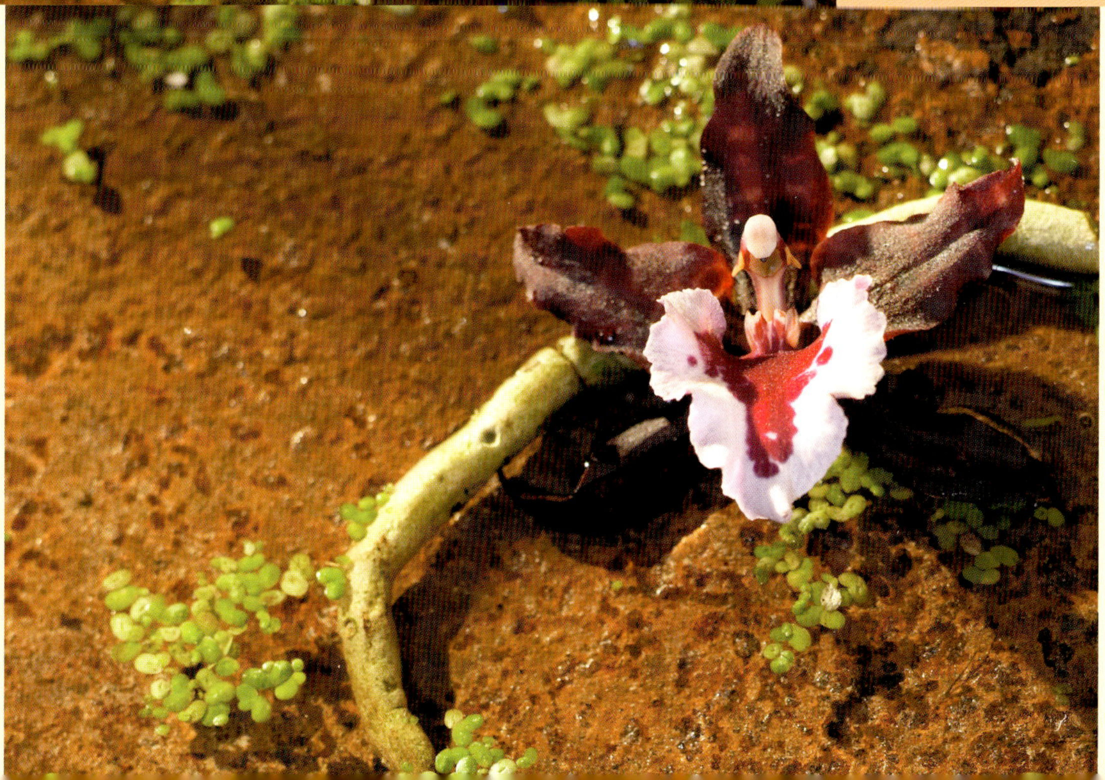

Fire

Feuer

Water
Wasser

Ein hoch aktuelles Thema, das vor allem viele Gestalter heutzutage in einer Epoche des Zuviel von allem auf der Suche nach dem Elementaren, Grundsätzlichen, dem Ursprünglichen beschäftigt. Wo finden sich die wahren Werte für ein lebenswertes Umfeld – ohne die letztendlich nutzlosen kommerziellen Ersatzhandlungen? Zählt die enge Freundschaft zu Blumen und Pflanzen nicht zu den elementaren Bedürfnissen des Menschen? Für mich eine unbestreitbare Tatsache, der ich meine ganze Kraft widme. Sind es nicht gerade Blumen und Pflanzen, die uns die Lebenselexiere Erde, Wasser und Luft sowie Licht und Wärme in all ihren unzähligen, phantastischen Ausformungen nahe bringen? Ist es nicht gerade diese Nähe, die uns mehr und mehr abhanden gekommen ist und die wir wieder mehr pflegen müssen? So repräsentieren hier die Masdevallia, Bromelien & Co aus der riesigen Familie der Orchideen mit ihren 26.000 Arten die ganze Bandbreite der Evolution zwischen Erde und Luft – auf der Basis von Wasser und Feuer. Abgesehen davon, dass fast das halbe Studio bei dieser Arbeit in Flammen stand, hat mich diese Arbeit sehr kleinmütig und noch einmal ein wenig mehr nachdenklich gemacht.

Earth
Erde

An extremely up to date topic, which concerns especially today many designers in a time of overall abundance while searching for elementary, basically and originally things. Where are the true values of an environment worth living – without finally being dependant on useless commercial alternative activities? Is a close friendship with flowers and plants not considered to be one of the most elementary needs of men? Personally I think that this is an undisputable fact to which I dedicate my entire energy. Isn't it precisely the flowers and plants which make the elixirs such as the earth, water and air as well as light and warmth accessible for us in all their indefinite, fantastic implementation? And isn't it exactly this proximity, which we have gradually lost und have to take more care of? In this context, the Masdevallia, Bromeliads and the like from the huge family of orchids with its 26000 species are representing here the whole range of evolution between earth and air – on the basis of water and fire. Besides the fact, that half of the studio was aflamed while realizing this arrangement, this work made me really half-hearted and a bit more contemplative.

Air
Luft

Natur & Technik

LERSCH | Individuelle Ansichten *Individual Views*

Stahl und Gewachsenes – eine Synthese, die eine hervorragende Balance schafft. Keine harmoniesüchtige, rührselige Landhaussuppe, keine Anbiederung sondern bereitwillige Übernahme von Formen, wie sie das Umfeld anbietet. Das Chaos der Stiele ist dabei der Ausdruck natürlicher Spontaneität des Lebendigen. Spannende Signale von Pflanzen, die in einem ansonsten statisch durchorganisierten, technischen Umfeld auf sich aufmerksam machen. Ich mag eigentlich Autos wenig bis gar nicht. Doch diese kühle Technikwelt aus Stahl, Chrom, Alu, Zink und Beton schafft die deutliche Polarität zum Vitalen, wie ich sie liebe. Als Hintergrund für das, was lebt.

Nature & Technology

Steel and plants – a synthesis which creates perfect balance without searching for exaggerating harmony, conventions or ingratiation. On the contrary, it willingly adopts forms, which the environment is offering. The chaotic stems reveal natural spontaneity of the living. This are exciting signals of plants, which incite attention in a usually static, well organized technical environment. Honestly, I don't like cars very much. However, this cool technical world of steel, chrome, aluminium, zinc and concrete provides – as a background for the living elements – the clear polarity to the vital, just the way I love it.

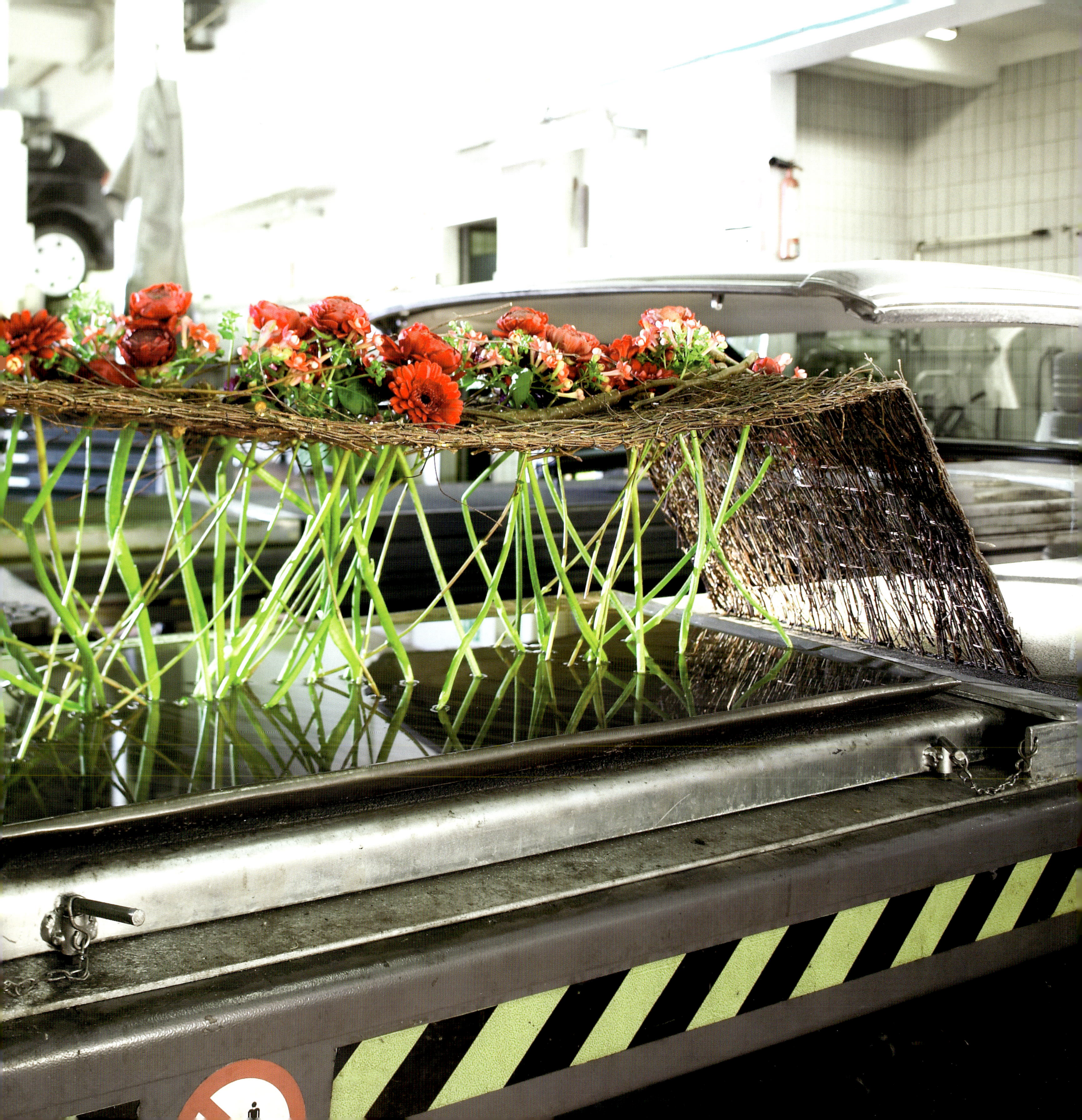

Der älteste uns überlieferte, kulturell motivierte Umgang mit der Pflanze ist die Grabbeigabe. Zum ersten Mal wird die Pflanze nicht zur Befriedigung der täglichen Bedürfnisse genutzt, sondern erfährt eine emotionale Bedeutung und wird als Ausdruck von Gefühlen verwendet. Die grenzenlose Stille und Traurigkeit, die uns in Momenten des Ablebens geliebter und geachteter Menschen umfängt, versuchen wir mit Licht und Weiß ein wenig zu erhellen. Ein klein wenig davon genügt schon als Lichtblick für den so wichtigen Trost und wirkt stärker als Berge von Farbe. Hier durchdringen zarte winterliche Blüten wie Allium neapolitanum, Ranunculus caucasicus und Jasminium nudiflorum das Gitterwerk aus winzigen Birkenholzstückchen, die mit Holzleim auf ein gebogenes Bronzenetz aufgeklebt sind. Das Arrangement mit seinen sehr modernen Kandelabern und extrem schlichten Kerzen möchte zeigen, dass die Symbolik der Trauer nicht unbedingt an altbackene Bilder und tradierte Klischees gebunden ist, sondern durchaus zeitgemäße Formen entwickeln kann.

Life & Death

The most ancient, traditional and culturally motivating utilization of plants is the burial object. For the first time, the plant is not used to satisfy daily needs, but gains an emotional importance utilized as a form of expressing emotions. We are trying to brighten up a bit with lights and white the indefinite atmosphere of silence and sadness, which is weighing on us in a moment of death of a beloved and respected person. Just a little bit of this is sufficient for a ray of hope for the comfort, which is so important. Its effect is much stronger than all the colours in the world could provide. In this arrangement delicate wintry blossoms, like Allium neapolitanum, Ranunculus caucasicus and Jasminium nudflorum are penetrating the network of tiny birch wood particles, which are stuck on a bronze grid with wooden glue. This arrangement with its modern candelabras and extremely decent candles wants to show that the symbolism of sympathy is not necessarily bound to dowdy images and traditional clichés but may absolutely develop also contemporary forms.

Leben
& Sterben

Ordnung kontra

Aus den gleichen filigranen Zweiglein zwei völlig gegensätzliche Anmutungen zu erzielen, war das Ziel. Zum einen entsteht durch Verwickeln ein chaotisches, sehr transparentes Netzwerk, zum anderen, spiralförmig auf einer Kugel geordnet, eine kompakte, geschlossene Form. Inspiration durch zwei kontrastierende Begriffe. Sie provozieren verschiedene Muster oder Gliederungen in einer einzigen Gestaltungsarbeit. Ein interessanter Ansatz für die Floristik, hierüber genauer nachzudenken. Denn er bietet eine weitere interessante Quelle für Inspirationen.

Chaos

Order versus *Chaos*

The aim was to create two completely contrasting impressions out of the similar filigree sprigs. Entangling creates on the one hand a chaotic, very transparent network on the other hand, a compact, cohesive form, spirally arranged on a bowl. Inspirations provided by two contrasting terms. They provoke different patterns and structures in just one single arrangement. This is a really interesting approach in floral design which should be considered more intensively as it offers an additional interesting source of inspirations.

Mengen schwarzer Cornusstäbe lassen durch ihre parallele Schrägneigung ein starkes, dynamisches Muster entstehen. Einfach in der Form, doch stark in der gemeinsamen Aussage. Davor tanzen die Individualisten: Orchideen, Sukkulenten, Bromelie und Araceaen. Faszinierende Exotik kontra heimatlichem Outdoorumfeld, bei dem das Einfache aber durchaus seinen Wert gegenüber dem für uns Edlen darzustellen weiß. Auf der einen Seite bescheidene Zurückhaltung, weil man sich auf die Stärke des gemeinsamen Auftritts verlässt – auf der anderen Seite Ego um jeden Preis. Die einen haben's, die anderen müssen sich ihren Platz erst hart erkämpfen.

Mono versus Mass

Plenty of black Cornus sticks provide a strong, dynamic pattern through their parallel angular inclination. Their shape is quite simple, but the common message it reveals more impressive. In front of this composition individualists enjoy their appearance: orchids, succulents, Bromeliads and Araceae – a fascinating exotic versus homelike outdoor surroundings in which the simple is absolutely competing with the elements, so noble in our eyes. On the one hand, this signifies modest retention relying on the common appearance – on the other hand we see ambition at all costs. Some already have it, while others have to struggle hardly to gain their place.

Mono
kontra Masse

Gregor Lersch

Professionelle Leidenschaft *Professional Passion*

8 | 9   Geheimnisvolle Wurzeln *Mysterious Roots*
Anthurium hookeri, Heliconia, Saccharum arundinaceum, Synadenium grantii, Tillandsia dyeriana, Vanda `Rothschildiana`

10 | 11   Erstaunliche Triebe *Astonishing Shoots*
Asparagus scandens var. deflexus, Betula pendula, Ceropegia sandersonii, Cucurbita, Hedera erecta

12 | 13   Dynamische Stiele *Dynamic Stems*
Cornus alba `Sibirica`, Disa uniflora, Epidendrum varicosum, Vanda `Rothschildiana`, Xanthorrhoea australis, Zantedeschia rehmannii

14 | 15   Aufregende Blätter *Exciting Leaves*
Agave americana, Anthurium hookeri, Crassula falcata, Kalanchoe tubiflora, Sansevieria kirkii, Testudinaria elephantipes

16 | 17   Faszinierende Blüten *Fascinating Blossoms*
Betula pendula, Fallopia japonica `Toscana`, Hippeastrum Cultivar, Nerine bowdenii

Meisterliches Handwerk *Master Trade*

20 | 21   Gebündelt zu starken Kompetenzen *Bundled to strong Competences*
Epidendrum radiatum, Epidendrum varicosum, Vanda `Rothschildiana`

22 | 23   Geknotet zu festen Verbindungen *Knotted to firm Combinations*
Ceropegia sandersonii, Cucurbita, Salix viminalis, Zantedeschia aethiopica

24 | 25   Geflochten zu erfolgreichen Synergien *Braided to successful Synergies*
Betula pendula, Odontoglossum Cultivar, Xanthorrhoea australis

26 | 27   Gewoben zu effizienten Netzwerken *Woven into efficient Networks*
Ceropegia sandersonii, Cocos nucifera, Odontoglossum, Phalaenopsis miriabilis, Rhipsalis robusta, Vanda `Rothschildiana`, Xanthorrhoea australis

28 | 29   Geschichtet zu neuen Dimensionen *Coated to new Dimensions*
Betula humilis, Euphorbia spinosa, Ludisia discolor, Phalaenopsis Cultivar, Vanda `Rothschildiana`, Xanthorrhoea australis

30 | 31   Gereiht zu überraschenden Aufstellungen *Ranked to astonishing Settings of Rows*
Hippeastrum `Lemon Lime`

Gestalterische Bekenntnisse *Creative Confessions*

34 | 35   Symmetrische Ruhe *Bundled to a solid Basis*
Dianthus caryophyllus, Helleborus niger, Pinus thunbergii

36 | 37   Asymmetrische Spannung *Asymmetric Tension*
Acer negundo, Aloe, Asparagus falcatus, Citrus sinensis, Epidendrum Cultivar, Heliconia caribaea, Hippeastrum Cultivar, Strelitzia reginae, Synadenium grantii

38 | 39   Dekorative Ansichten *Decorative Views*
Betula pendula, Euphorbia spinosa, Hippeastrum vittatum, Hypericum, Ornithogalum arabicum, Papaver nudicaule, Ranunculus asiaticus, Tulipa Cultivar

40 | 41   Vegetative Erkenntnisse *Vegetative Insights*
Euphorbia spinosa, Hedera helix, Hippeastrum, Hippeastrum `Toscana`, Thymus vulgaris, Tulipa Cultivar

42 | 43   Formal-lineare Fantasien *Formally linear Fancies*
Alocasia macrorrhiza, Aloe ciliaris, Anthurium andraeanum, Ensete ventricosum, Euphorbia mammilaris `Cristata`, Heliconia mariae, Hoya linearis, Nicolaia elatior, Saccharina arundinarium, Zygocactus

44 | 45   Einsichtige Strukturen *Insightful Structures*
Oncidium microchilum, Paphiopedilum Cultivar, Phalaenopsis Cultivar, Tetraria terminalis

46 | 47   Gewagte Konstruktionen *Risky Constructions*
Phalaenopsis `Lissabon`, Rhipsalis capilliformis, Strongylodon, Tetraria terminalis

48 | 49   Beeindruckende Texturen *Impressive Textures*
Ceropegia linearis subsp. woodii, Masdevallia infracta, Tetraria terminalis

50 | 51   Innovative Objekte *Innovative Objects*
Chamaerops humilis, Cotyledon, Crassulaceae, Disa uniflora

52 | 53   Monochrome Raffinesse *Monochromatic Finesse*
Betula pendula, Ceropegia, Zantedeschia rehmannii

54 | 55   Farbige Lust *Colourful Delight*
Campanula medium, Celosia argentea var. cristata, Delphinium cultorum, Gerbera jamesonii, Hypericum, Lavandula latifolia, Limonium suworowii, Picea abies, Rosa Cultivar, Sandersonia aurantiaca, Tanacetum parthenium, Veronica officinalis

56 | 57   Bunte Leidenschaft *Coloured Passion*
Corylus avellana, Grevillea robusta, Hedera helix, Olea europaea, Punica granatum, Ranunculus asiaticus, Tulipa `Cairo`, Viburnum opulus `Sterile`, Zantedeschia rehmannii

Ganz persönliche Gefühle *Very private Emotions*

60 | 61   Frühlingshaft-verspielt *Spring-like Plays*
Camellia japonica, Citrus limon, Crassula obliqua, Olea europaea, Papaver nudicaule

62 | 63   Sommerlich-berauschend *Summer-like Exhilaration*
Cornus kousa, Fragaria ananassa, Paeonia lactiflora

64 | 65   Herbstlich überschwänglich *Autumn-like Exuberance*
Cattleya Cultivar, Cucumis, Hypericum, Mahonia japonica, Punica granatum, Raphia, Strongylodon

66 | 67   Winterlich-zart *Winter-like Delicateness*
Carlina acaulis, Lunaria annua, Miscanthus sacchariflorus, Pinus strobus, Senecio cacaliaster, Usnea filipendulina

68 | 69   Heillos romantisch *Unlimited Romanticism*
Euphorbia spinosa, Hedera helix, Ranunculus asiaticus, Viburnum opulus `Sterile`

70 | 71   Erregend sinnlich *Sensual Excitements*
Rosa `Isa`, Vaccinium corymbosum, Zantedeschia `Christal Blanche`

72 | 73   Inspirierend sexy *Sexy Inspirations*
Anthurium `Red Magic`, Ensete ventricosum, Euphorbia mammilaris `Cristata`, Heliconia `Sexy Pink`, Saccharum arundinaceum, Salix purpurea `Gracilis`, Tetraria terminalis

74 | 75   Maßlos opulent *Excessive Abundance*
Anthurium andraeanum, Citrus, Crocosmia Cultivar, Euphorbia spinosa, Gerbera jamesonii, Hedera helix, Lycopersicon esculentum, Papaver nudicaule, Punica granatum, Rosa Cultivar, Vitis vinifera, Zantedeschia rehmannii

76 | 77   Minimalistisch reduziert *Minimalist Reductions*
Hoya linearis, Oncidium bicallosum, Phalaenopsis Cultivar, Tetraria terminalis

78 | 79   Heimat – Wein und nochmals Wein *Homeland – Wine and Wine again*
Heuchera Cultivar, Vitis vinifera

80 | 81   Heimat – Efeu und Wein *Ivy and Wine*
Hedera helix, Rubus flagellaris, Vitis vinifera

82 | 83   Heimat – Weide und Wein *Homeland – Willow and Wine*
Gypsophila repens 'Rosea', Hedera helix, Lilium longiflorum, Paeonia lactiflora, Rosa Cultivar, Vitis vinifera

84 | 85   Heimat – Gras und Moos und Wein *Homeland – Grass and Moss and Wine*
Alchemilla mollis, Carex, Rosa Cultivar, Salix, Vitis vinifera

Individuelle Ansichten *Individual Views*

88 | 89   Elementar wichtig *Basic Importance*
Ammi majus, Asparagus scandens var. deflexus, Betula pendula, Hedera helix, Tulipa `Cairo`

90 | 91   Heiß geliebt *Precious Treasures*
Dendrobium nobile, Spathiphyllum Cultivar, Vanda `Rothschildiana`

92 | 93   Neu entdeckt *New Discoveries*
Anthurium clarinervium, Ceropegia sandersonii, Cryptocereus anthonyanus, Cornus alba `Sibirica`, Phalaenopsis Cultivar, Synadenium grantii, Tillandsia usneoides

94 | 95   Natürlich gewachsen *Naturally Grown*
Allium neapolitanum, Betula pendula, Fallopia, Hedera helix `Erecta`, Ranunculus asiaticus, Thymus vulgaris

96 | 97   Architektonisch konstruiert *Architectural Constructions*

Alocasia macrorrhiza, Jasminum nudiflorum, Zantedeschia aethiopica

98 | 99 Themen – Trends – Tendenzen *Topics – Trends – Tendencies*
Aloe arborescens, Anthurium clarinervium, Encyclia radiata, Hoya linearis, Leucadendron argenteum, Licaste, Odontoglossum Cultivar, Phalaenopsis Cultivar, Rhipsalis capilliformis, Rhipsalis clavata, Vanda `Rothschildiana`

100 | 101 Feuer – Wasser – Erde – Luft *Fire – Water – Earth – Air*
Cattleya Cultivar, Clematis vitalba, Cocos nucifera, Hippeastrum vittatum, Hippophae rhamnoides, Masdevallia candida, Phalaenopsis miriabilis, Rhipsalis Cultivar, Tillandsia ionantha, Tillandsia xerographica

102 | 103 Natur & Technik *Nature & Technology*
Betula pendula, Bouvardia Cultivar, Gerbera jamesonii, Ranunculus asiaticus

104 | 105 Leben & Sterben *Life & Death*
Allium neapolitanum, Betula pendula, Jasminium officinale, Ranunculus asiaticus

106 | 107 Ordnung kontra Chaos *Order versus Chaos*
Betula alba, Encyclia radiata, Phalaenopsis Cultivar, Synadenium grantii

108 | 109 Mono kontra Masse *Mono versus Mass*
Anthurium, Beaucarnea recurvata, Cornus alba `Sibirica`, Masdevallia veitchiana, Testudinaria elephantipes, Tillandsia dyeriana, Vanda `Rothschildiana`

110 | 111 Tempo in der Stadt *Speed in the City*
Rosa sericea subsp. omeienses, Tetraria terminalis, Zantedeschia rehmannii

112 | 113 Beschaulichkeit auf dem Land *Rural Tranquillity*
Jasminium officinale, Limonium suworowii, Papaver nudicaule, Vitis vinifera, Heu / *hay*

114 | 115 Engagement bei der Arbeit *Commitment at Work*
Aristea africana, Begonia serratipetala, Hippeastrum `Raeggae`, Hoya australis, Rhipsalis, Rhipsalis clavata, Salix

116 | 117 Feier: Mit Freunden *Celebrating: With Friends*
Citrus limon, Craspedia globosa, Oncidium varicosum, Rhipsalis bassifera

118 | 119 Aufblühen im Rampenlicht *Flourishing in the limelight*
Anthurium Cultivar, Clianthus formusus, Cornus alba `Sibirica`, Helleborus argutifolius, Leucospermum cordifolium, Tillandsia

Engagierte Synergien *Committed Synergies*

122 | 123 Kopfstand der Kontraste *Contrasts upside Down*
Gregor Lersch links / *on the left*: Alocasia sanderiana, Prunus spinosa, Zantedeschia `Black Forest`
Klaus Wagener rechts / *on the right*: Betula pendula, Bouvardia Cultivar, Carlina acaulis, Helleborus orientalis, Muscari botryoides, Ornithogalum thyrsoides, Prunus spinosa, Symphoricarpos albus, Viburnum opulus, trockene Gräser / *dried grasses*

124 | 125 Erkennbare Parallelen *Visible Parallels*
Gregor Lersch links / *on the left*: Betula pendula, Ceropegia sandersonii, Encyclia radiata, Ranunculus asiaticus, Tulipa `Super Parrot`, Vanda `Rothschildiana`, Wurzeln / *roots*
Klaus Wagener rechts / *on the right*: Agave nucifera, Cocos nucifera, Dipsacus sativus, Fenestraria terminalis, Foeniculum, Lilium `Casablanca`, Sedum nussbaumerianum, Viburnum rhytidophyllum, Xylomele australis, Wurzeln / *roots*

126 | 127 Harmonie der Gegensätze *Harmony of the Contrasts*
Gregor Lersch und / *and* Klaus Wagener: Clematis vitalba, Cornus alba `Sibirica`, Hedera helix, Ranunculus asiaticus, Zantedeschia `Chrystal Blanche`, trockene Gräser / *dried grasses*

128 | 129 Verbindung von Kompetenzen *Combination of Competencies*
Gregor Lersch und / *and* Klaus Wagener:
Ceropegia linearis subsp. woodii, Crataegus, Hippeastrum `Showmaster`, Hoya linearis, Lychnis viscaria, Proboscidea louisianica, Rosa `Black Baccara`, Rosa polyantha, Tulipa Cultivar, Vanda `Rothschildiana'

130 | 130 Zusammenspiel der zwei Gesichter *Interaction of the two Faces*
Gregor Lersch und / *and* Klaus Wagener: Vitis vitifera, Zantedeschia aethiopica, Zantedeschia rehmannii

72 | 73   Sexy-provokant   *Sexy Provocations*
Aechmea fasciata, Allium sativum, Eucalyptus lehmannii, Guazuma ulmifolia, Hedera helix, Nelumbo nucifera, Nerine bowdenii, Petroselinum crispum, Rosa 'Aqua', Schinus molle, Tillandsia argentea, Tillandsia cyanea

74 | 75   Opulent-dekadent   *Abundant Decadence*
Links / *left*: Ammi majus, Celosia argentea, Chrysanthemum Cultivar, Cornus alba 'Sibirica', Dahlia Cultivar, Gerbera jamesonii, Helianthus annuus, Hydrangea macrophylla, Ligustrum vulgare, Panicum, Protea barbigera, Rosa Cultivar, Zea mays
Mitte / *middle*: Allium sphaerocephalon, Anis Frucht / *anis fruit*
Rechts / *right*: Ceropegia linearis subsp. woodii, Chrysanthemum Cultivar, Dahlia Cultivar, Dianthus caryophyllus, Ligustrum vulgare, Nigella damascena, Punica granatum, Rosa Cultivar, Zea mays

76 | 77   Reduziert-pointiert   *Trenchant Reductions*
Allium moly, Asclepias physocarpa, Dianthus caryophyllus, Echeveria, Geranium x cantabrigiense, Glyceria maxima 'Variegata', Helleborus orientalis, Hyacinthus orientalis, Lunaria annua, Ophiopogon japonicum, Ornithogalum thyrsoides, Pulsatilla vulgaris, Stachys byzantina, Tillandsia usneoides

78 | 79   Heimat: Wiese   *Homeland: Meadow*
Agropyron, Agrostis, Carex, Lolium, Phleum, diverse Gräser / *various grasses*

80 | 81   Heimat: Sonnenblume   *Homeland: Sunflower*
Helianthus annuus

82 | 83   Heimat: Buche   *Homeland: Beech*
Chrysanthemum Cultivars, Fagus sylvatica

84 | 85   Heimat: Zuckerrübe   *Homeland: Sugar Beet*
Angelica archangelica, Beta vulgaris, Chrysanthemum Cultivars, Cornus alba 'Sibirica', Punica granatum, Sedum telephium

Individuelle Ansichten   *Individual Views*

88 | 89   Elementar wichtig   *Basic Importance*
Chamaecyparis, Lonicera henryi, Phoenix dactylifera, Quercus germanica, Sambucus nigra, Tillandsia usneoides, Tolmiea menziesii, Tulipa Cultivar

90 | 91   Heiß geliebt   *Precious Treasures*
Dicentra spectabilis, Fritillaria meleagris, Helleborus orientalis, Miscanthus, Muscari armeniacum, Pulsatilla vulgaris, Viola wittrockiana

92 | 93   Neu entdeckt   *New Discoveries*
Amaranthus caudatus, Aristea africana, Heuchera x brizoides, Zantedeschia aethiopica

94 | 95   Natürlich gewachsen   *Naturally Grown*
Schale links / *left bowl*: Acorus gramineus, Allium christophii, Anthrinum majus, Astilbe x arendsii, Gomphrena globosum, Iris Cultivar, Lavandula angustifolia, Leucobryum glaucum, Luzula sylvatica, Nemesia caerulea, Ornithogalum
Schale rechts / *right bowl*: Agapanthus africanus, Alyssum spinosum, Aquilegia flabellate, Heuchera sieboldiana, Iris Cultivar, Leucobryum glaucum, Nemesia, Tiarella cordifolia, Xanthorrhoea australis

96 | 97   Architektonisch konstruiert   *Architectural Constructions*
Ceropegia, Sterculia quinqueloba, Tetraria terminalis, Tulipa Cultivars, Viburnum opulus, Vinca major, Xanthorrhoea australis, Xerophyllum tenax

98 | 99   Themen – Trends – Tendenzen   *Topics – Trends – Tendencies*
Links / *left*: Averrhoa carambola, Leucospermum cordifolium, Malus, Papaver orientalis, Quercus suber, Ranunculus asiaticus, Scabiosa stellata
Mitte / *middle*: Aloe vera, Asclepias fruticosa, Bambusa multiplex, Euphorbia x martinii, Nelumbo nucifera, Pandanus odoratissimus, Protea neriifolia, Zantedeschia elliottiana
Right / *right*: Chrysanthemum Cultivar, Citrullus lanatus, Craspedia globosa, Salix caprea, Viburnum opulus 'Sterile'

100 | 101   Feuer – Wasser – Erde – Luft   *Fire – Water – Earth – Air*
Feuer / *Fire*: Anthurium andraeanum, Heliconia stricta, Protea neriifolia, Punica granatum
Wasser / *Water*: Ageratum houstonianum, Eucharis amazonica, Hyacinthus orientalis, Iris 'Blue Magic', Muscari armeniacum, Ophiopogon jaburan
Erde / *Earth*: Fritillaria michailovskyi, Hedera helix, Ornithogalum dubium, Papaver nudicaule, Ranunculus asiaticus, Salix 'Golden Curls', Tulipa Cultivar
Luft / *Air*: Gypsophila paniculata, Lysimachia clethroides, Nerine bowdenii, Spiraea x arguta, Tulipa Cultivars

102 | 103   Natur & Technik   *Nature & Technology*
Galanthus nivalis, Leucophyta brownii, Salix caprea, Schinus molle

104 | 105   Leben & Sterben   *Life & Death*
Cocus nucifera, Fagus sylvatica, Galanthus nivalis, Muscari armeniacum, Narcissus tazetta, Scilla bifolia

106 | 107   Ordnung kontra Chaos   *Order versus Chaos*
Betula pendula, Castanea sativa, Crataegus, Pinus nigra, Protea sulphurea, Ranunculus asiaticus, Reedstäbe / *reed sticks*

108 | 109   Mono kontra Masse   *Mono versus Mass*
Links / *left*: Anigozanthos flavidus, Cornus alba 'Sibirica', Heliconia, Larix decidua, Salix udensis 'Sekka'
Oben rechts / *top right*: Salix x sepulcralis 'Chrysocoma', Tulipa Cultivar
Unten rechts / *bottom right*: Anthurium andraeanum, Laminaria cloustonii, Sisymbrium officinale

110 | 111   In der Stadt – hoch hinaus   *In the City – starting up*
Allium, Anthurium andraeanum, Hedera helix, Laminaria cloustonii, Musa x paradisiaca, Odontoglossum Cultivar, Stomanthe sanguinea 'Triostar', Tacca chantrieri

112 | 113   Auf dem Land – buntes Treiben   *In the Countryside – life full of colours*
Ageratum houstanianum, Ammi majus, Betula alba, Calendula officinalis, Fritillaria meleagris, Hyacinthus orientalis, Hypericum x inodorum, Lathyrus odoratus, Muscari armeniacum, Narcissus Cultivars, Papaver nudicaule, Primula denticulata, Salix caprea, Tulipa Cultivars, Viburnum opulus, diverse Gräser / *various grasses*

114 | 115   Bei der Arbeit   *At Work*
Rechts / *right*: Begonia Cultivars, Dianthus caryophyllus, Echinacea purpurea, Gloriosa superba, Hypericum androsaemum
Mitte / *middle*: Anthurium andraeanum, Crocosmia x crocosmiiflora, Protea lacticolor, Xanthorrhoea australis
Links / *left*: Banisteriopsis caapi, Dianthus caryophyllus, Fagus sylvatica, Gerbera jamesonii, Rosa Cultivars

116 | 117   Feier: Mit Freunden   *Celebrating: With Friends*
Craspedia globosa, Fritillaria imperialis, Gypsophila paniculata, Hydrangea macrophylla, Lilium Cultivar, Nerine bowdenii, Oncidium Cultivar, Paeonia Cultivar, Prunus triloba, Rosa Cultivar, Salix x sepulcralis 'Chrysocoma', Tolmiea menziesii, Viburnum opulus

118 | 119   Bühne: Im Rampenlicht   *Stage: In the Limelight*
Allium, Anthurium andraeanum, Dendrobium Cultivar, Eucharis amazonica, Helleborus niger, Spiraea x arguta, Stillingia, Xylomelum pyriforme, Zantedeschia rehmannii

Engagierte Synergien   *Committed Synergies*

122 | 123   Kopfstand der Kontraste   *Contrasts upside Down*
Klaus Wagener links / *on the left*: Cornus alba 'Sibirica', Hedera helix, Helleborus orientalis, Hyacinthus orientalis, Hydrangea macrophylla, Larix kaempferi, Tulipa 'Super Pappot', Moos / *moss*
Gregor Lersch rechts / *on the right*: Caryota, Ceropegia sandersonii, Phalaenopsis Cultivar, Vanda Rothschildiana

124 | 125   Erkennbare Parallelen   *Visible Parallels*
Klaus Wagener links / *on the left*: Anthurium andraeanum, Anthurium veitchii, Cocos nucifera, Fenestraria terminalis, Hedera helix, Nelumbo nucifera
Gregor Lersch rechts / *on the right*: Betula pendula, Cocos nucifera, Hippeastrum 'Lemon Line', Leucophyta brownii, Zantedeschia 'Chrystal blanche'

126 | 127   Harmonie der Gegensätze   *Harmony of the Contrasts*
Klaus Wagener weiß / *white*: Betula pendula, Cocos nucifera, Cryptocereus anthocyanus, Fenestraria terminalis, Gossypium arboreum, Lilium 'Casablanca', Lunaria annua, Musa x paradisiaca, Pinus pinaster
Gregor Lersch rot / *red*: Agave sisalana, Alocasia sanderiana, Anthurium andraeanum, Brassica rubra, Cocos nucifera, Fenestraria terminalis, Hedera helix, Nelumbo nucifera

128 | 129   Verbindung von Kompetenzen   *Combination of Competencies*
Klaus Wagener und / *and* Gregor Lersch: Bouvardia Cultivar, Ceropegia linearis subsp. woodii, Grevillea, Helleborus asiaticus, Heuchera americana, Mattiola incana, Muehlenbeckia complexa, Papaver orientale, Ranunculus asiaticus, Tanacetum parthenium, Sinapis alba, Viburnum tinus

130 | 130   Zusammenspiel der zwei Gesichter   *Interaction of the two Faces*
Klaus Wagener und / *and* Gregor Lersch: Vitis vitifera, Zantedeschia aethiopica, Zantedeschia rehmannii

Klaus Wagener

Professionelle Leidenschaft *Professionelle Leidenschaft*

8 | 9 Geheimnisvolle Wurzeln *Mysterious Roots*
Aruncus sinensis, Brassica napus, Cynara scolymus, Dahlia pinnata, Epilobium angustifolium, Hydrangea aspera, Hydrangea macrophylla, Lonicera henryi, Macleaya cordata, Sambucus melanocarpa

10 | 11 Erstaunliche Triebe *Astonishing Shoots*
Acer carpinifolium, Aloe vera, Ananas comosus, Kniphofia uvaria, Leucospermum cordifolium, Luzula campestris, Musa x paradisiaca, Rheum officinale, Saccharum, Tulipa gesneriana, Zantedeschia aethiopica

12 | 13 Dynamische Stiele *Dynamic Stems*
Argyreia nervosa, Aruncus sinensis, Banksia coccinea, Berzelia abrotanoides, Chrysanthemum Cultivar, Dahlia pinnata, Foeniculum vulgare, Helianthus annuus, Heliconia vellerigera, Hypericum androsaemum, Kerria japonica, Leucadendron discolor, Rosa multiflora, Salix alba, Vinca major, Zea mays

14 | 15 Aufregende Blätter *Exciting Leaves*
Anthurium andraeanum, Anthurium crystallinum, Aristea confusa, Begonia Cultivar, Ctenanthe amabilis, Cotinus coggygria, Eucalyptus polyanthemos, Kalanchoe thyrsiflora, Lunaria annua, Nepenthes Cultivar, Odontoglossum Cultivar, Peperomia caperata, Populus alba, Punica granatum, Strelitzia reginae, Tillandsia xerographica, Zea mays

16 | 17 Faszinierende Blüten *Fascinating Blossoms*
Cornus alba, Epimedium x versicolor, Hippeastrum vittatum, Macleaya cordata, Salix alba

Meisterliches Handwerk *Master Trade*

20 | 21 Gebündelt zur soliden Basis *Bundled to a solid Basis*
Chrysanthemum Cultivar, Cocos nucifera, Cornus alba, Cotoneaster dammeri, Echinacea purpurea, Miscanthus floridulus, Usnea filipendula

22 | 23 Geknotet zu Netzwerken *Knotted Networks*
Ananas comosus, Anthurium andraeanum, Asclepias fruticosa, Clematis vitalba, Echinacea purpurea, Phalaenopsis amabilis, Platanus x hispanica, Protea compacta, Scabiosa stellata, Sinapis arvensis, Zantedeschia rehmannii

24 | 25 Geflochten zu Schützendem *Braiding for Protection*
Asclepias fruticosa, Berzelia abrotanoides, Betula pendula, Helleborus niger, Pinus pinaster, Salix alba, Tillandsia xerographica

26 | 27 Gewoben zu Texturen *Woven Textures*
Agave americana, Banksia ashbyi, Craspedia globosa, Crocosmia x crocosmiiflora, Equisetum giganteum, Eucalyptus, Gossypium herbaceum, Phormium tenax, Zantedeschia rehmannii

28 | 29 Geschichtet zu neuen Dimensionen *Coated to new Dimensions*
Actinidia deliciosa, Cocos nucifera, Betula pendula, Brassica oleracea, Chrysanthemum Cultivar, Clematis tangutica, Euonymus europaeus, Hydrangea aspera subsp. sargentiana, Pandanus odoratissimus, Parthenocissus inserta, Pinus nigra, Punica granatum, Rosa multiflora, Sedum spectabile

30 | 31 Gereiht zu Allianzen *Ranking to Alliances*
Aechmea fasciata, Brassica oleracea, Chaenomeles japonica, Coccoloba uvifera, Rudbeckia hirta, Scabiosa stellata, Stachys byzantina, Vriesea splendens, Xanthorrhoea australis, diverse Wildblumen-fruchtstände / *diversified infructescences of wild flowers*

Gestalterische Bekenntnisse *Creative Confessions*

34 | 35 Symmetrische Ruhe *Bundled to a solid Basis*
Rechts / *right*: Dianthus caryophyllus, Olea europaea
Links / *left*: Dianthus caryophyllus, Fritillaria imperialis

36 | 37 Asymmetrische Spannung *Asymmetric Tension*
Coccoloba uvifera, Helichrysum bracteatum, Lunaria annua, Viburnum rhytidophyllum

38 | 39 Dekorative Ansichten *Decorative Views*
Agave americana, Allium giganteum, Anthurium crystallinum, Ceropegia sandersonii, Curcuma alismatifolia, Dianthus caryophyllus, Ensete ventricosum, Euonymus europaeus, Fritillaria imperialis, Helleborus niger, Hydrangea macrophylla, Papaver nudicaule, Phalaenopsis Cultivar, Prunus cerasifera, Rhododendron yakushimanum, Rosa Cultivar, Smilax rotundifolia, Stachys byzantina, Tulipa gesneriana, Zantedeschia aethiopica

40 | 41 Vegetative Erkenntnisse *Vegetative Insights*
Achillea millefolium, Celastrus angulatus, Gaura lindheimeri, Lapsana communis, Nemesia Cultivar, Oxalis, Phleum, Sedum spectabile, Moos / *moss*

42 | 43 Formal-lineare Fantasien *Formally linear Fancies*
Aechmea fasciata, Aechmea primera, Asclepias fruticosa, Guzmania wittmackii, Strelitzia reginae, Tillandsia xerographica, Tillandsia cyanea, Vriesea 'Polonia', Vriesea splendens

44 | 45 Einsichtige Strukturen *Insightful Structures*
Astrantia major, Fritillaria meleagris, Lathyrus odoratus, Magnolia x soulangeana, Pieris 'Forest Flame', Tetraria terminalis, Tulipa gesneriana

46 | 47 Gewagte Konstruktionen *Risky Constructions*
Hedera helix, Helleborus niger, Magnolia x soulangiana, Miscanthus purpurascens, Scabiosa stellata, Tetraria terminalis

48 | 49 Innovative Objekte *Innovative Objects*
Anthurium andraeanum, Clematis vitalba, Fagus sylvatica, Lilium 'Casablanca', Lunaria annua, Phalaenopsis Cultivar, Quercus suber, Rhodocoma gigantea, Stachys byzantina, Viburnum rhytidophyllum, Zantedeschia aethiopica

50 | 51 Beeindruckende Texturen *Impressive Textures*
Allium aflatunense, Anthurium andraeanum, Celosia Cultivars, Crataegus altaica, Curcuma alismatifolia, Dianthus caryophyllus, Lilium longiflorum, Passiflora caerulea, Quercus suber, Schinus molle

52 | 53 Monochrome Raffinesse *Monochromatic Finesse*
Dianthus caryophyllus, Gypsophila paniculata, Helleborus orientalis, Hippeastrum vittatum, Hyacinthus orientalis, Lagurus ovatus, Lilium longiflorum, Ornithogalum arabicum, Tillandsia xerographica, Tulipa Cultivar, Trockenzweige / *Drywood*, "Mitsumatazweige" / "Mitsumata" bunches

54 | 55 Farbige Lust *Colourful Delight*
Astrantia major, Cordyline terminalis, Fritillaria assyriaca, Fritillaria Cultivar, Helleborus orientalis, Hydrangea macrophylla 'Mirai', Magnolia x soulangiana, Prunus cerasifera, Pulsatilla vulgaris 'Rubra', Ranunculus asiaticus, Saccharum, Tulipa Cultivars, Tulipa gesneriana

56 | 57 Bunte Leidenschaft *Coloured Passion*
Carex muskingumensis, Zinnia elegans, "Reed Stäbe" / *reed sticks*

Ganz persönliche Gefühle *Very private Emotions*

60 | 61 Frühlingshaft-verspielt *Spring-like Plays*
Amelanchier canadensis, Fritillaria meleagris, Gypsophila paniculata, Helleborus orientalis, Hydrangea aspera, Prunus cerasifera 'Nigra', Tulipa gesneriana 'Fancy Frills', Tulipa gesneriana 'Queen of Marvel', Viola x wittrockiana

62 | 63 Sommerlich-frisch *Summer Breeze*
Antirrhinum majus, Dahlia pinnata, Delphinium elatum, Eremurus stenophyllus, Gypsophila paniculata, Hydrangea macrophylla, Tetraria terminalis

64 | 65 Herbstlich-melancholisch *Autumn's Melancholy*
Brassica oleracea var. acephala, Clematis vitalba, Crataegus laevigata, Euonymus europaeus, Hydrangea arborescens 'Annabelle', Nelumbo nucifera, Rhus typhina, Rudbeckia hirta, Scabiosa stellata, Sedum spectabile, Zea mays

66 | 67 Winterlich-erstarrt *Winter's Freeze*
Carlina acaulis, Lunaria annua, Miscanthus sacchariflorus, Pinus strobus, Senecio cacaliaster, Usnea filipendulina

68 | 69 Romantisch-ländlich *Rural Romanticism*
Hedera helix, Pulsatilla vulgaris, Viola x wittrockiana

70 | 71 Sinnlich-körperlich *Sensual Material*
Links / *left*: Allium sativum, Betula pendula, Celosia argentea var. cristata, Ceropegia linearis subsp. woodii, Cotinus coggygria, Dahlia pinnata, Origanum vulgare, Panicum virgatum 'Fountain', Rosa Cultivar 'Grand Prix', Sambucus caerulea
Rechts / *right*: Dahlia x hortensis, Hydrangea macrophylla, Sambucus caerulea

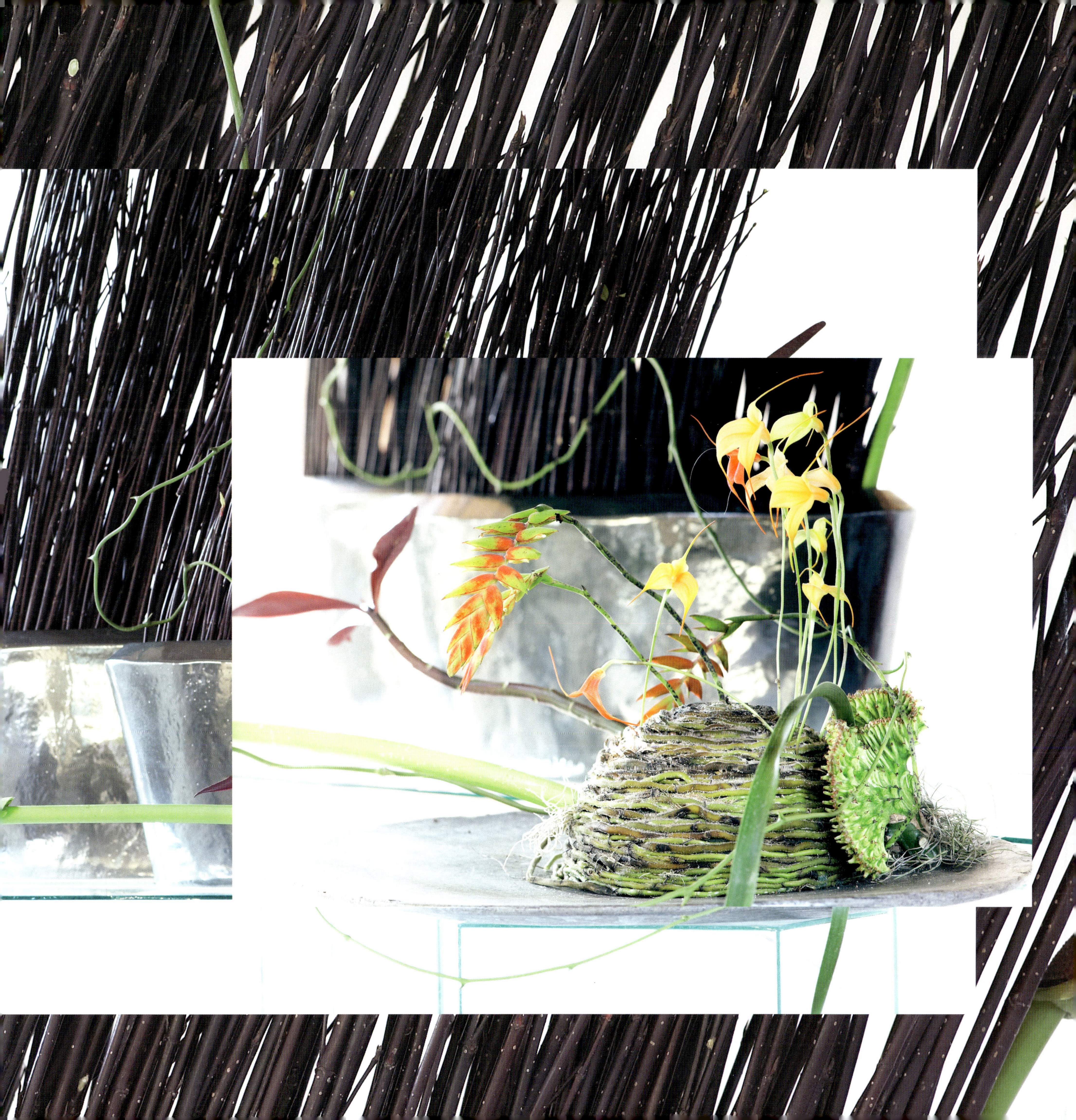

LERSCH | Individuelle Ansichten *Individual Views*

110 | 111

Tempo in der Stadt

Die Dramaturgie zum Thema „Tempo" erscheint zunächst ein wenig ironisch: alte Damen mit Gehhilfen, das Stadt- (oder soll ich besser sagen: Dorf-)original mit Jahre alter Seidenblumenfülle an Bord seines alten Rades, Mütter mit Kinderwagen. Sie waren es hauptsächlich und nicht die Geschäftigen und Arbeitenden, die in der Fußgängerzone am späten Nachmittag an diesem Werkstück vorbei flanierten, das sich dynamisch in sich selbst zu drehen scheint. Beinahe wie ein Hamsterrad. Eine Antwort auf unsere schnelllebige Gesellschaft: die von vielen geforderte Verlangsamung unserer Zeit? Zeit kann man nicht verändern. Aber den Umgang mit ihr. Denn wir sollten uns schon überlegen, welche Lebensqualität dahinter steckt, wenn man heute Abend noch schnell in Deutschland eine Ausstellung eröffnet, um übermorgen Früh um Neun vor einer Seminarrunde in Tokio zu stehen. Das Internet mit seiner Just-in-Time-Dynamik mal ganz außen vorgelassen. Vielleicht können uns ja die Blumen ganz vorsichtig auf den Weg bringen. Mich inklusive. Oder ist das zu ironisch?

Speed in the City

The dramaturgy of the topic "speed" seems at first quite ironic: In contrast to business people and employees it was predominantly the old ladies with their walkers decorated with old silk flowers and mothers with their buggies who – while strolling in the pedestrian zone during the late afternoon – passed this arrangement which seems to rotate dynamically around itself – almost like a hamster wheel. Could a slow-down of our time, being demanded by so many people, be a probable response to our fast growing society? You can't change the time as such, but the way you deal with it. However, we should think about the quality of life of someone who opens an exposition rapidly the same night in Germany in order to participate in a workshop the day after tomorrow morning at nine in Tokyo. The internet, with its just-in-time-dynamism, is ignored in this case. Maybe the flowers could show us, including myself, cautiously the way out. Or is that too ironic?

Ländliche Umgebung ist ein gutes Stück Erinnerung an die Kindheit. An den Heuboden beim Bauern Jupp in der Nachbarschaft, wo wir uns Heuschlachten lieferten. An Hans Willi, an Claudia, Wolfgang und Erika. An eine schlichte und rustikale, aber auch sonnenbeschienene und heitere Welt. Die Stimmung von damals ist für mich noch greifbar. Der Weinberg direkt hinter der Scheune – daher die Reben. Die Wiese noch dazwischen. Die Kugel als geborgenes Zentrum. Der große Eisenring ist das einzige sichtbare, technische Hilfsmittel. Ansonsten besteht alles andere aus Gewachsenem, aus Handwerk und Formgebung und symbolisiert die kleine, beschauliche, auf sich selbst bezogene, ländliche Welt mit ihrer Freiheit, Wildheit und Spontaneität der Kindheit.

Rural Tranquility

The rural environment is an essential part of my childhood. I still remember the hayloft of farmer Jupp from our neighbourhood where we used to have our battles in the hay. But also Willi, Claudia, Wolfgang and Erika are running through my thoughts. It was a chaste and rustic but also sunny and gay time. The mood at that time is still present today: I see the vineyard just behind the barn – that's the reason for the vines – and the meadow in-between. The bowl symbolizes a centre of security. The big iron ring is the only visible technical aid. All the rest however, consists of plants, technical devices, shaping techniques and symbolizes the small, contemplative, self-concentrated, rural world with its freedom, ferocity and spontaneity of childhood.

Beschaulichkeit

den Land

LERSCH | Individuelle Ansichten *Individual Views*

114 | 115

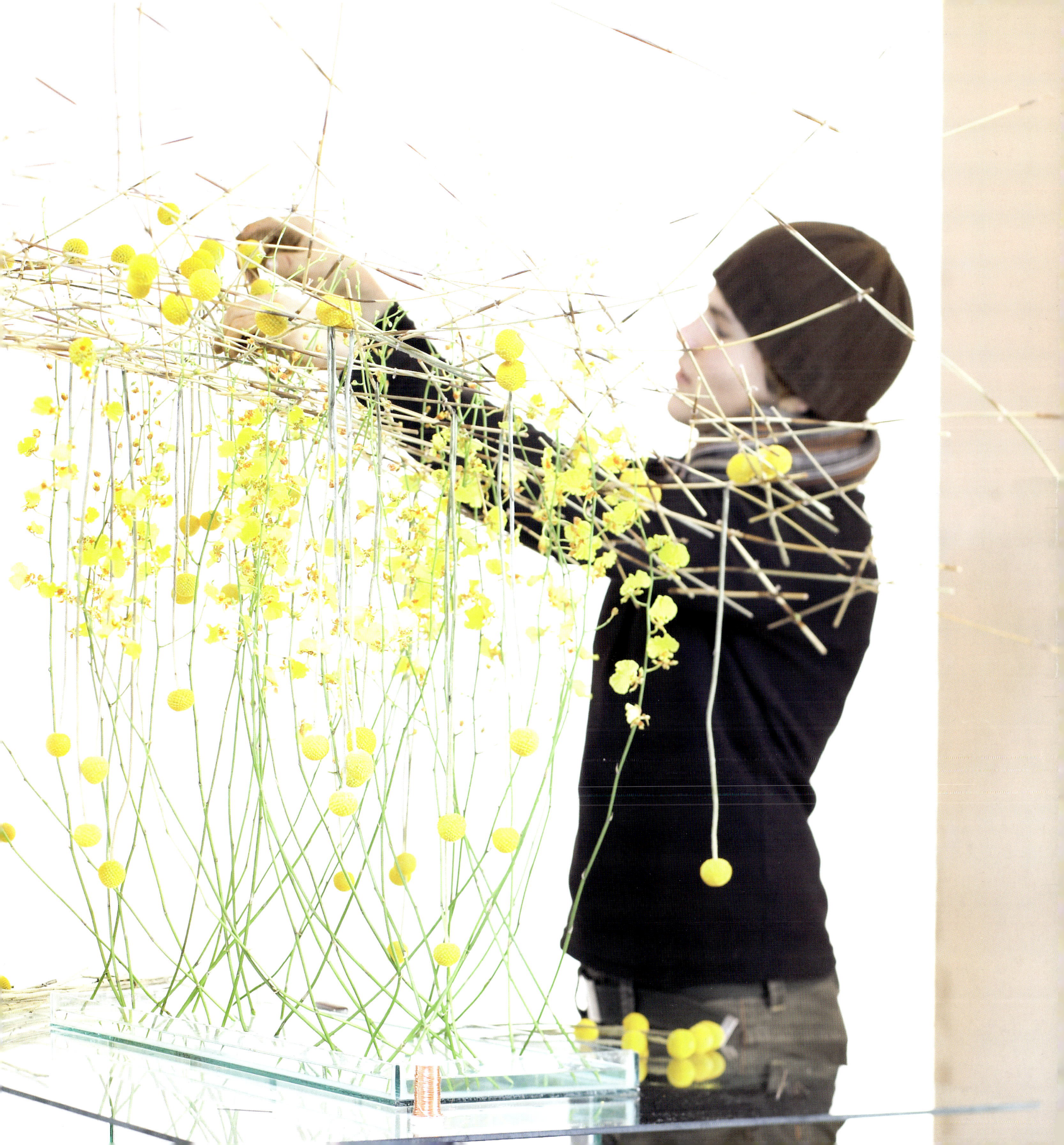

Floristik ist eine Tätigkeit wie viele andere, wo nicht nur die hohe Schule der Gestaltung Spaß machen darf, sondern in der man auch die vielen vorbereitenden und begleitenden Arbeiten mit Engagement, wenn auch sicherlich nicht immer mit reiner Freude zu machen hat. Denn nur so gelingen letztendlich auch die gestalterischen Highlights. Die Schönheit edler Gefäße beispielsweise, die Floralien erst wirklich zur Geltung kommen lassen, kann sich nur entfalten, wenn man das Schleppen und Tragen, das Reinigen und Bruchvermeiden als eine notwendige und heilige Aufgabe ansieht, durch die eine Gestaltungsarbeit am Ende ihre ganze Wirkung entfalten kann.

Commitment at Work

Floristry is a profession like many others with its pros and cons. A florist should not only enjoy designing but prove commitment also for all the preparatory working necessary to accomplish such an arrangement. Of course, this does not always mean pure fun. This is thus the only way to achieve such creative highlights. A container's beauty, which for example emphasizes the impact of the flora, can only be displayed if tasks like carrying, cleaning, preventing from breaking are regarded as necessary and holy in order to let an arrangement finally display its entire effect.

Engagement

Feiern mit Freunden

Halogenlicht-Installationen waren hier das Vorbild: Anlagen aus Kabeln und Lichtquellen mit hell strahlenden kleinen Birnen. So entstand ein sehr transparentes Netz, das locker und in – bei mir selten vorkommendem – Gelb die Gäste überdacht. Es ist vorgefertigt und dann im Raum an den oberen Bereichen der Wände fest verspannt. Zarteste Gestalten recken sich dem Konstrukt entgegen, um auch wiederum von ihm gehalten zu werden. Ich mag diese kleinen Runden, wo alle miteinander sprechen können. Oder aber die ganz langen Tische, die ich in Flandern und in Spanien schon sehr früh zu schätzen gelernt habe.

Celebrating with Friends

Halogen lamp installations served as the role model in this case: devices of cables and light sources with small bright bulbs. In this manner a very transparent grid, which loosely covers the guests in a yellow, which I rarely use in my constructions, is created. It is prefabricated and then firmly distorted at the upper parts of the walls. The most delicate creatures are stretching towards the construction in order to be sustained by it. I like these small round tables where everyone can speak with each other. Or the very small ones, I had learnt to appreciate very early in Flanders or Spain.

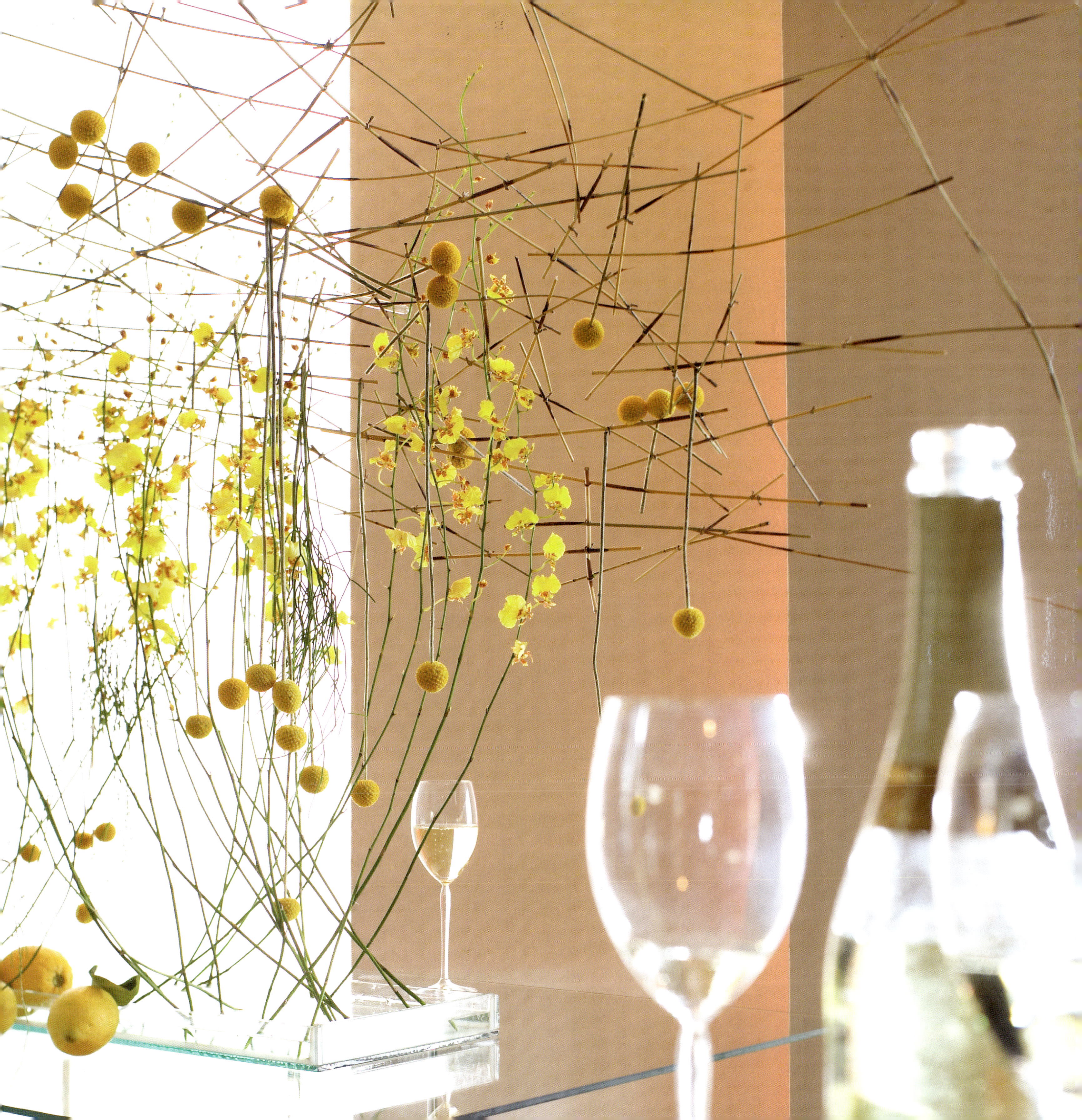

Aufblühen im Rampen

Der Stress der Vorbereitung, die Nervosität vor dem Auftritt, die Anspannung, ob alles ausreichend vorbereitet ist – auf der Bühne ist das alles verflogen. Vielleicht auch deswegen, weil hier doch mehr die Blumen zählen, die Arbeiten, die floralen Arrangements. Blüten verlieren eben selten in den Augen der Menschen, vor allem nicht in den Händen verantwortungsbewusster Gestalter. Blumen und Pflanzen sind die eigentlichen Stars einer floristischen Präsentation. Eher stört hier der Versuch der Vermassung, die ihren Untergang bedeuten könnte und die ich in all meinen Berufsjahren vehement bekämpft habe. Florale Kultur basiert auf einer Jahrtausende alten Entwicklung und bildet einen unverzichtbaren Bestandteil unseres kulturellen Lebens. Sie muss nur neu interpretiert werden in einer Zeit, in der die Medien unsere Kommunikation beherrschen. Es ist unumgänglich, sich ihrer zu bedienen und zu neuen Formen der Darstellung zu kommen. Also Bühne frei für die Stars aus fünf Kontinenten.

Flourishing in the Limelight

The stressful period of preparation, the excitement before the performance and the agitation if everything is well prepared vanish on stage. A probable reason could be that the flowers, the work and the floral arrangements are more important here. Flowers are always winning people's hearts and especially if they are put in the hands of responsible designers. Flowers and plants are the actual stars of a floral presentation. The attempt of dimensioning, which could be its ruin and which I have fought vehemently during all my years as a professional florist, could be a handicap here. Floral culture is based on a development of thousands of years and constitutes an indispensable part of our cultural life. In a time where the media dictates our communication it must indeed be reinterpreted. We cannot prevent us from using flowers and getting to new types of presentation. So let the stars from five continents get on stage.

licht

Engagierte Synergien

Verschiedenste Themen getrennt voneinander zu interpretieren und die Ergebnisse gemeinsam zu präsentieren, ist die eine Sache. Gemeinsam an ihnen zu arbeiten, eine ganz andere. Da ist Abstimmung notwendig und man muss auch schon mal seine eigenen Intentionen zurückstecken. Nämlich dann, wenn man wirklich durch die Verbindung von zwei kreativen Kompetenzen zu neuen Ergebnissen kommen will. Zweifellos eine große Herausforderung. Doch sie hat mir jede Menge Inspiration vermittelt und darüber hinaus noch viel Spaß bereitet, was man den Arbeiten wie auch den Bildern aus der Produktion deutlich ansehen kann, wie ich meine.

Committed Synergies

It is a complete difference to interpret separately the most different subjects and present their results commonly than working on these differences together. This requires coordination and the ability to make compromises and neglect thus one's own intentions. This is especially the case if new results want to be achieved by the combination of two creative competencies. Without any doubt, this is a big challenge. But it gave me a lot of inspirations and more than

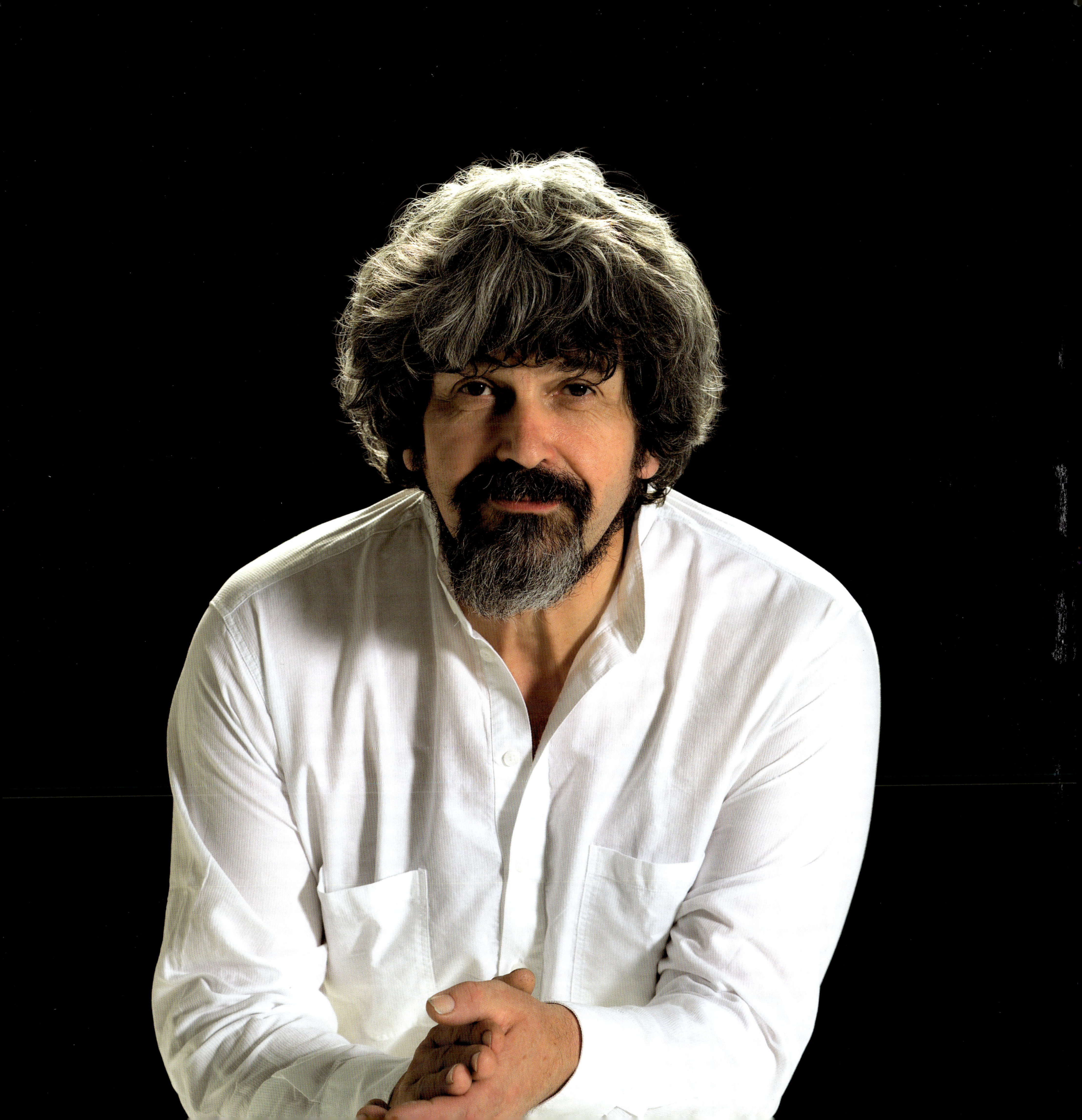

Kopfstand der Kontraste

GREGOR LERSCH : Während Klaus den Kopfstand wörtlich nimmt und seine grünen und weißen Blüten um den Hexenbesen tanzen lässt, interpretiere ich ihn auf meine Weise und zerlege die ruppigen Schlehenzweige in feine Teilchen, um sie dann zu einer fast weich erscheinenden Matte neu zusammen zu fügen. Interessant, wie unterschiedlich die Gedankengänge sind, allerdings bei einer weitgehenden Übereinstimmung in gestalterischen Grundsatzfragen. Für mich eine echte Bereicherung meiner Arbeit.

Contrasts upside down

GREGOR LERSCH : Whereas Klaus takes the word headstand literally by letting his green and white blossoms dance around the witch's brush I have my own interpretation while dismantling the abrasive Hawthorn in fine particles in order to combine it again to an almost soft seemingly meadow. It is quite interesting how different our thoughts can be, yet widely conform concerning designing principles. Personally, I think this is a real enrichment of my work.

WAGENER | Engagierte Synergien Committed Synergies

Erkennbare Parallelen

GREGOR LERSCH : Zunächst einmal prallen hier extrem konträr wirkende Energien aufeinander. Zum einen ein Sich-nach-oben-Stemmen, zum anderen ein massenhaftes Nach-unten-Fallen. Interpretation von zwei sehr unterschiedlichen Persönlichkeiten. Doch auch hier stellt sich heraus, dass wir in unserer grundsätzlichen Auffassung von Floristik gar nicht so weit voneinander entfernt sind, wie manch einer vielleicht glauben könnte. Diese Erkenntnis hat gut getan. Gerade hinsichtlich einer gemeinsamen Offensive für den Berufsstand.

Visible Parallels

GREGOR LERSCH : At first, extremely contrary-acting energies are colliding here: on the one hand a way of stemming upwards-movements on the other hand heavy falling down-movements - interpretations resulting from two very different personalities. But even here it turns out that our basic interpretation of floristry is not that different from each other how it may seem to one or another. Realizing this, made me really happy, and precisely concerning a common offensive for our profession.

Harmonie der Gegensätze

GREGOR LERSCH : Ich habe mich mit dieser Kunststoff-Amöbe auf etwas eingelassen, was ich noch nie getan, nie angerührt, nie in meiner Welt gesehen habe. Trotzdem war es eine der vielen guten Erfahrungen aus dieser gemeinsamen Arbeit, dass nämlich der Wille, gemeinsam mit einem anderen Gestalter zu arbeiten, auch solche Spannungen überwinden kann. Für mich war es allerdings auch die Bestätigung: Das ist nicht mein Weg. Aber hätte ich mich nicht darauf eingelassen, könnte ich es auch nicht so definitiv von mir weisen.

Harmony of the Contrasts

GREGOR LERSCH: With this artificial Amoeba I got involved with something I have never done, never touched and never seen before for all my life. Nevertheless this was one of many positive experiences of this common work, proving that my will to work with another designer can surmount even such tensions. However, it was also a confirmation for me that this was not my way. But if I hadn't tried it I would not have been able to reject it with such conviction.

WAGENER | Engagierte Synergien Committed Synergies

Verbindung von Kompetenzen

GREGOR LERSCH : Das Zusammenkommen über einen Kranz, eine der traditionsreichsten Formen der Blumenbindekunst, darzustellen, ist fast eine logische Folge. Da verschmelzen zwei Halbkreise zu einem Ganzen und schaffen Synergie. Als Symbol für eine gemeinsame Initiative, die neue Potenziale zugunsten einer intensiveren Floralkultur auf allen Ebenen freisetzen möchte.

Zusammenspiel der 2 Gesichter

GREGOR LERSCH : Der Abschluss und Höhepunkt einer gemeinsamen Arbeit. Und das meine ich so, wie ich es sage.
Ich akzeptiere das Ergebnis ohne Vorbehalt, auch wenn es ganz anders aussieht als bei mir. Denn man ist durchaus bereit, das eigene Ego hinten an zu stellen, wenn man erfahren hat, dass da jemand ist, der ebenso wie man selbst Entscheidendes für die Entwicklung des Floral Design tun will. Zumal, wenn man weiß, dass der andere es kann. Wenn auch anders.

Interaction of the two faces

GREGOR LERSCH : The termination and highlight of our common work. And I mean what I say. I accept the result without any reservation, even if it looks completely different than my work. Having once learned that there is someone next to me who is also willing to achieve decisive things for the development of floral design, we are ready to make compromises. Especially when we know that the other person is capable, even though in a different way.

Gregor Lersch

LERSCH | WAGENER | Engagierte Synergien Committed Synergies

130

Combination of Competencies

GREGOR LERSCH : Presenting our cooperation through a wreath as one of the most traditional forms of floral bundling is almost a logical consequence. It is a symbol for two half circles merging to a whole and creating thus synergy: A common initiative, which wants to set free new potentials on all levels in favour of a more intensive floral culture.

Zusammenspiel der 2 Gesichter

KLAUS WAGENER : Hier, am Höhenpunkt dieses außergewöhnlichen Projektes, empfinde ich große Freude und Zufriedenheit. Auf der Basis von gegenseitiger Achtung und hohem Respekt haben wir im kultivierten Miteinander etwas Neues und Ungewöhnliches entstehen lassen. Gegensätzlichkeit treibt an zum Wunsch nach höchster Perfektion! Diese knisternde und jederzeit spürbare Spannung war stets unsere dynamische Kraftquelle. Im gegenständlichen Zusammentreffen unserer Überzeugungen entlädt sie sich in nicht erwartete Harmonie. Gestalterisch und persönlich. Wir sind gemeinsam am Ziel angekommen.

Interplay of the two faces

KLAUS WAGENER : Now, at the summit of this extraordinary project I feel great satisfaction and joy.
Thanks to our well-balanced cooperation we could create something new and unusual on the basis of mutual respect and high esteem.
Contrariness incites the wish in us for highest perfection! This crackling tension, noticeable at anytime, has always been our dynamic source of energy, which turns into unexpected harmony the moment our workings and thus convictions coincide. This concerns our way of designing but also our private life. Finally, we have reached the target in common.

Klaus Wagener

WAGENER | LERSCH | Engagierte Synergien Committed Synergies

Combination of Skills

KLAUS WAGENER : The ability to realize skills, enhance these and constantly have new things being created out of the flow proves a real expertise. Any progress requires external impulses by others. The fly wheel of creativity is well activated especially when such two experts come together. Providing directness and mutual appreciation, these skills complement one another to a complete entity like Ying and Yang. Thanks to Gregor Lersch, who became a colleague, friend, competitor, adversary and leading part due to our common profession, this common project, a heart's desire, offered us the opportunity to pause in a world full of attraction and creation - beyond any requirements claimed by our professional everyday life. In this case, floristic skills could evolve to the profession's own sake and shall now emanate on all those, who commit themselves to the floristic profession.

Verbindung von Kompetenzen

KLAUS WAGENER : Können erkennen, dieses weiter zu entwickeln und aus dem Fluss heraus stetig Neues entstehen zu lassen, zeugt von Kompetenz. Jeglicher Progress bedarf der Impulse von außen und anderen. Vor allem, wenn zwei Könner ihres Fachs zusammen kommen, wird das Schwungrad der Kreativität kräftig angestoßen. Offenheit und gegenseitige Wertschätzung vorausgesetzt, ergänzen sich diese Kompetenzen wie Yin und Yang zu einem perfekten Ganzen. Durch Gregor Lersch, der mir seitens der Profession Kollege, Freund, Konkurrent, Widerstreiter und Protagonist ist, wurde mit diesem gemeinsamen Projekt als Herzenswunsch auch ein Innehalten in eine persönliche Welt voller Ausstrahlung, Kreation gestattet – fern aller Anforderungen, die der Berufsalltag abfordert. Kompetenz durfte um ihrer selbst willen erblühen und soll nun ausstrahlen auf alle, die sich der Floristik verschrieben haben.

Harmony of the Contrasts

KLAUS WAGENER : *The basic rules of design according to German floristry create a clear framework within creative designing work is realized. Whether this concerns opposites, like light and heavy, huge and delicate, white and black or opposed colours, it depends on a designer's skills to cleverly combine opposites in order to create harmony. Almost intuitively and benefiting from the abundance of experiences, Gregor Lersch and I have worked together hand in hand while complementing one another in a harmonic way. It was an exciting collaboration leading to **a harmonic result.***

LERSCH | Engagierte Synergien Committed Synergies

Harmonie der Gegensätze

KLAUS WAGENER : Die gestalterischen Grundregeln, wie sie die deutsche Floristik festschreibt, schaffen nachvollziehbar einen Rahmen, innerhalb dessen gestalterisch-kreatives Wirken stattfindet. Ob es das Spiel von leicht zu schwer, massig zu zart, von Weiß und Schwarz oder von gegensätzlichen Farben ist – es liegt im Können des Gestalters, Gegensätzliches wohldosiert mit einander zu kombinieren, damit Harmonisches entsteht. Geradezu intuitiv und aus der Fülle an Erfahrungen schöpfend, arbeiteten Gregor Lersch und ich Hand in Hand und ergänzten uns auf harmonische Weise. Ein spannendes Miteinander, das zu einem harmonischen Ergebnis führte.

Visible Parallels

KLAUS WAGENER : It is really surprising to see how many things develop simultaneously. But someone, who lives consciously with one's eyes open, absorbing new flows and tendencies while facing the challenges of the **present**, will often achieve similar results. Parallel evolvements of two personalities of different characters are possible if their **basic values are corresponding**. Passion and credibility, authenticity and independence are characteristics that I have in common with **Gregor Lersch**.

Erkennbare Parallelen

KLAUS WAGENER : Erstaunlich festzustellen, dass vieles gleichzeitig entsteht. Doch wer wachen Auges in der Zeit lebt, wer Strömungen und Tendenzen aufnimmt und sich den Herausforderungen der Gegenwart stellt, wird oft zu ähnlichen Ergebnissen gelangen. Parallele Entwicklungen zweier Persönlichkeiten mit unterschiedlichen Ausprägungen können entstehen, wenn es bei den Grundwerten Übereinstimmungen gibt. Leidenschaft und Glaubwürdigkeit, Authentizität und Unabhängigkeit sind Eigenschaften, die Gregor Lersch und mich verbinden.

LERSCH | Engagierte Synergien Committed Synergies

Contrasts upside down

KLAUS WAGENER : Contrasts or opposites attract. But it is far more than that, because only differences make similarities visible. This dualism reinforces the respective energies and novelties and allows extraordinary things to be created. Together with Gregor Lersch I realized through our common creative work that we have the same attitude despite different designing characteristics. After having argued, justified, checked and weighed up, we have finally found to each other. This created a floral dispute, which incited us and which we enjoyed a lot.

Kopfstand der Kontraste

KLAUS WAGENER : Kontraste oder Gegensätze ziehen sich an. Mehr noch, erst durch Unterschiedlichkeit wird auch Gemeinsamkeit deutlich. In dieser Polarität potenziert sich die jeweilige Energie und Neues, Außergewöhnliches kann entstehen. In der gemeinsamen Kreativarbeit spürten Gregor Lersch und ich, dass wir trotz unterschiedlicher gestalterischer Ausprägungen die gleiche Auffassung vertreten. Wir diskutierten, wir rechtfertigten, wir überprüften und wägten ab und fanden zueinander. Der floristische Disput war da. Das spornte an und machte viel Spaß.

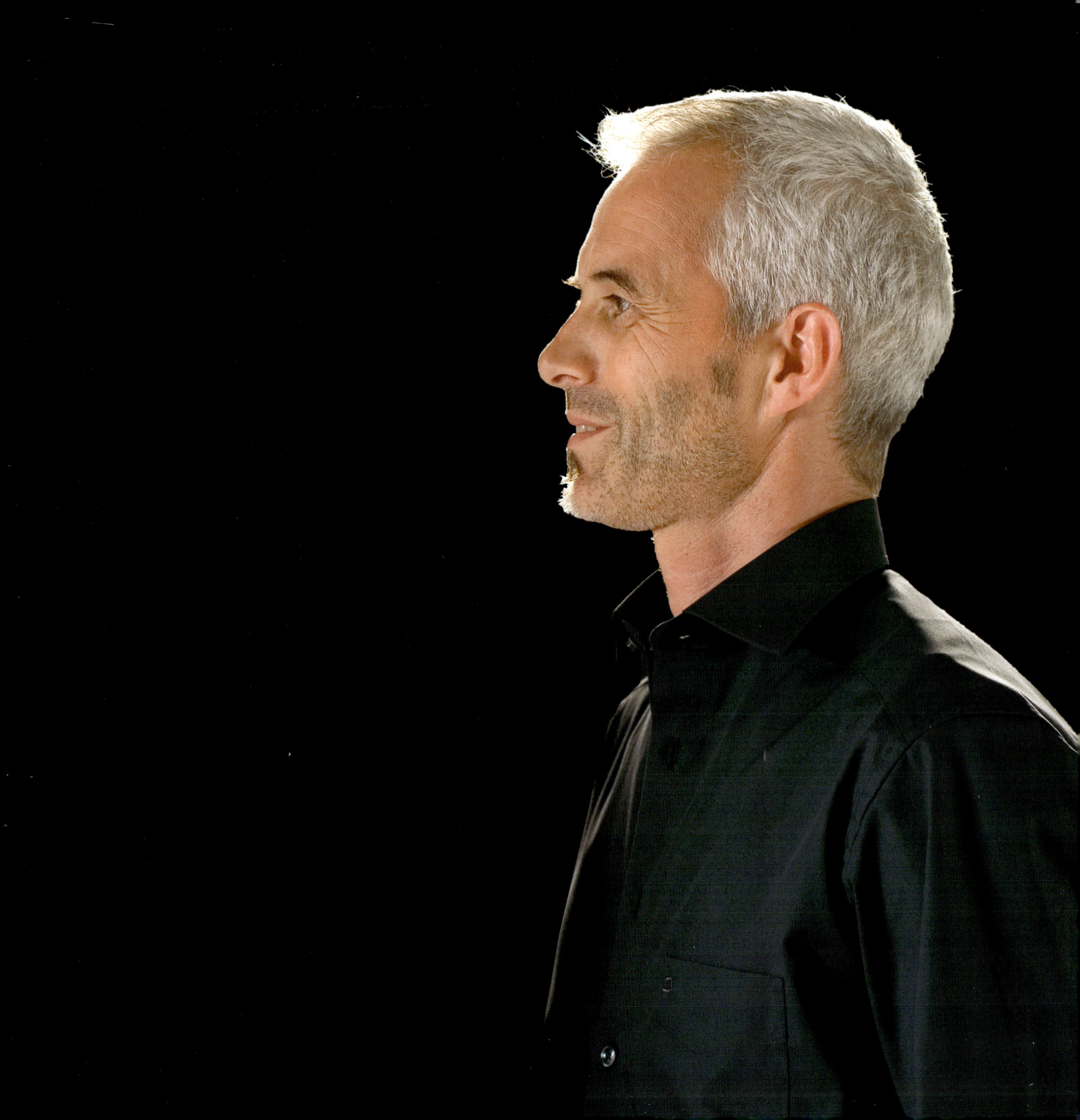

Engagierte Synergien

Berufliche Lebensläufe und kreativ-gestalterische Entwicklungen sind bei Zeitgenossen häufig im Detail unterschiedlich, doch im Großen und Ganzen ähnlich. Das stellten auch Gregor Lersch und ich fest. In unseren ersten Jahren der beruflichen Eigenständigkeit engagierten wir uns beide für den Berufsverband der Floristen, wir waren gleichermaßen auf den floristischen Bühnen präsent. Mit dem zunehmenden Radius der Aktivitäten, mit der steigenden Verantwortung in den eigenen Unternehmen verloren wir uns jedoch über Jahre hinweg aus den Augen. Nun, in der Lebensmitte nach recht unterschiedlichen, rast-losen wie arbeitsreichen Jahren, sowie nach vielen Erfolgen auf beiden Seiten, begegneten wir uns wieder. Und wir stellten fest, dass uns nach wie vor die Begeisterung für alles Florale und Kreative sowie der Respekt vor Blume und Pflanze eint. Die Idee, unsere Erfahrungen nun zu bündeln und zu einem gemeinsamen Projekt zusammenwachsen zu lassen, war geboren.

Committed Synergies

Professional careers and creative designing evolutions of the people of our time are often different in detail, but on the whole similar. That's what I and Gregor Lersch have also realized. During the first years of our professional independence, we both got involved with the staff association for florists and were both equally present at floral shows. We have lost track of each other over the last years due to rising activities and to increasing responsibilities in our own companies. Now, in the middle of our lives, after years full of restless, busy days with rather different events have passed and after each of us has achieved a lot, we have met each other once again. And we realized that our enthusiasm for the entire floral world and all creativity as well as the respect for flowers and plants still unites us. That's when the idea of bundling our experiences, which should grow together to a common project, was born.

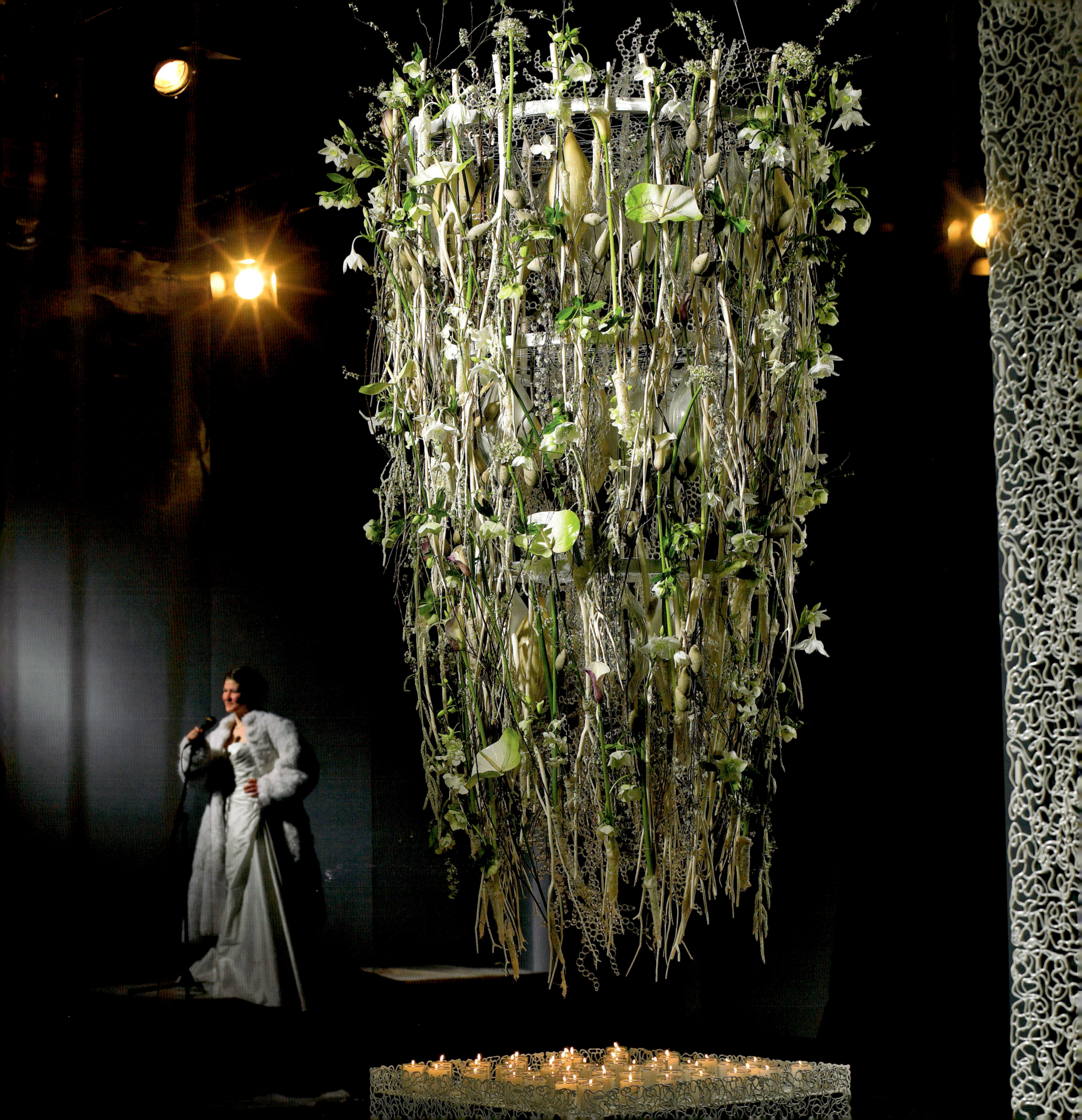

Bühne: Im Rampenlicht

Weiß ist Balsam für Reiz überflutete Seelen. Sich fallen zu lassen und einem Anblick hinzugeben, der sinnlich-purer Genuss ist, lässt Raum und Zeit eins werden. Die Welt draußen wird klein und unbedeutend, nur der Moment zählt.

Stage: In the Limelight

White is balm for all the souls being saturated by impulses. Relaxing and indulging oneself in a view full of purely sensual pleasure makes time and place become one. The world outside appears to be small and insignificant, only the moment is important.

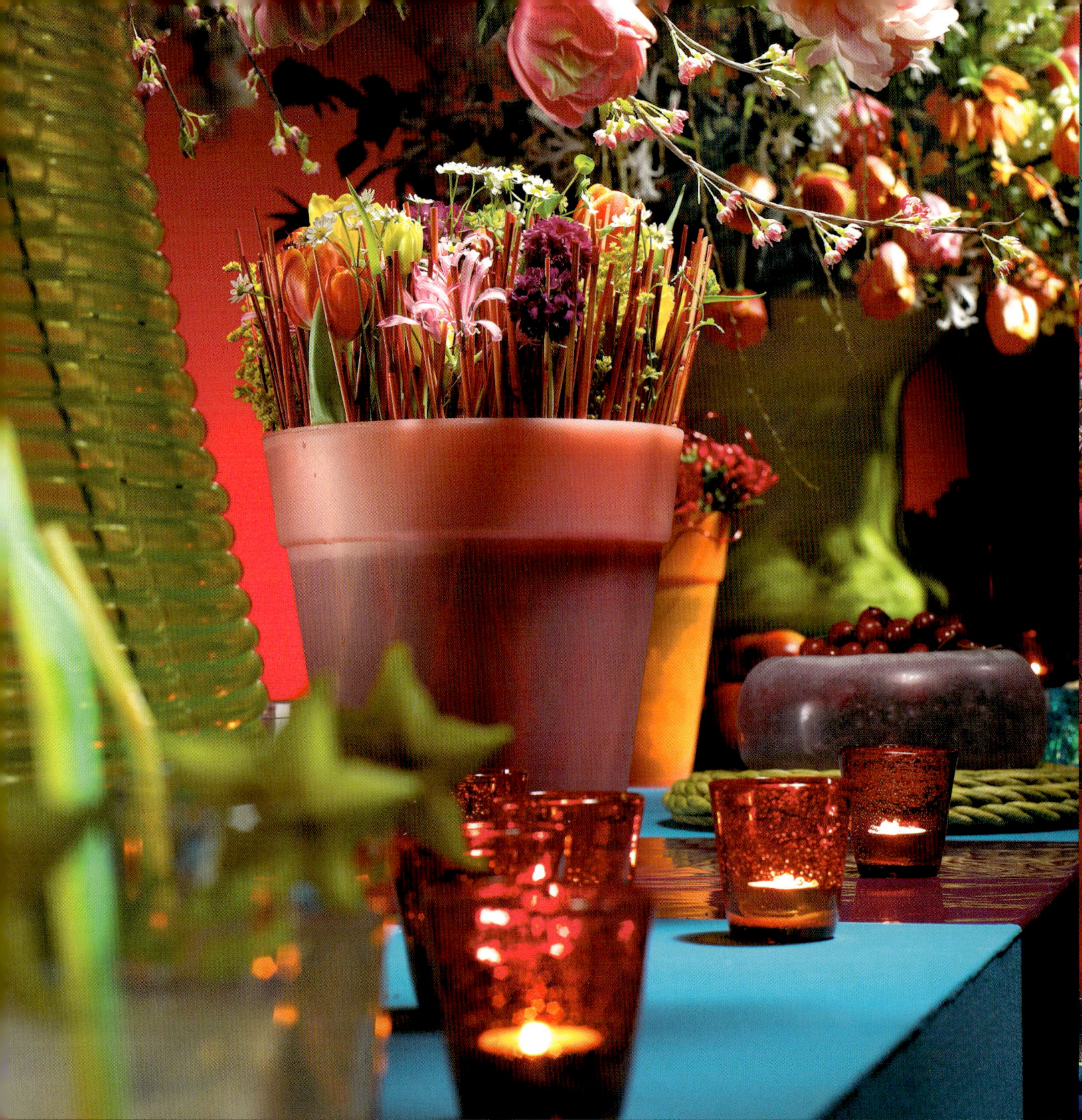

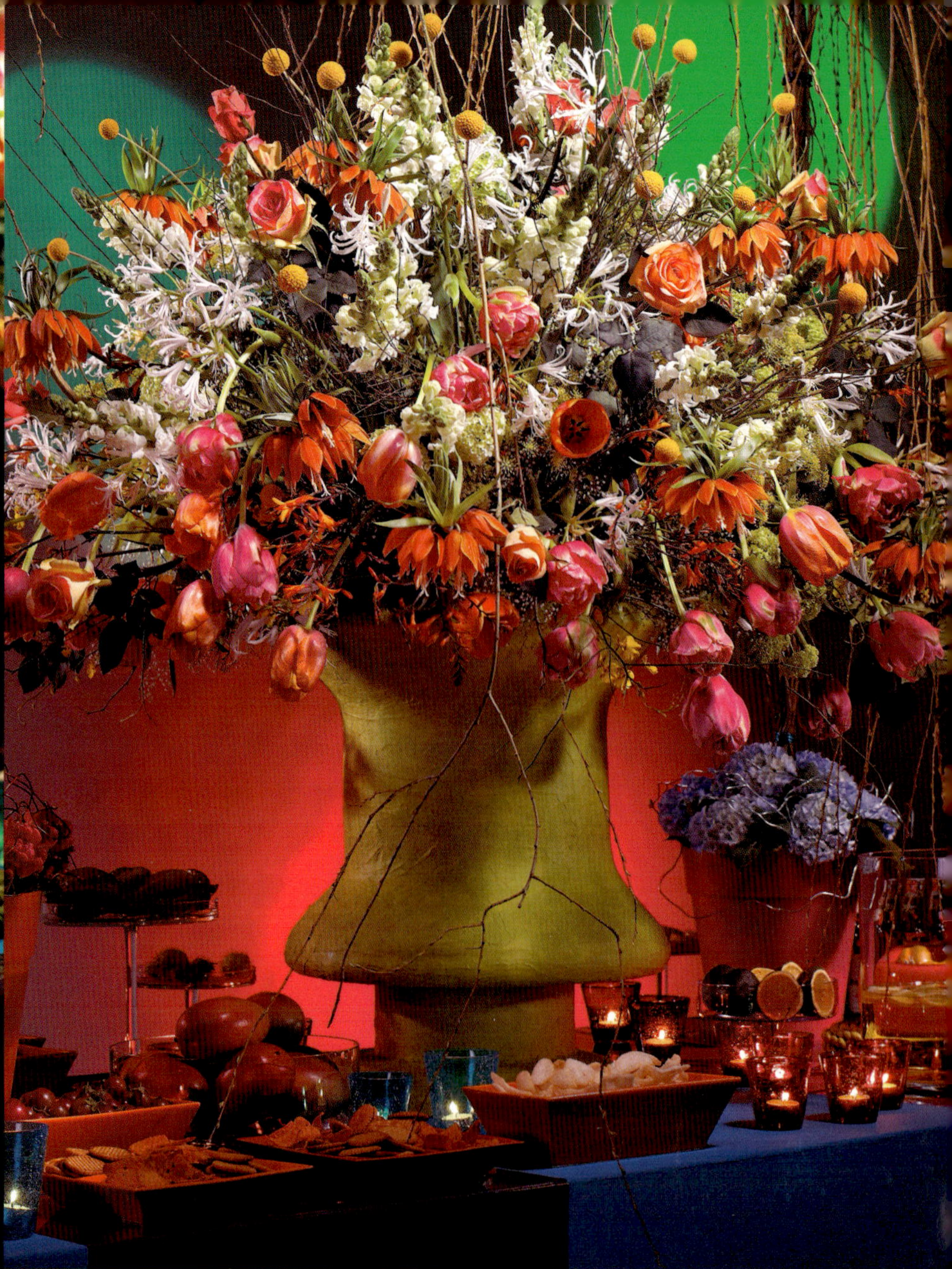

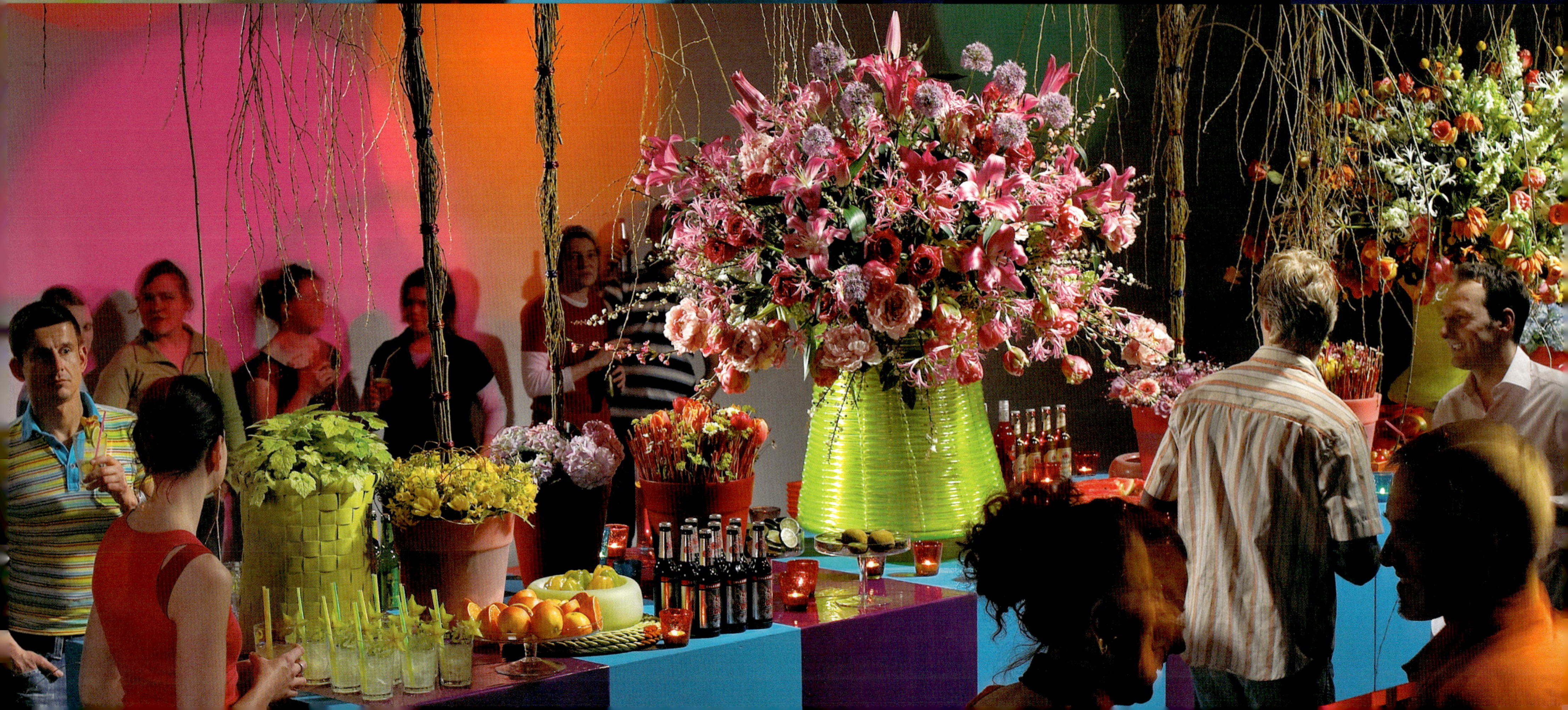

Der neue Luxus bittet Blütenpracht und Farbenvielfalt zu Tisch. Statt Hektik und Oberflächlichkeit bestimmen Genießen und Spaß die Feste und Feiern mit Freunden. Wenn sich das Leben so von seiner unterhaltsamsten Seite zeigen soll, betören Blumen die Atmosphäre und das Ambiente. So schön und einfach kann das Leben sein!

Celebrating: With Friends

The new luxury of flowerage and the diversity of colours are served on table. Instead of hectic and superficiality, joy and fun are dominating the festivities among friends. When life is supposed to show its most entertaining side, certain flowers determine the atmosphere and ambience. Life can be so beautiful and easy!

Feier: mit Freunden

Teamwork

Jobsharing

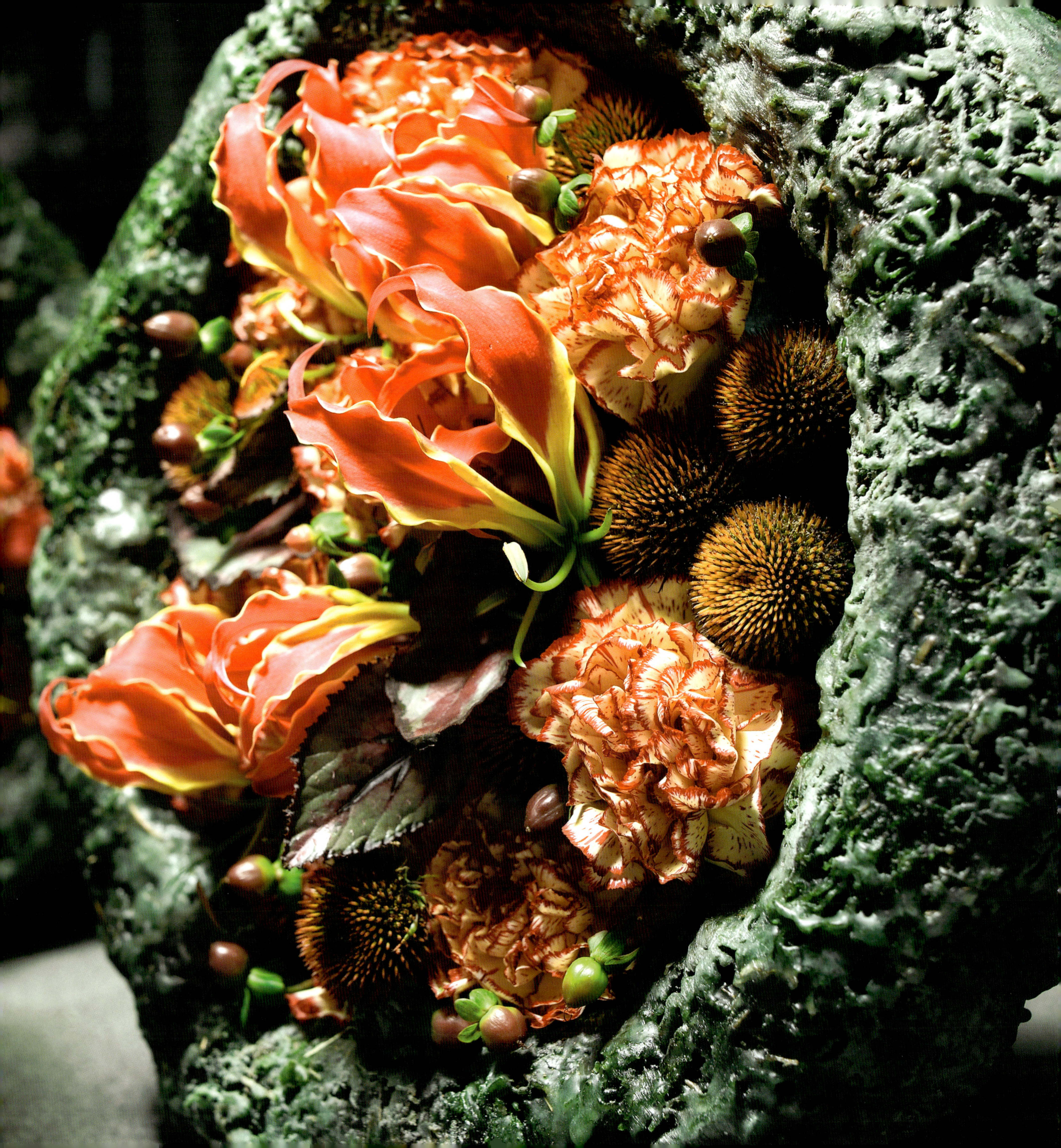

114 | 115

WAGENER | Individuelle Ansichten *Individual Views*

Bei der Arbeit: Manpower
At work

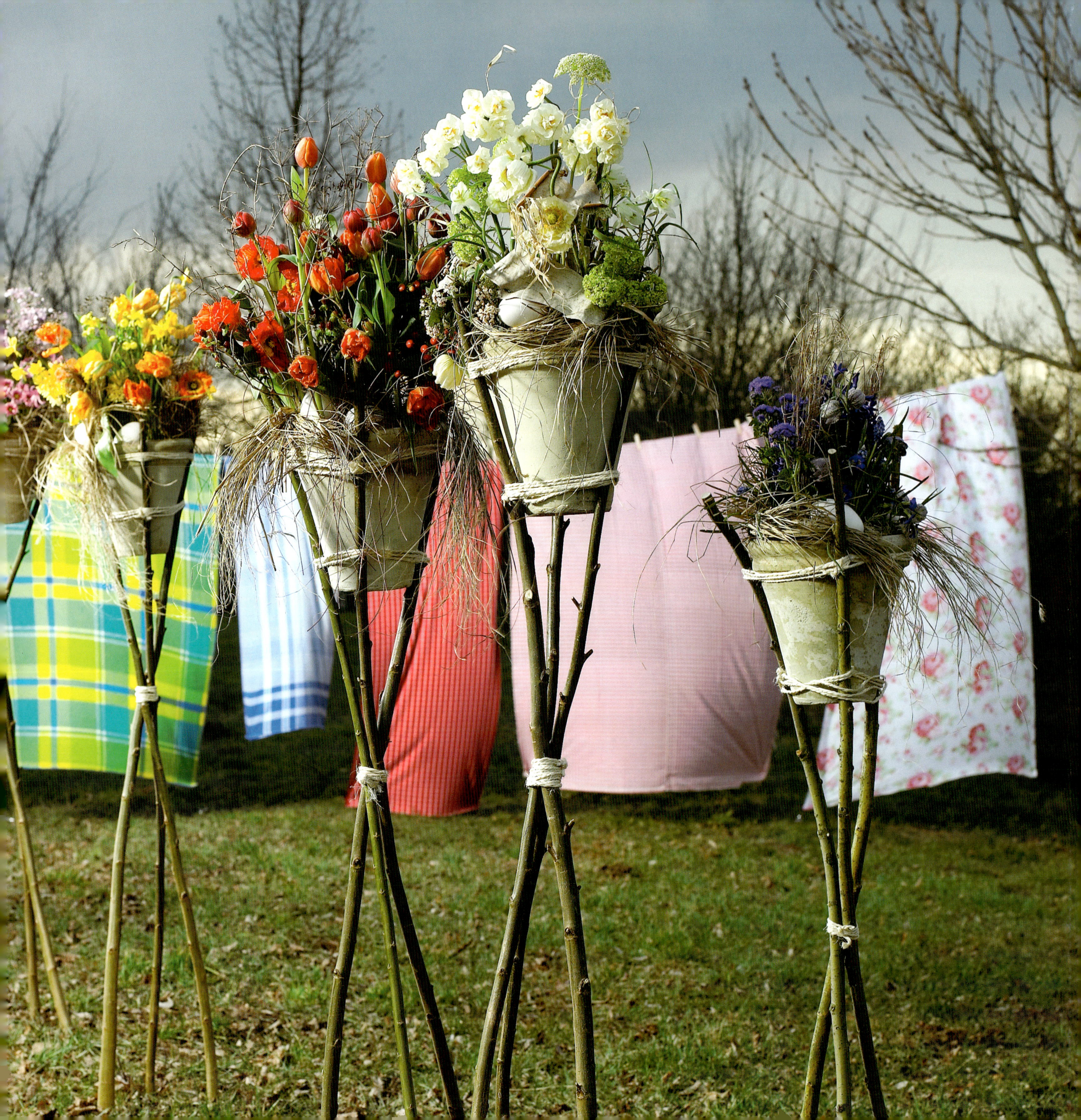

Auf dem Land – buntes Treiben

Eine neue Romantik ist das modische Leitthema. Nach Zeiten des Glanz und Glamours reift die Sehnsucht nach Tradition und Rückbesinnung. Inspirationen geben ländlich-bäuerliche Sitten, wie der Waschtag. Die bunten Tücher stehen für das vielgestaltige Leben auf dem Lande und machen Lust, Konventionelles unkonventionell zu präsentieren.

In the Countryside – life full of colours

A new form of romanticism is the modern key topic. After a time of glamour the longing for traditions and recollection is emerging. Rural customs, like the washing day are inspiring. The coloured cloth represent the multiform life in the countryside and invites to present conventional elements in an unconventional way.

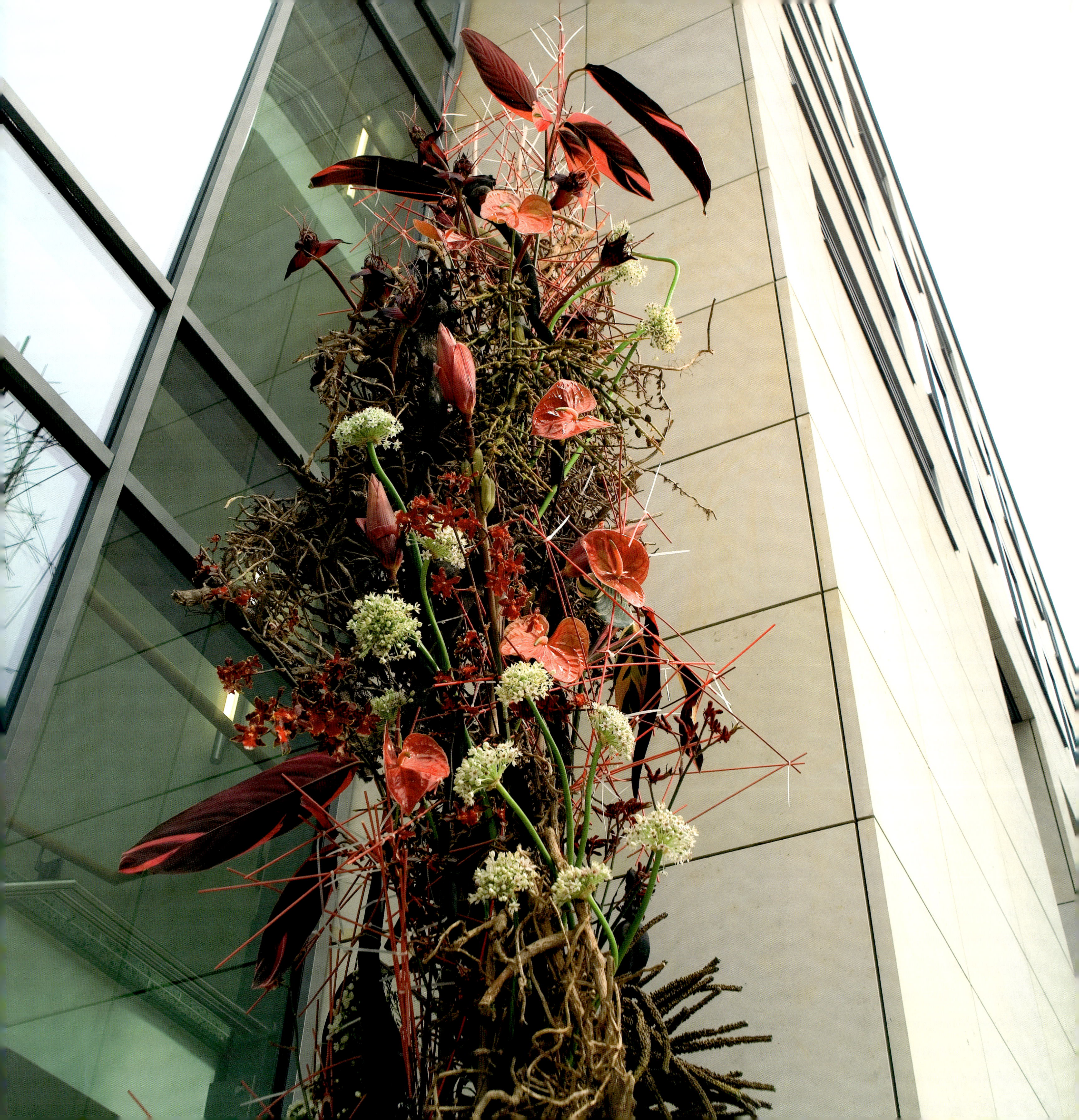

In der Stadt – hoch hinaus

Blüten adeln Glas und Marmor. Floraldesign als Lebensadern moderner Architektur sind Oasen für die Seele Millionen der Natur entfremdeter Menschen. Leben in Harmonie und Einklang mit dem Umfeld ist eine Frage des Zusammenwirkens von zeitgemäßer Urbanität und lebenswerter Ausgestaltung. Die Zukunft sollte blühenden und grünenden Städten gelten.

In the City – starting up

Blossoms ennoble glass and marble. Floral designs represent the life veins of modern architecture and thus an oasis for the soul of millions of people alienated from nature. Living in harmony with the environment depends on the conformity between contemporary urbanism and liveable design. The future should be dedicated to blooming green towns.

Solisten in Gegenüberstellung zur Masse oder Leicht-Schwer-Kontraste schaffen spannungsvolle Inszenierungen. Die Kunst ist es, die richtige Gewichtung zu finden, die Balance zwischen einem Zuviel und einem Zuwenig auszutarieren. Das erfordert Fingerspitzengefühl und Augenmaß vom Kreativen, sowie Mut, einmal gegen den Strom der Konformität zu gestalten.

Mono versus Mass

Floral soloists contrasted to the mass or light-heavy contrasts create exciting productions. Checking the right weighting and finding the balance between too much and too little makes the difference. This requires a sure instinct and a sense of visual judgement, as well as the courage to oppose once all conformities when designing.

Mono kontra Masse

108 | 109

WAGENER | Individuelle Ansichten *Individual Views*

Ordnung kontra Chaos

Die Ordnung hilft uns, das Chaos zu regeln. Erst gewählte Prinzipien und der gestalterische Eingriff lassen im scheinbar Ungeordneten der Natur Strukturen erkennen. Gebändigt durch Begrenzungen, ändert sich der Blick auf Gewohntes und offenbart Altbekanntes neu. Solche subtilen gestalterischen Eingriffe, die selbst kaum erkennbar werden, mag ich ganz besonders.

Order versus Chaos

The order helps us settle the chaos. Thanks to selected principles and creative actions nature's apparent disorder gets visible structures. Being restrained by limitations, we change our view of familiarities while the well-known is revealed in a new form. Such subtly creative actions, which are hardly recognizable as such, are my favourites.

106 | 107   WAGENER | Individuelle Ansichten *Individual Views*

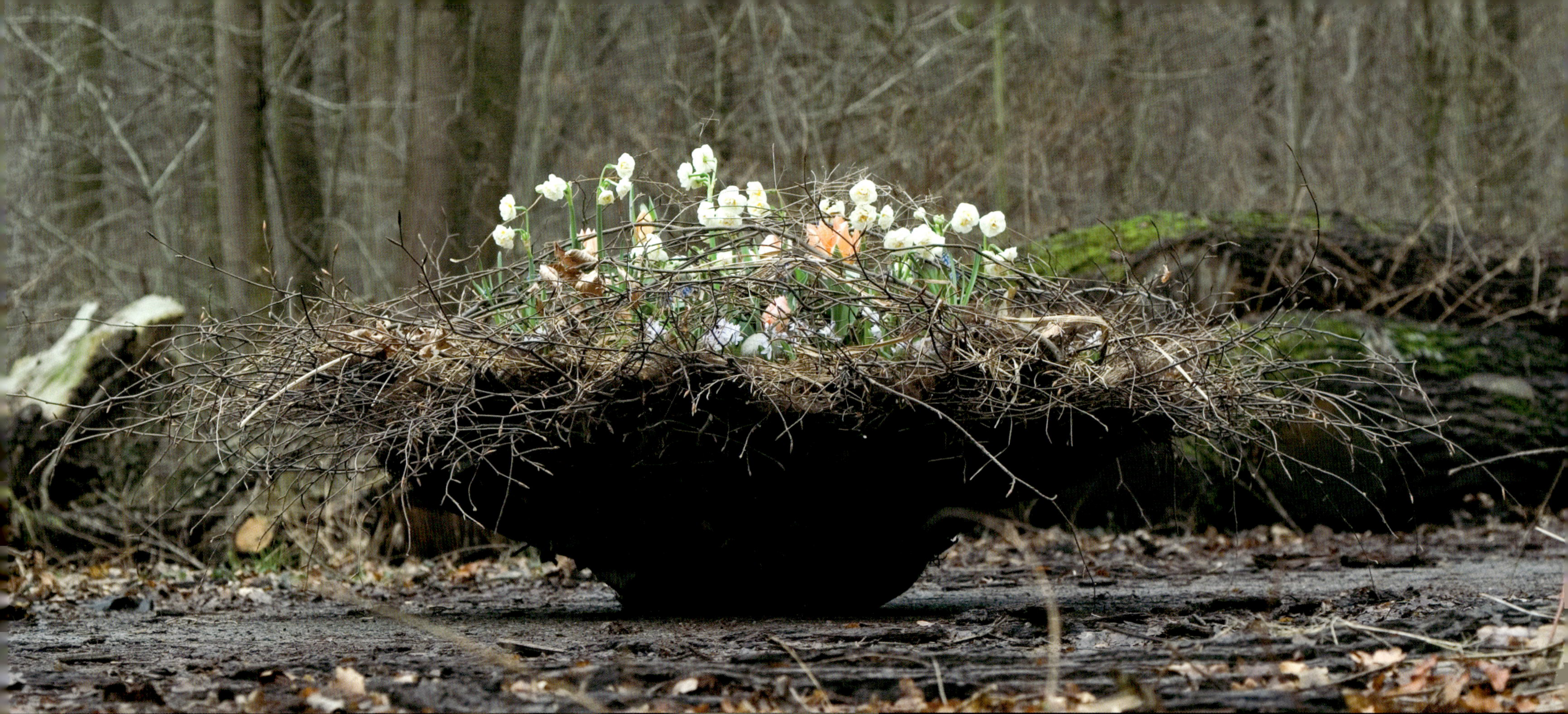

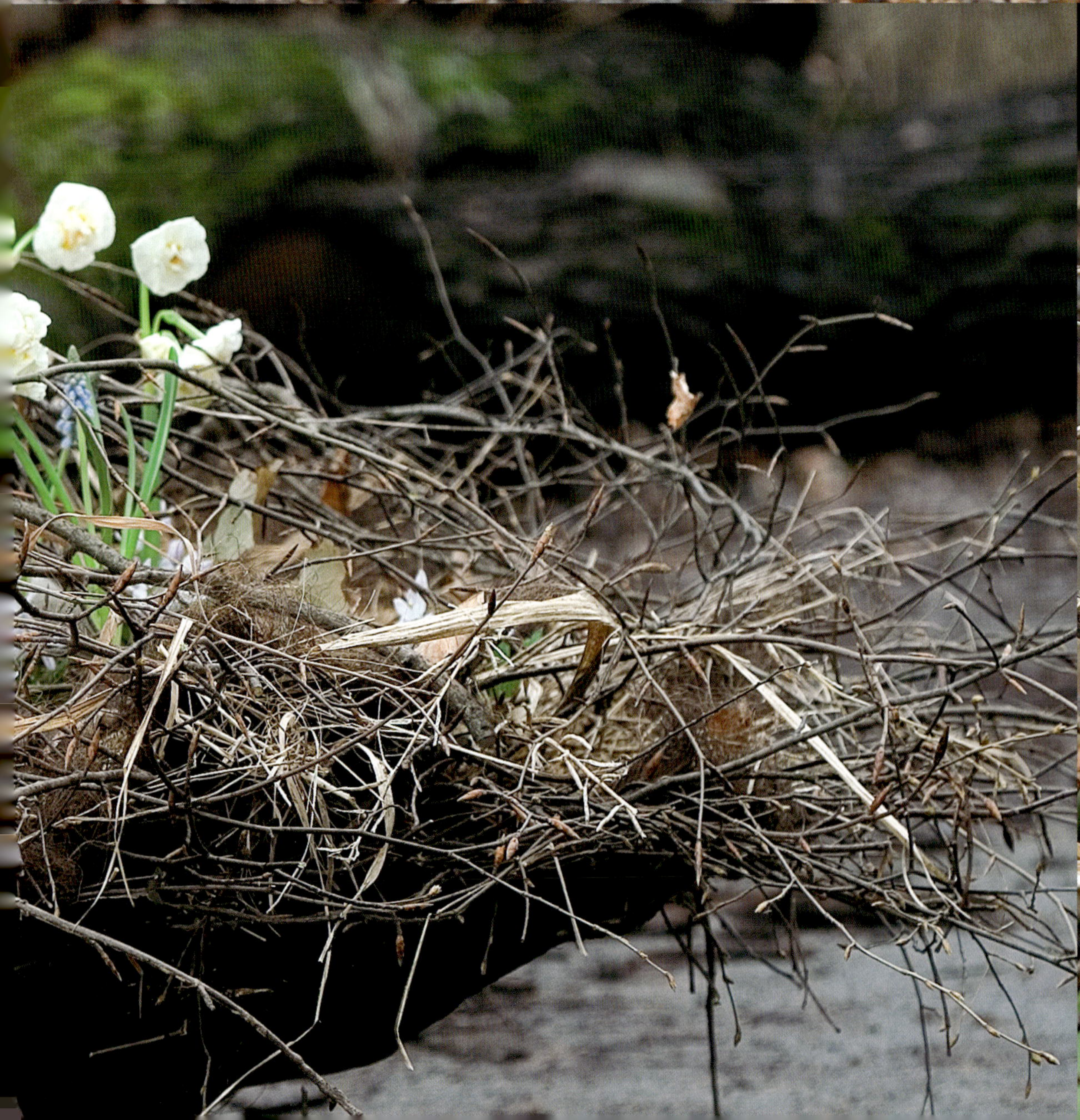

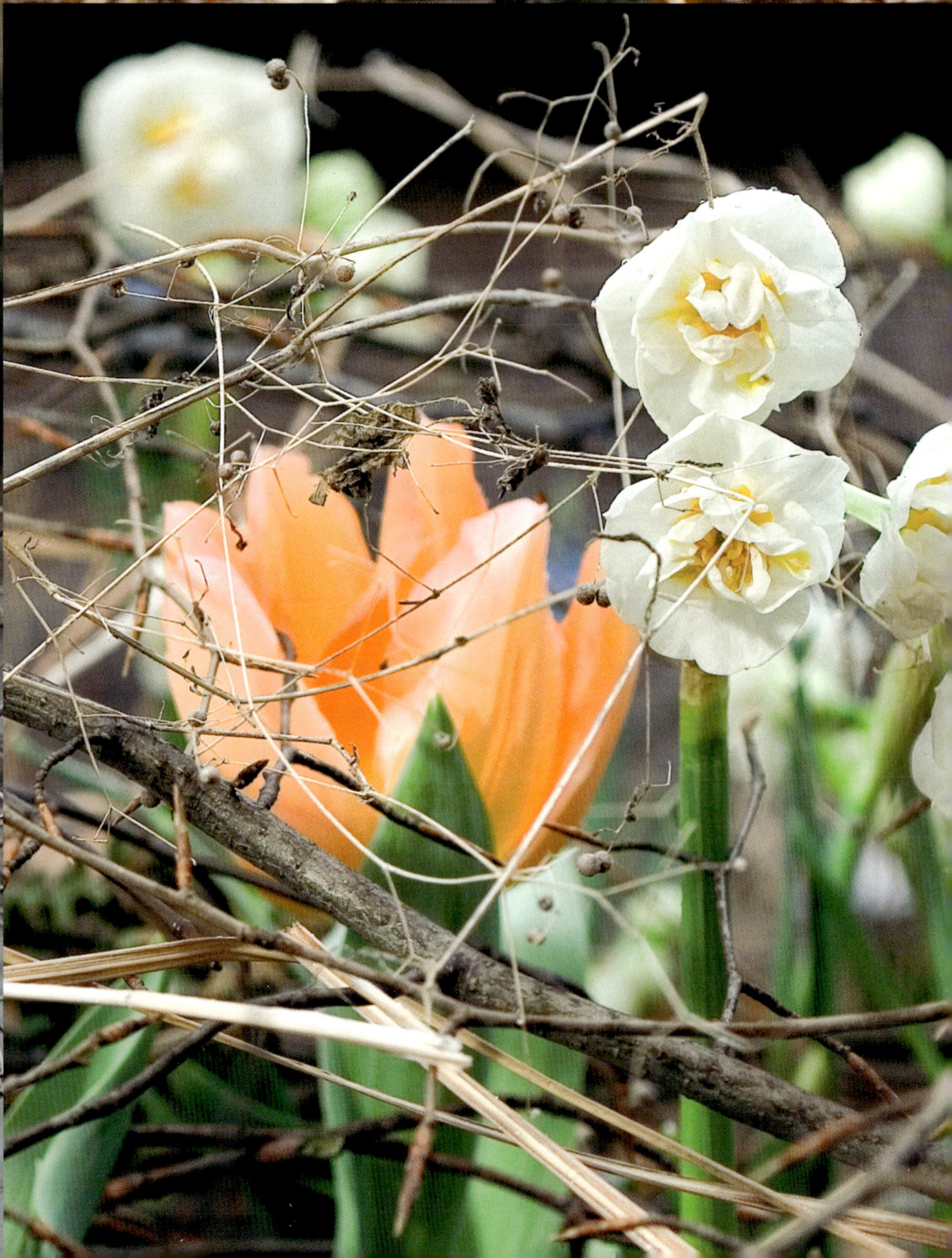

Leben & Sterben

An der Schwelle vom Winter zum Frühjahr, beim Wechsel vom alten in das neue Jahr oder beim Miteinander von Trockenem, Abgestorbenem mit Frischem, Sprießendem wird das Rad des Lebens sichtbar. Das eine geht aus dem anderen hervor, das Leben beginnt mit dem Tod. Ein Kreislauf, dem sich nichts und niemand entziehen kann.

Life & Death

The wheel of life becomes obvious on the threshold from winter to spring, from the change of the old into a new year and also in the combination of dry, dead elements with fresh, shooting ones. Something begins when something else ends, life begins with death. The cycle of life unavoidable by nothing and no one.

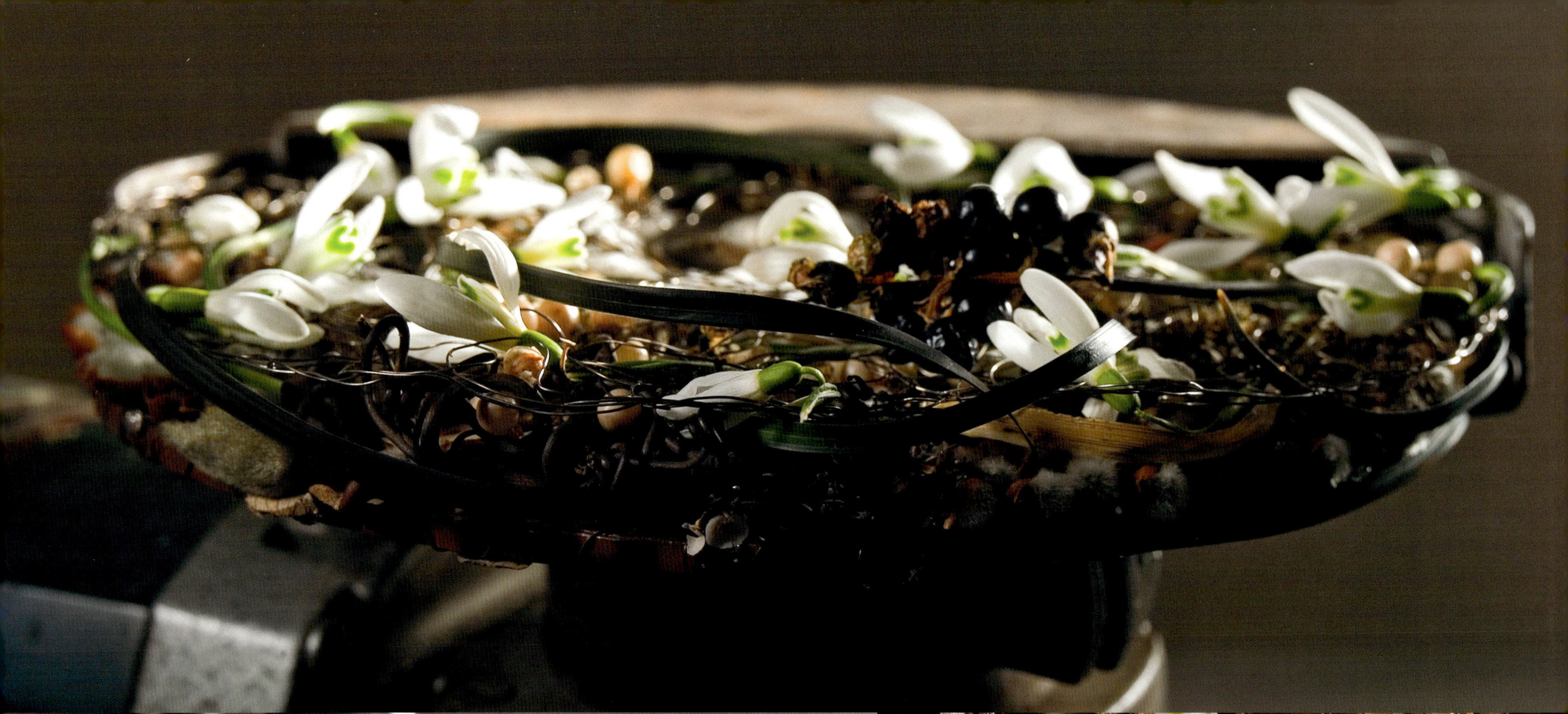
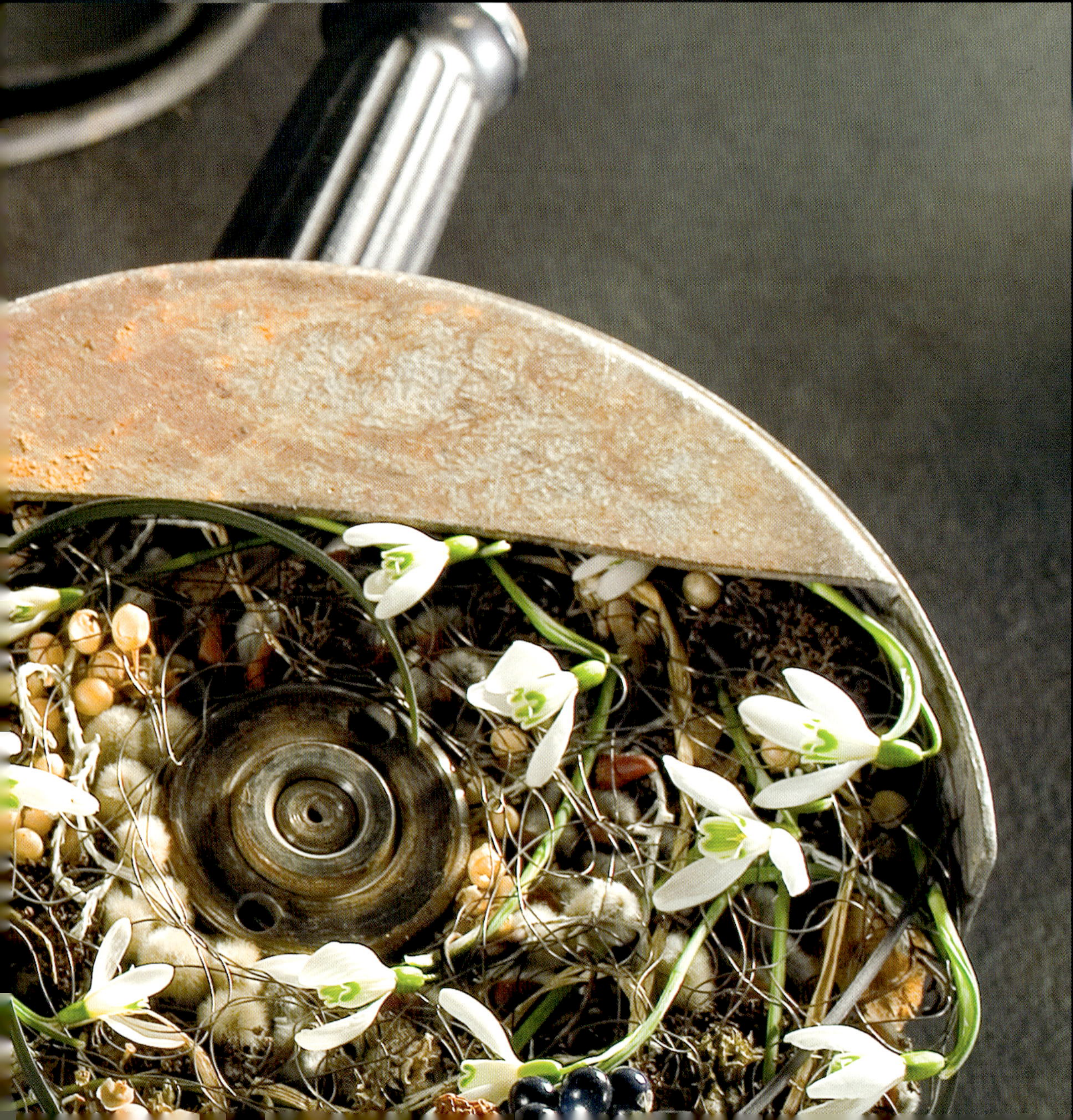
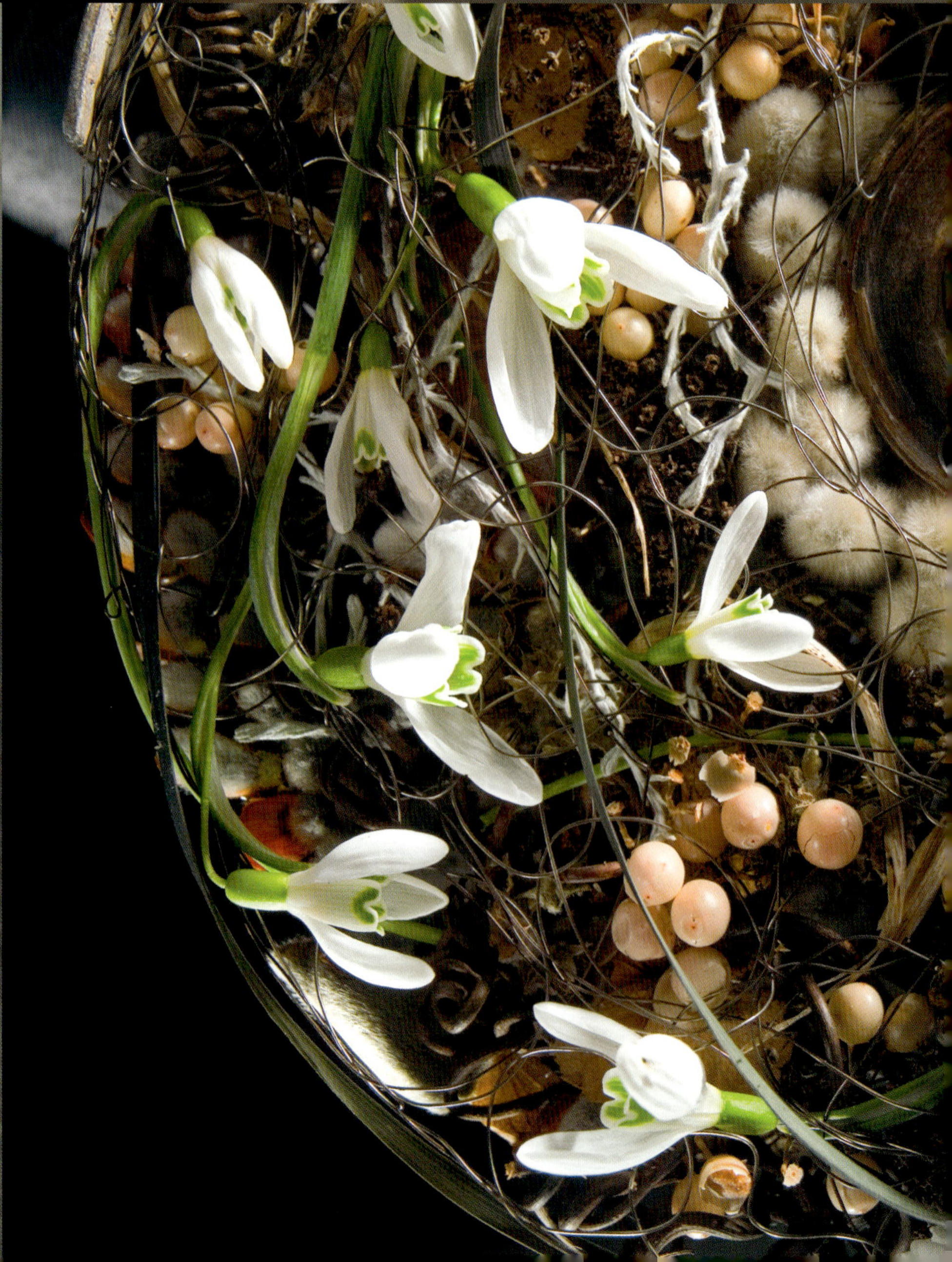

Natur & Technik

So zart und bescheiden die Solisten selbst, so kraftvoll ist das Konzert im Ganzen. Wenn Natur und Technik eine Symbiose eingehen, drängt sich die Frage auf, wer hier wen dominiert. Gestalterische Grenzgänge, die mich reizen.

Nature & Technology

Whereas the floral soloists are fragile and modest, their bloomy concert as a whole is full of energy. Whenever nature and technology build a symbiosis we ask ourselves which one is dominating? This are creative limits that appeal to me.

Erd-bewegung

krümelig – Erdbeben – bodenständig – Erdball – Lehm – braun – umgraben – erden – Erdkruste – Wurm – Erddrehung – Wurzel

Earth Rotation

crumbly – earth quake – rooted to the soil – globe – loam – brown – digging over – to earthen – earth's crust – worms – earth rotation – roots

Luft-schloss

nichts – schweben – aufsteigen – Ballon – Wind – Sturm – Flugzeug – luftleer – leicht – fliegen – Luftfahrt – Höhenluft – Luftgeist

Air Castle

nothing – floating – rising – balloon – wind – storm – airplane – vacuum – light – flying – aviation – mountain air – sylphals

Feuer- topf

WAGENER | Individuelle Ansichten *Individual Views*

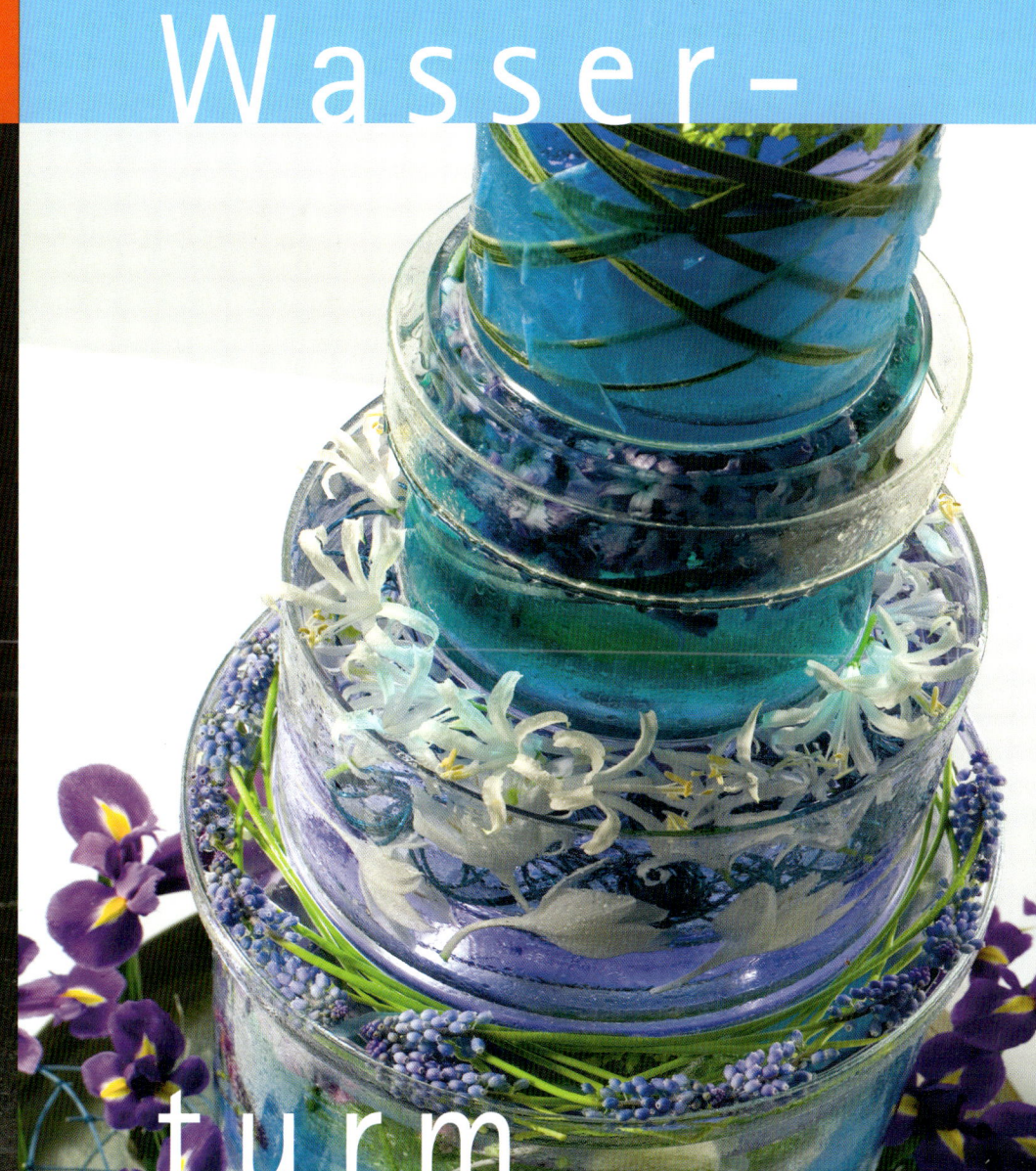

heiß – glutrot – gefährlich – Flammen – Feuerwehr – Ofen – Feuergefecht – Vulkan – Hitze – Hochofen – brennen – Lagerfeuer – Feuerteufel

Fire Pot

hot – fiery red – dangerous – flames – fire brigade – oven– gunfight – volcano– height – blast furnace – burning – campfire – firebug

Wasser- turm

nass – blau – fließend – spritzen – abtauchen – erfrischend – Tropfen – Fontäne – Brunnen – Meer – Regen – Durst – Wolken – Wasserglas – trinken

Water Tower

wet – blue – flowing– splashing – plunging – refreshing – drops – fountain – ocean – rain – thirst – clouds – tumbler – drinking

Trends

Die Renaissance der Ornamentik bei Lifestyle- und Konsumprodukten macht auch vorm Floraldesign nicht Halt. Diese neue Dekorativität ist vielseitig und flexibel einsetzbar. Mal wird Florales ornamental geschmückt, mal ist es schon selbst das Ornament, eben Magic Ornaments!

The renaissance of ornaments with lifestyle and consumer products also affects the floral design. This new multifunctional form of decorations proves to be flexibly applicable. Sometimes a floral design is decorated with ornaments, whereas other times it's the design itself, which is the ornament, exactly magic ornaments!

Tendenzen

Es kündigt sich eine neue Ruhe und Gelassenheit in der Gestaltung an. Alle Kreativen dieser Welt sind auf der Suche nach dem zeitlosen Design von morgen. Der Wunsch nach Authentizität einerseits, aber auch Sinngebung und Spiritualität lässt uns Floristen aufs Wesentliche blicken, eben eine luxuriöse Askese!

A new form of silence and serenity is being pronounced. All creations of the world are looking for the timeless design of tomorrow. Our desire for authenticity on the one hand, but also for interpretation and spirituality lets us florists concentrate on the essential, namely a luxurious abstinence.

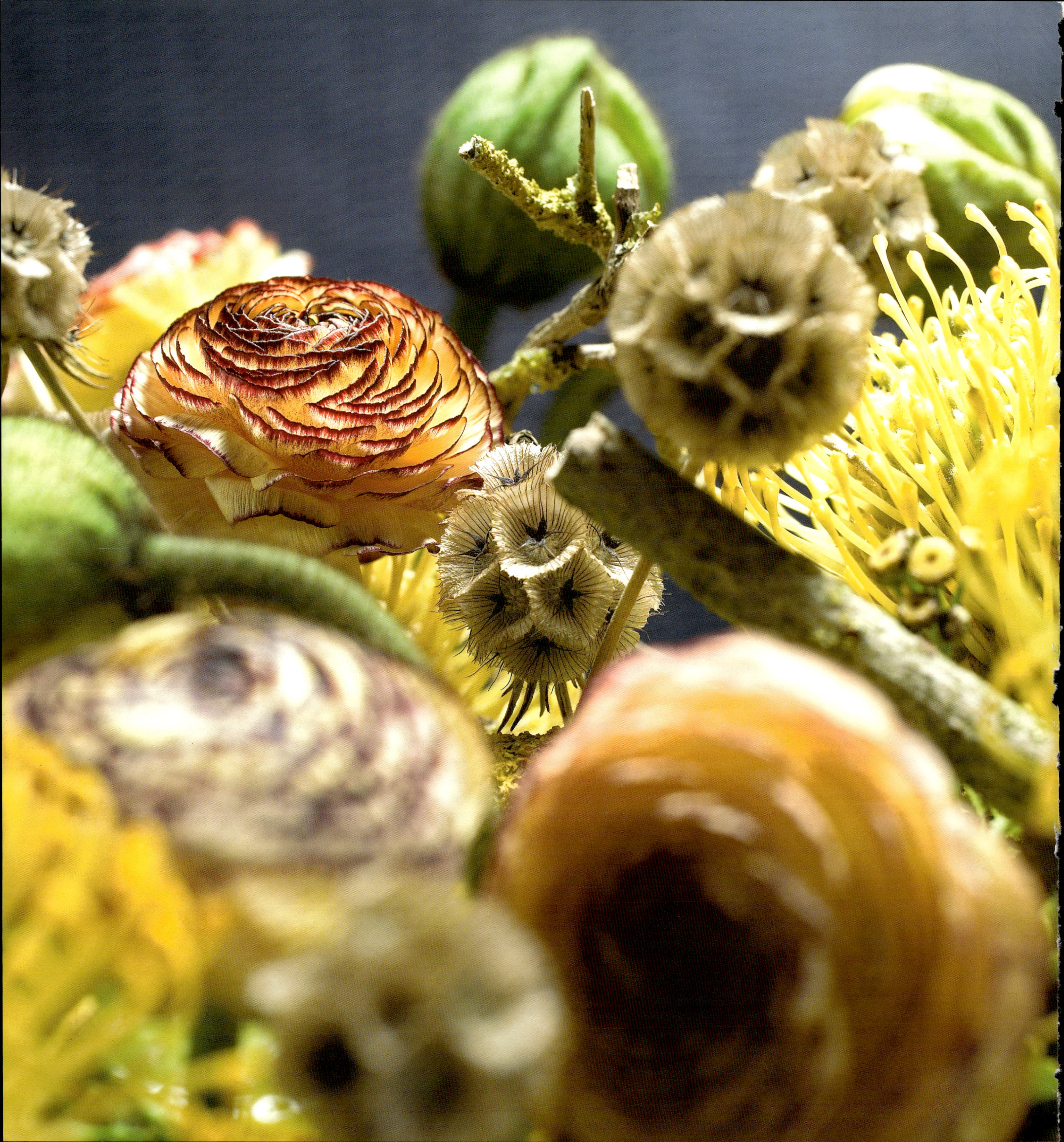

Themen
Topics – Trends – Tendencies

Die Haptik ist ein neues Thema in der Floristik. In einer Epoche, in der die Fülle an Reizeinwirkungen keine Grenzen kennt, darf Floraldesign neben dem Optischen auch den Tastsinn ansprechen. So erschließen sich Kreationen mit mehreren Sinnen. Neben Werkstoff und Material werden deren Oberflächen und Strukturen bedeutsam, eben das florale Profil!

Haptics is a new topic in floristry. In a time of borderless effects of impulses, floral designs may also appeal to the sense of touch besides the optical senses. Thus, several senses are seized by creations. Besides materials, it's their surfaces and structures, and precisely the floral portrait, which gains in importance!

Architektonisch konstruiert

Den absolut perfekten rechten Winkel wird man – zumindest als Prinzip – in der Natur vergeblich suchen. Somit bleibt dieser der von Menschenhand konstruierten Technik vorbehalten. Bringt man jedoch beides zusammen, ergibt sich ein reizvoller Kontrast, der modernen Ansprüchen genügt. Konstruiertes bringt den Gegensatz des Natürlichen zur Geltung, Florales überwindet ganz selbstverständlich die Grenzen der Technik.

Architectural Constructions

You won't find a right angle in nature – at least as a rule. It remains a manually constructed technique. If you combine, however, natural and technical forms you will get a charming contrast, which meets modern demands. A technical construction emphasises the contrast to a natural one and thus floral constructions surmount naturally technical borders.

Ausgangspunkt aller gestalterischen Darstellungen eines Floraldesigners ist die Natur. Sie ist Ursprung, Vorbild und Lehrer zugleich. Unerreichbar in ihrer Einzigartigkeit, sind unsere Interpretationen lediglich Versuche, sie in ihrer Komplexität zu erfassen. Ein Aspekt, der für mich dabei so natürlich wie faszinierend ist, ist der der Parallelität. Die himmelwärts wachsenden, sich vertikal erhebenden Blumen und ihre Begleiter stellen damit einen kleinen Naturausschnitt dar, sozusagen einen idealisierten Garten.

Natural Growth

Nature is the basis of all creative designs. It is at the same time the origin, the role model and the mentor. In the context of its unreachable uniqueness, our interpretations are only attempts to seize its complexity. Parallelism is an aspect, I consider to be both, naturally and fascinating. The flowers and their companions rising vertically to the sky represent thus a small portrait of nature, somehow an idealized garden.

Natürlich gewachsen

Mit der Zeit ändern sich Wahrnehmung und Empfindung. Die Kalla, die zu meiner Ausbildungszeit als typische Beerdigungsblume galt, weiß ich mittlerweile als eine Blüte voller Charakter und erlesener Eleganz zu schätzen. Die Reinheit ihrer klaren Form, der glatte, unbeblätterte, dickfleischige Schaft und ihre vornehme, distanzierte Ausstrahlung faszinieren mich, die Entdeckung ihrer Biegsamkeit animiert mich heute, dreißig Jahre später, zu grafisch-formalen Gestaltungen voller Ästhetik und Transparenz.

New Discoveries

Time makes change our perceptions and feelings. Nowadays, I appreciate the Calla, which used to be a typical funeral flower during my apprenticeship, as a blossom full of character and exquisite elegance. I am fascinated by its pure and clear shape as well as by its even, leafless and juicy bole. Today, 30 years later, the discovery of its flexibility animates me to create graphically formal designs full of aesthetics and transparency.

Neu entdeckt

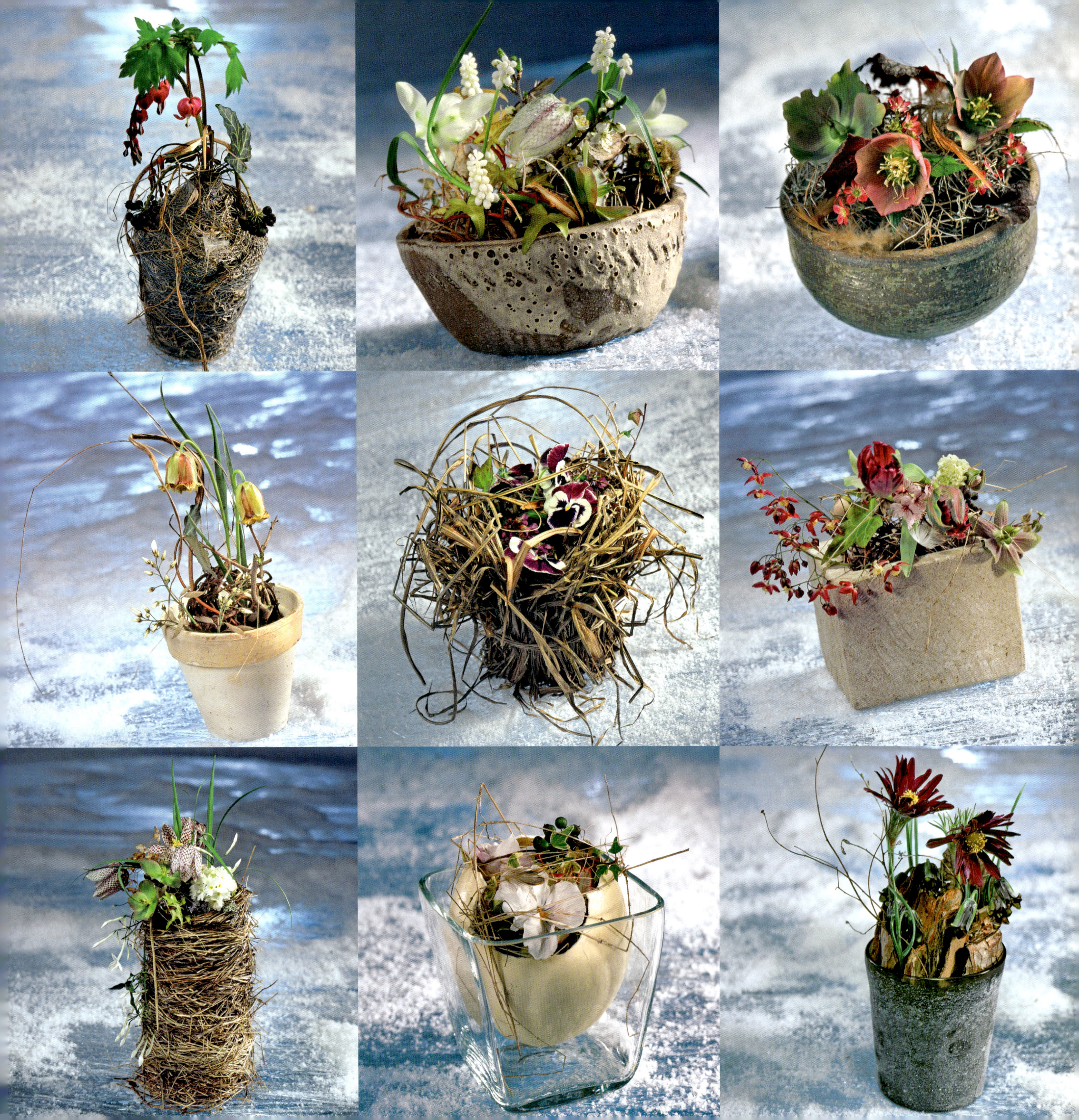

Heiß geliebt

Schätze aus der Vergangenheit, liebgewonnene Fundstücke von Spaziergängen, Kleinode aus dem eigenen Garten – all das, woran das Herz hängt, verbindet sich in Kleinstarrangements wie der Inhalt einer Schatztruhe. Manchmal ist es nur eine Blume, die ich ihrer Einfachheit wegen liebe, und die keiner aufwändigen Gestaltung bedarf. Die blühenden Kleinigkeiten werden so zu heiß geliebten Kostbarkeiten.

Precious Treasures

Treasury from the past, beloved funds gained through walkways, gems of one's own garden, everything the heart is attached to, is combined to tiny arrangements like the content of a treasure chest. Sometimes it's just a simple flower that I am fond of, because of its simplicity and because it doesn't require a complex designing. The blooming odds and ends become thus precious treasures.

Erkennen, was schön und einmalig ist, auch den Blick für das scheinbar Unscheinbare zu haben sowie wachen Sinnes die Natur zu beobachten, sind für mich als Gestalter Voraussetzungen, um selber Individuelles schaffen zu können. Jedes Teil eines Ganzen will sorgfältig erkannt und platziert sein: ein bizarr gewachsener Ast, eine imposante Wurzel, ein getrockneter Fruchtstand. Doch die Attribute einer modernen Welt bleiben nicht außen vor. Erst im Miteinander mit ihnen entstehen für mich spannungsvolle Inszenierungen, die den Geist der Zeit atmen.

Basic Importance

The ability to recognize beauty and uniqueness, to have a sense of apparently unimportant things and to observe nature with wake senses is the basis for all of us designers in order to realize an individual creation on our own. Each part of a whole needs to be carefully recognized and positioned: a bizarrely grown branch, an impressive root, a dried infructescence. But the accessories of a modern world are not left outside. Only a combination of these engenders exciting productions that breathe the spirit of the time.

Elementar wichtig

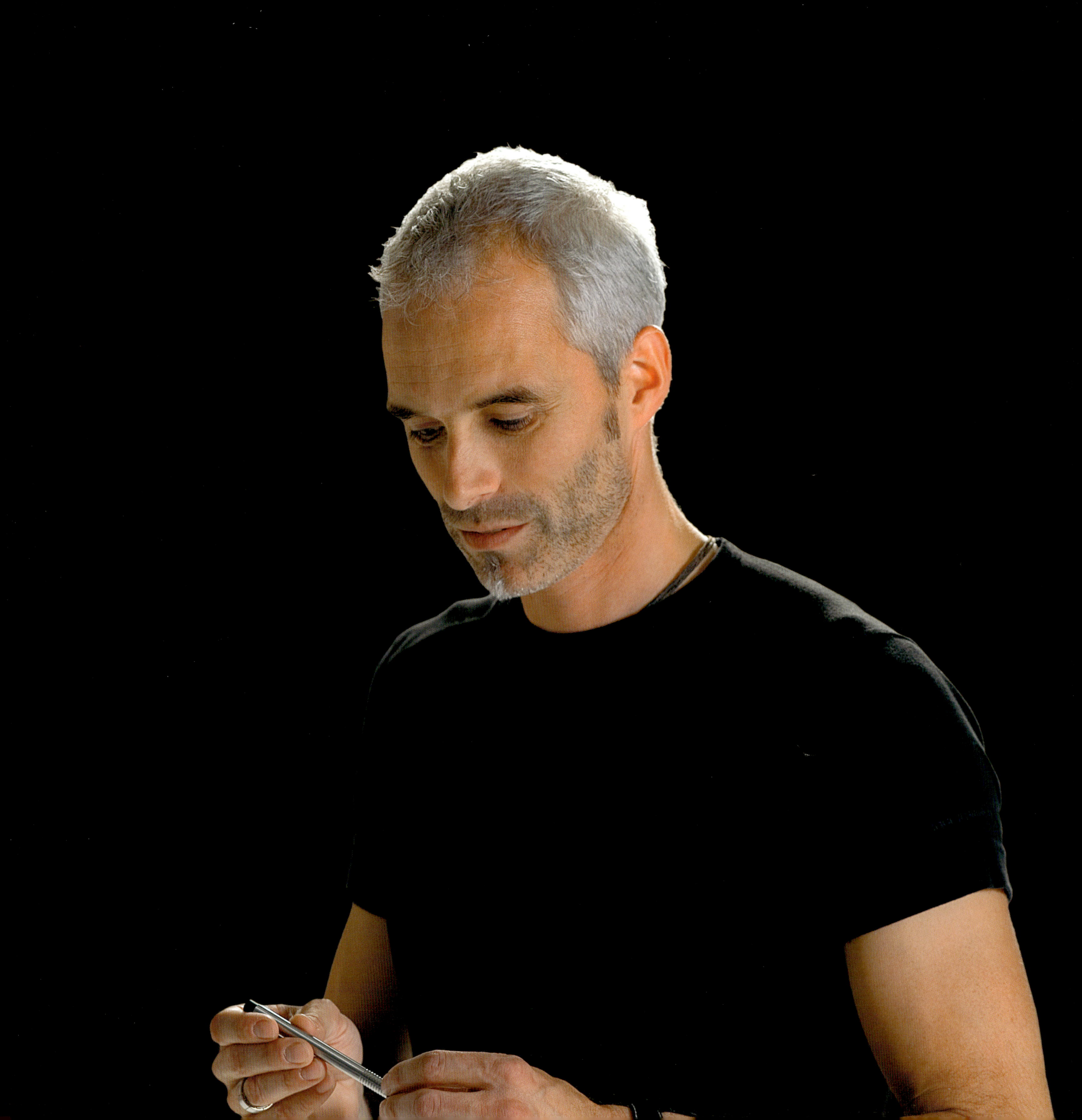

Individuelle Ansichten

Blumen und Pflanzen sind für mich etwas Einmaliges. Jede von ihnen hat ihren eigenen Charakter und damit eine eigene Faszination. Sich mit diesem „Lächeln der Natur" zu verbünden und damit einen immer neuen gestalterischen Ausdruck zu finden, ist meine Berufung und persönliche Erfüllung. Dennoch: Floristik will für Menschen gemacht sein, und ihnen muss man in ihrer Zeit begegnen. Deshalb sollten florale Kreationen nicht losgelöst vom gesellschaftlichen Wandel oder ungeachtet der sich ständig verändernden Designvorstellungen entstehen. Dies ist mir einerseits Verpflichtung, anderseits liegt hierin meine immerwährende Inspirationsquelle. Erkennen, Umsetzen, Genießen sind für mich deshalb die drei großen Schritte auf dem Weg zu einer Floristik, die Menschen erreichen und begeistern, Lebensqualität steigern und ein Lebensumfeld gestalten will.

Individual Views

Flowers and plants are something unique for me. Each of them has its own character and thus its own fascination. My vocation and personal fulfilment is to embrace this "smile of nature" and thus to find a new creative expression. However, floristry is meant for people and the time they live in. Therefore, floral designs should not be created apart from social changes or regardless of the permanently changing visions of design. On the one hand, this means responsibility to me, but on the other hand this is my everlasting source of inspiration. Therefore I think that recognizing, realizing and enjoying are the three big steps on the way of creating a floral arrangement, which wants to reach and enthusiast people, enhance the quality of life and create a living environment.

Heimat: Zuckerrübe

Wenn der Winter naht und die trüben, kalten Tage beginnen, kehrt bei uns eine ganz besondere Ruhe ein. Die Felder entlang der Weser sind dann abgeerntet und haben ein braunes Kleid angezogen. Doch die Natur hat vorgesorgt und ihre gesammelte Energie kreativ verpackt. Jetzt ist Runkelrübenzeit. Die urigen Gesellen werden als Viehfutter zu Mieten gehäuft oder in die Fabriken zur Zuckergewinnung gefahren. Für uns Kinder damals die Zeit der gruseligen Rübengesichter, denen ein flackerndes Wachslicht schauderhaft das Innere erleuchtete. Halloween auf dem Lande.

Homeland: Sugar Beet

If winter is getting close and the cloudy, cold days begin, a particular silence is coming. The fields along the Weser have been harvested and put on a brown coat. But nature is prepared and has put all of its collected energy in creations. Now it's the time for beets. The quaint companions are piled as animal fodder or brought to factories for the extraction of sugar. For us children, it was the time of creepy beet heads, with a flickering candle that dreadfully illuminates its interior. Halloween in the countryside.

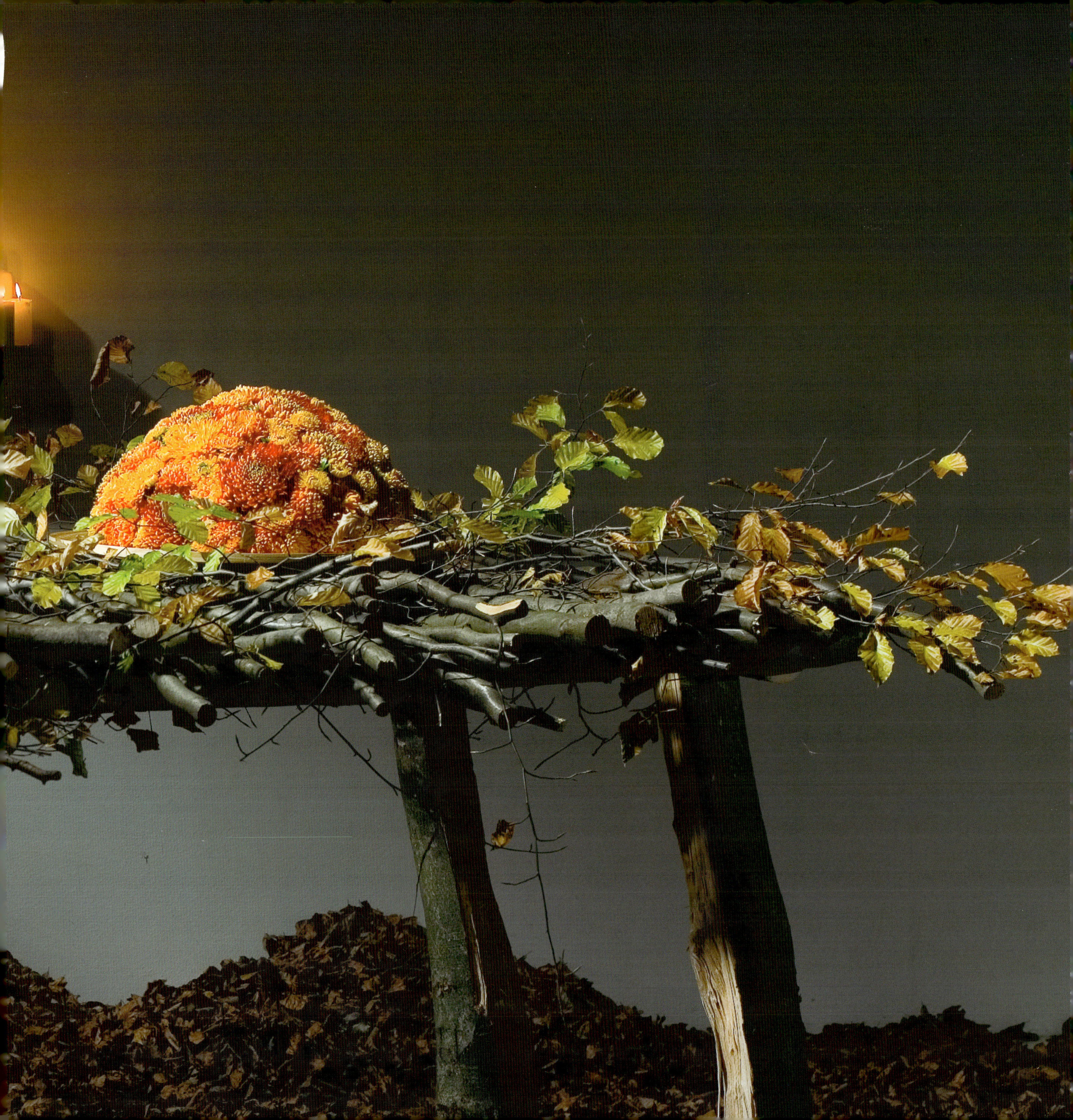

Wie kein anderer Baum dominiert die Buche mit ihren mächtigen Kronen die Bergketten meines Heimatlandes. Wird es Herbst, leuchten die Höhenzüge goldgelb und laden zu ausgiebigen Wanderungen ein. Diesen Gabentisch der Natur sehe ich für mich gedeckt. Ich liebe das glatte, gräuliche, leicht pockige Holz, das im Jahresverlauf von Hellgrün über Dunkelgrün, dann von Gelb bis Braun changierende Laub sowie die mit bräunlichen Spitzen besetzten Äste. Die Buche hält mir vor Augen, wo meine Wurzeln sind und welches Dach mich schützt.

Homeland: Beech

Like no other tree, the beech with its powerful crowns is dominating the mountain chains of my homeland. When autumn is getting near, the range of hills shine in yellow golden colours inviting us to extensive walks. In my eyes, the table for nature is set. I love the smooth, grey-like, slightly pock-like wood, the foliage changing its colour in the course of the year from bright green to dark green, then from yellow to brown as well as the branches set up with their small brown-like tops. The beech makes me aware of my roots and of the roof, which protects me.

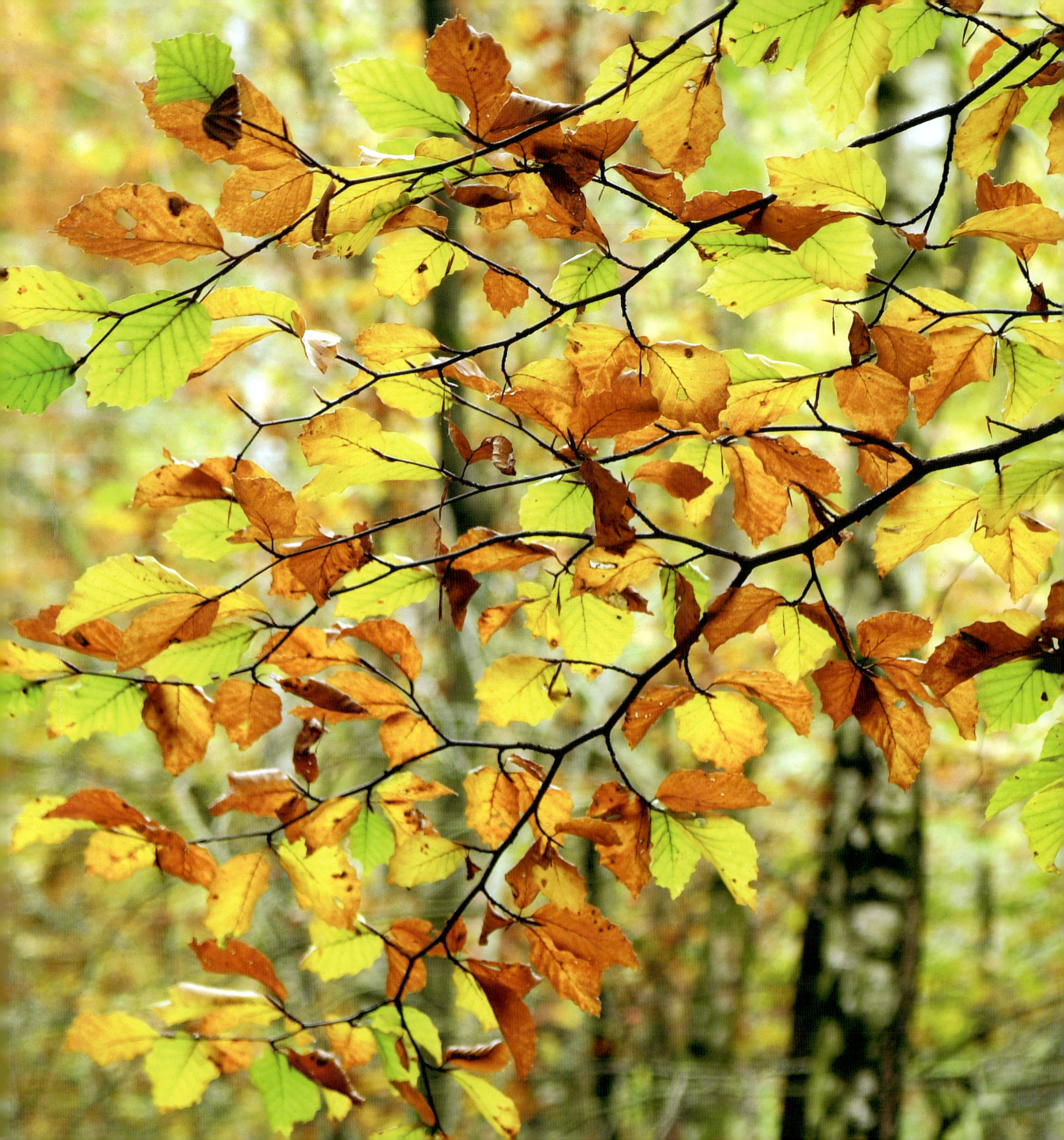

Heimat: Buche

WAGENER | Ganz persönliche Gefühle Very private Emotions

82 | 83

Heimat: Sonnenblume

Strahlende Höhepunkte übers Jahr stellen die gelbblühenden Blumen dar. Zuerst begeistern die mit fettem Löwenzahn besäten Auen im April und Mai. Dann die leuchtenden, wogenden Rapsfelder im Mai und Juni. Und schließlich im Hochsommer die vor Kraft strotzenden, majestätischen Sonnenblumen. Ihre Strahlkraft einerseits, aber auch die Schönheit ihrer dicht an dicht mit Kernen besetzten Blütenböden werden zu Fundstücken bei meinen Streifzügen durch die sommerwarme Landschaft.

Homeland: Sunflower

Yellow flowers are the sunny highlights throughout the year. At first, alluvial forests covered with thick dandelion fulfil us with enthusiasm In April and May. Then from May to June we are fascinated by shining and surging rape fields and finally at the height of the summer by powerful, majestic sunflowers. Their shining energy, but also the beauty of blossom's floors covered with dense seeds become finds in the course of my wanderings through a warm summer landscape.

Der Fluss in meiner Heimat, die Weser, mäandert sanft durch saftige Wiesen vorbei an verwunschenen Auwäldern. Beim Verweilen und Rasten im frischgrünen Gras folgt der Blick den Wolken, die der Wind am blauen Himmel wie Schafe vor sich hertreibt. Eine Landschaft, die mir ans Herz gewachsen ist, wo ich entspannen und neue Kraft für meinen Alltag sammeln kann.

Homeland: Meadow

The river of my homeland, the Weser, meanders softly through hefty meadows passing by enchanting alluvial forests. While dwelling and having a rest in the fresh green grass, the eyes are raised to the blue sky, following clouds, which are droved like sheep by the wind. A landscape, of which I have grown fond of, is the place where I can relax and collect new energy for my everyday life.

Heimat: Wiese

WAGENER | Ganz persönliche Gefühle *Very private Emotions*

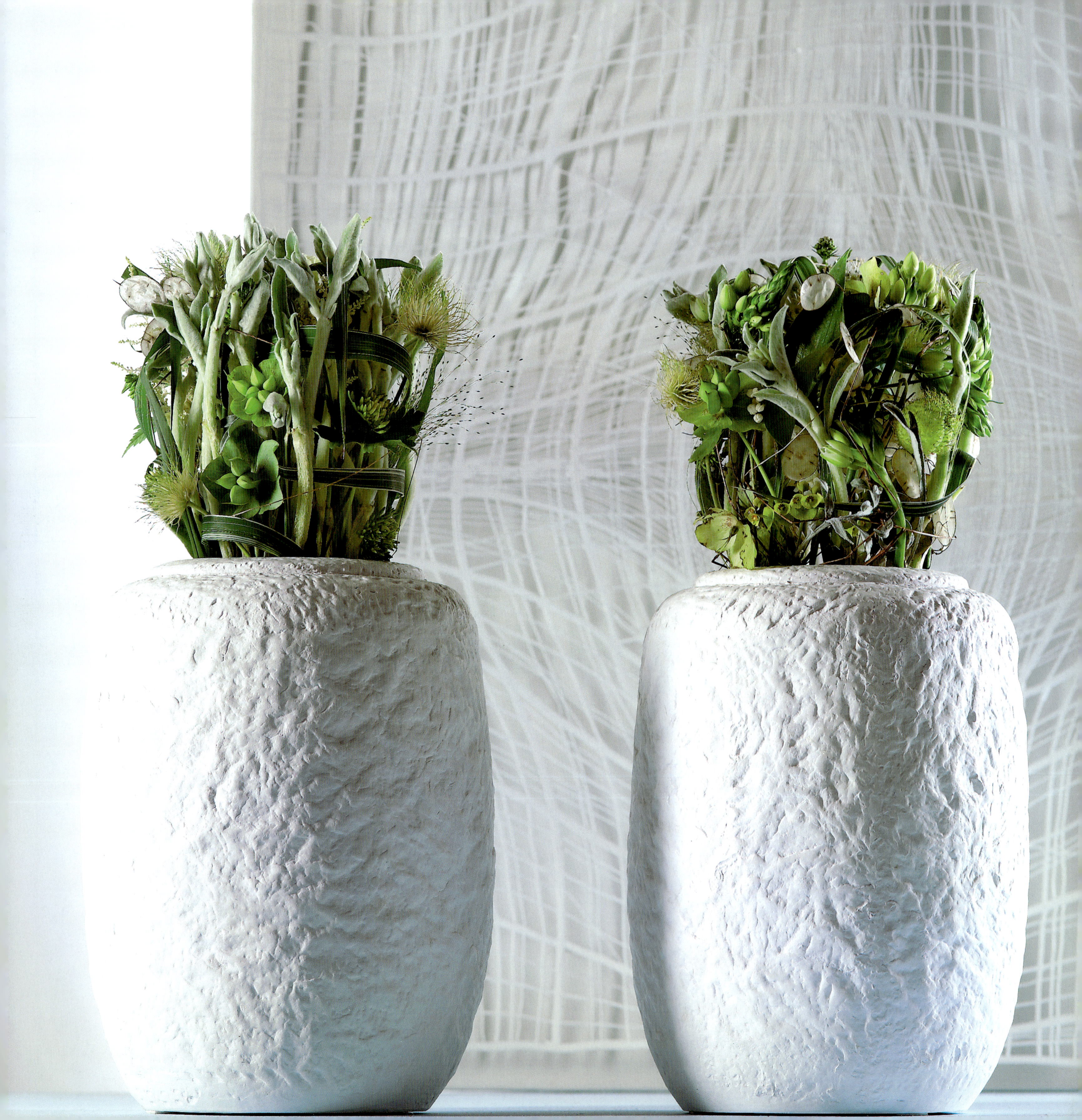

Die Reduktion von Farbe und Form belässt Strukturen ihren Auftritt. Wo Farbe zurückhaltend und bescheiden bleibt, wo das Einzelne und die Bewegungslinie sich der Form unterordnen, wirken für mich Oberflächen um so intensiver. Die Gestaltung funktioniert nach dem Prinzip: Weniger ist mehr!

Trenchant Reductions

Reducing colours and forms makes structures keep their appearances. For me, surfaces have a more intensive effect when colours are used with restriction and modesty and when individuality and movement lines are subordinated to formal aspects. According to the design's characteristic principle, less is more!

Reduziert-
pointiert

In der verschwenderischen Vielzahl von Blüten und Fruchtformen, Gräsern, Ranken und Zweigen wird der Reichtum der Natur zur Schau gestellt, die florale Fülle zum puren Luxus. Eine derartige Prachtentfaltung ist spektakulär und verführerisch zugleich. Nahezu jede Stilepoche hat diese Glanzpunkte. Doch wo das Maß der Dinge liegt und in welchem Moment Schönheit und Genuss in Sucht und Dekadenz umschlagen, muss jede Zeit immer wieder neu für sich definieren.

Abundant Decadence

The abundant diversity of nature is exhibited through the extravagant multitude of blossoms, fruit forms, grasses, twines and branches – floral wealth becomes pure luxury. Such a glorious evolvement is spectacular and seductive at the same time. Almost any stylistic era has such highlights. However, in any period the measure of all things and the moment of turning from beauty and pleasure to addiction and decadence has to be redefined once again.

ns
Opulent-dekadent

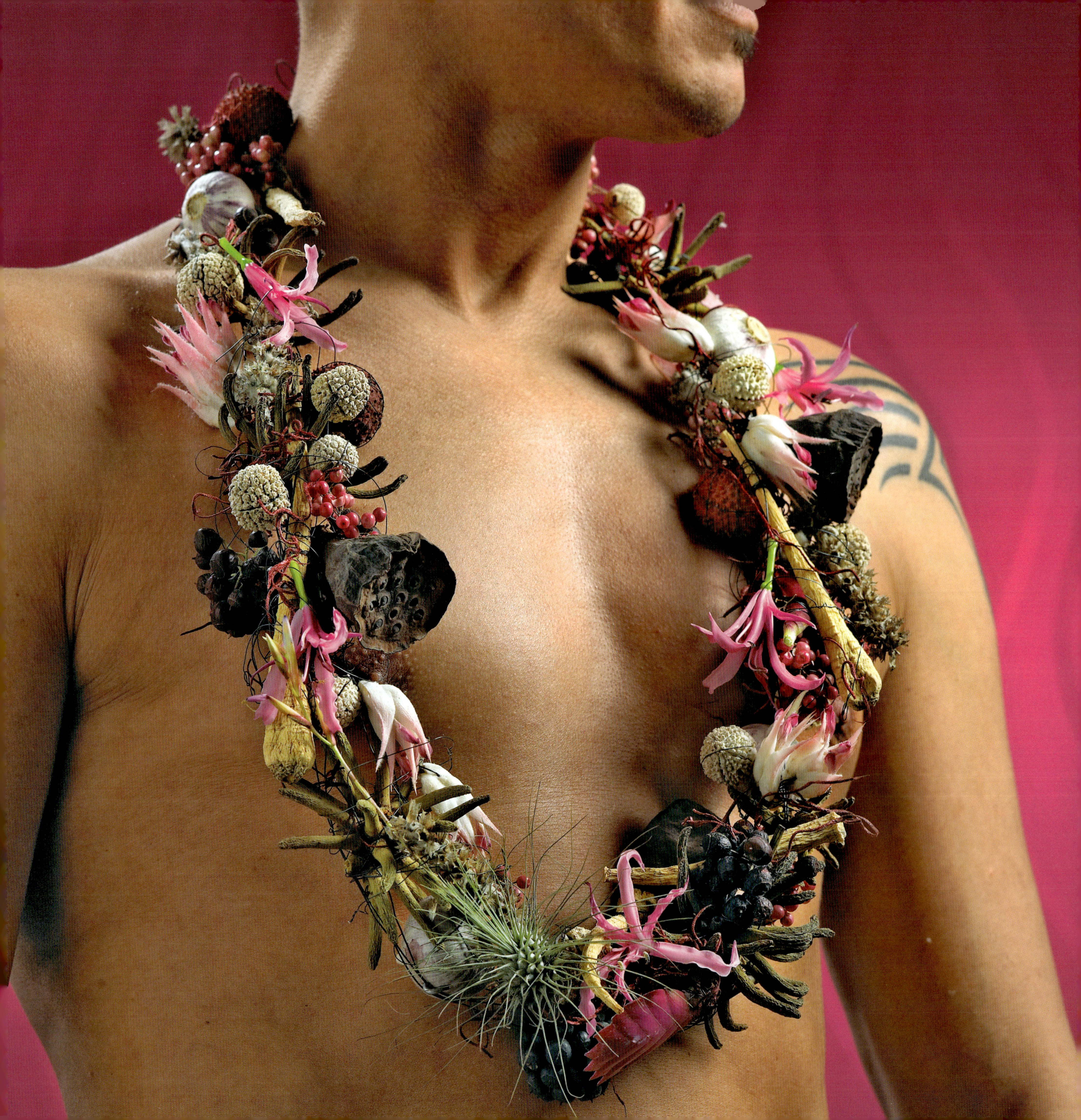

Sexy-provokant

WAGENER | Ganz persönliche Gefühle Very private Emotions

72 | 73

Sexy Provocations

In der Regel halten sich Blüten, Triebe und Fruchtformen auf Distanz zu uns Menschen. Berühren sie allerdings unseren Körper, entsteht Provozierendes, Erotisches. Blüten streicheln die Haut, Dornen schmerzen, Fasern kribbeln. Es stellt sich die Frage der eigenen körperlichen Nähe oder Distanz.

In general, blossoms, shoots and fruit forms keep the distance to us humans. However, if they get in contact with our body, something provocative, erotic is created. Blossoms caress the skin, thorns hurt and fibres itch. The question is, whether we prefer their proximity or distance.

Unsere Natur ist unendlich reich an grandiosen Farben und Formen. Sie betört uns durch Duft und beeindruckt durch feinsinnige Details. Greifen diese Eigenschaften perfekt ineinander, entsteht eine Komposition von großer Kraft und Tiefe. Der Faszination für diese vergängliche Pracht aus eleganten Blüten, formvollendeten, sinnlichen Früchten und betörenden Farben erliege ich jedes Jahr aufs Neue.

Sensual Material

Our nature is composed of endlessly terrific colours and forms, bewitching us with perfumes and impressing us through subtle details. If these characterstics are perfectly combined, a composition of great energy and depth emerges. Every year, I succumb again to the fascination of this transitory grace of elegant blossoms, perfect, sensual fruits and infatuating colours.

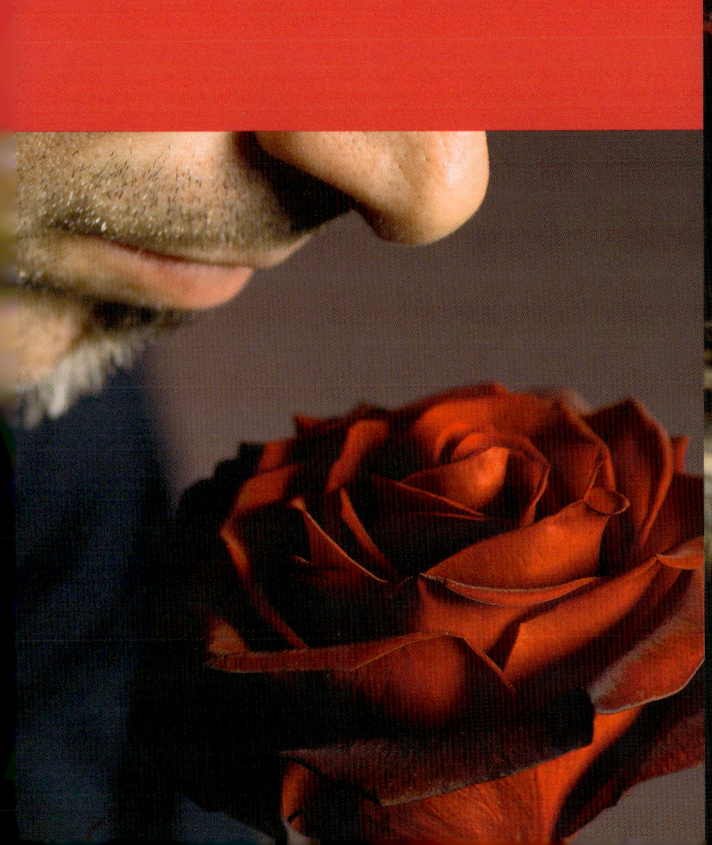

Sinnlich-körperlich

WAGENER | Ganz persönliche Gefühle Very private Emotions

70 | 71

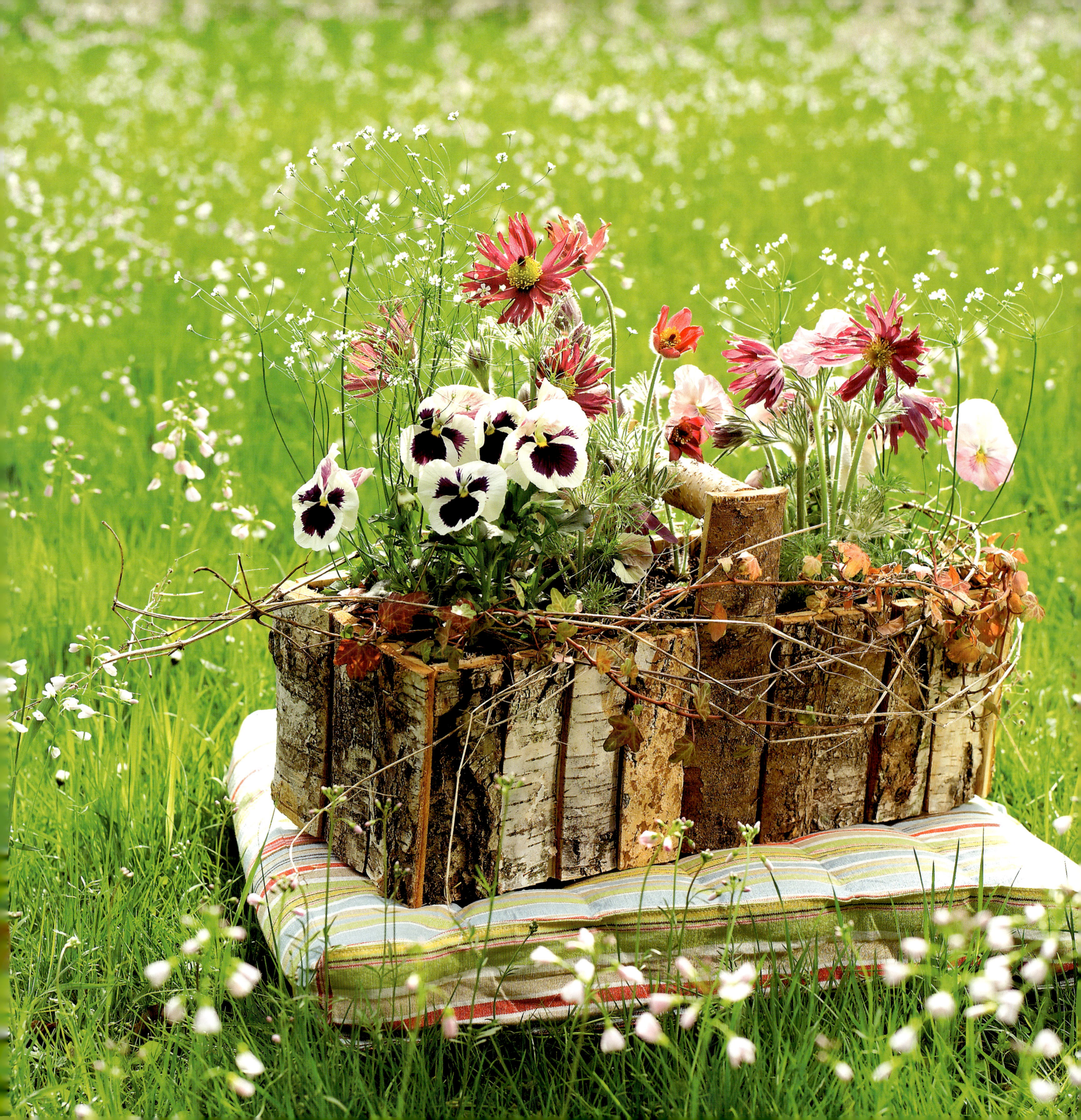

Romantisch-ländlich

Romantik verbindet sich für mich mit einer Liebe zu meiner Heimat und seiner ländlichen Gegend. Der Blick in den Garten oder das Paradies der mich umgebenden Natur zeigt Blütengesichter voller Liebreiz und Charisma. Jede einzelne Blume will betrachtet sein und weckt in uns die Sehnsucht nach Harmonie und Geborgenheit. Ihr Anblick zaubert ein Lächeln auf unser Gesicht und weckt die Freude über so viel Glück, der Natur so nahe sein zu dürfen.

Rural Romanticism

My idea of romanticism is combined with the love for my homeland and its rural environment. Looking into the garden or nature's paradise surrounding me reflects blooming faces full of grace and charisma. Any single flower needs to be contemplated and evokes a longing in us for harmony and security. Its appearance makes us smile and gives lots of pleasure: being this close to nature makes us really lucky.

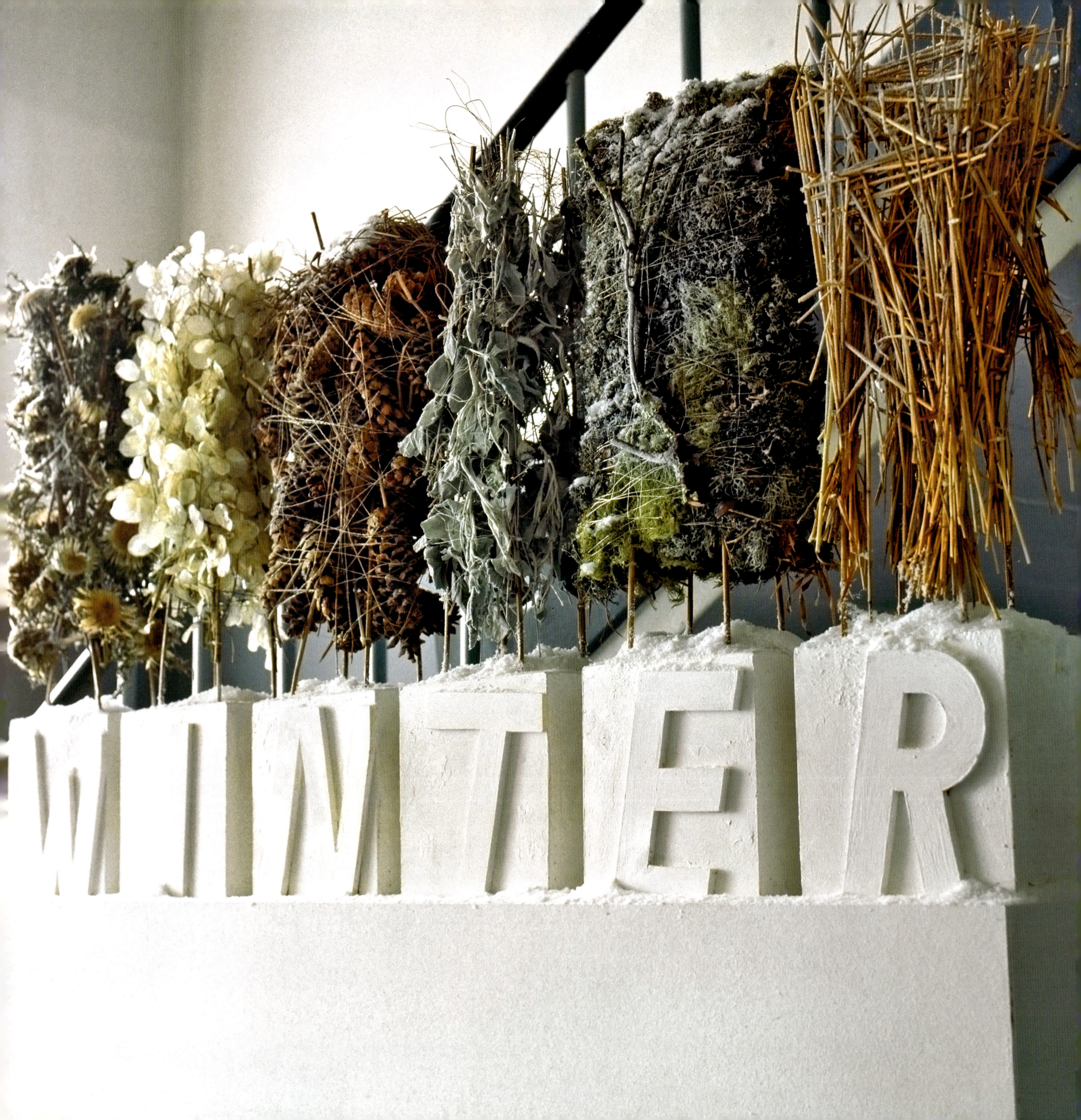
WINTER

Winterlich-erstarrt

Wenn die Natur vor dem Frost erstarrt, entstehen faszinierende Welten. Aus den Blättern, Zweigen und Blüten ist das Leben gewichen und hinterlässt winterstarre Hüllen. Diese fordern geradezu den Gestalter in mir heraus. Meine Winterkreationen stellen dann Strukturen und Formen in den Fokus, lassen Fasern und Schuppen wirken oder den Charme von Farblosem oder Verblichenem sich entfalten. Diese Jahreszeit steht für mich nicht für das Laute und Farbenfrohe, sondern für das Zurückhaltende und Unscheinbare, was erst beim Gesucht- und Entdecktwerden seinen besonderen Reiz entfaltet.

Winter's Freeze

When nature is freezing, fascinating worlds emerge: lifeless leaves, branches and blossoms disappear leaving winter-like rigid covers. As an artistic creator, I feel especially challenged by this. In my winter creations, structures and forms are focused, fibres and scales left to have an effect and uncoloured or pale elements left for blossoming. I think that this season does not represent "sounds and colours", but "restriction and inconspicuousness". Its particular charm is only discovered by exploring and searching.

Herbstlich-melancholisch

Der Herbst, wie er sich in dem Landstrich gebärdet, in dem ich lebe, ist leicht melancholisch und verschlossen. Über Wiesen und Wälder senkt sich abendlicher Nebel, seine Feuchtigkeit benetzt abgeerntete Felder und die braune Laubdecke unter kahlen Bäumen. Für mich eine reizvolle Jahreszeit, um warm verpackt durch die zur Ruhe kommende Natur zu streifen. Kleinode sind die letzten Leuchtfeuer des Herbstes: prächtige Pfaffenhütchen oder rotorange Hagebutten am Waldsaum.

Autumn's Melancholy

The autumn, I experience within the district I am living in, is a bit melancholic and reserved. The evening fog puts his layer on meadows and forests; its moistureness covers harvested fields and brown mulch under bare trees. Personally, I think this is a charming season to stroll through resting nature. Gems are the last bonfires of autumn: graceful spindle trees or red-orange bright rose hips, to be found at the border of the forest.

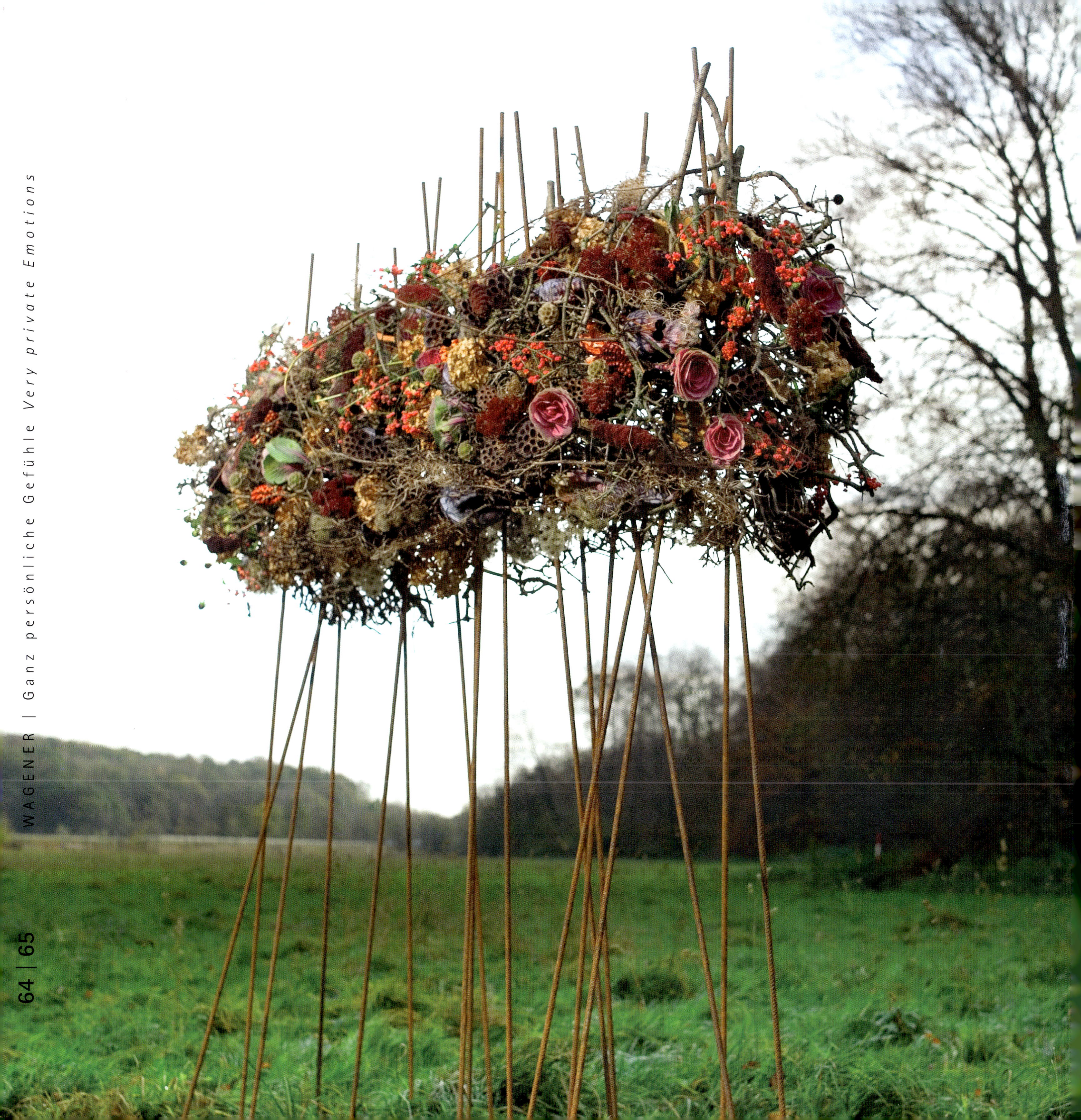

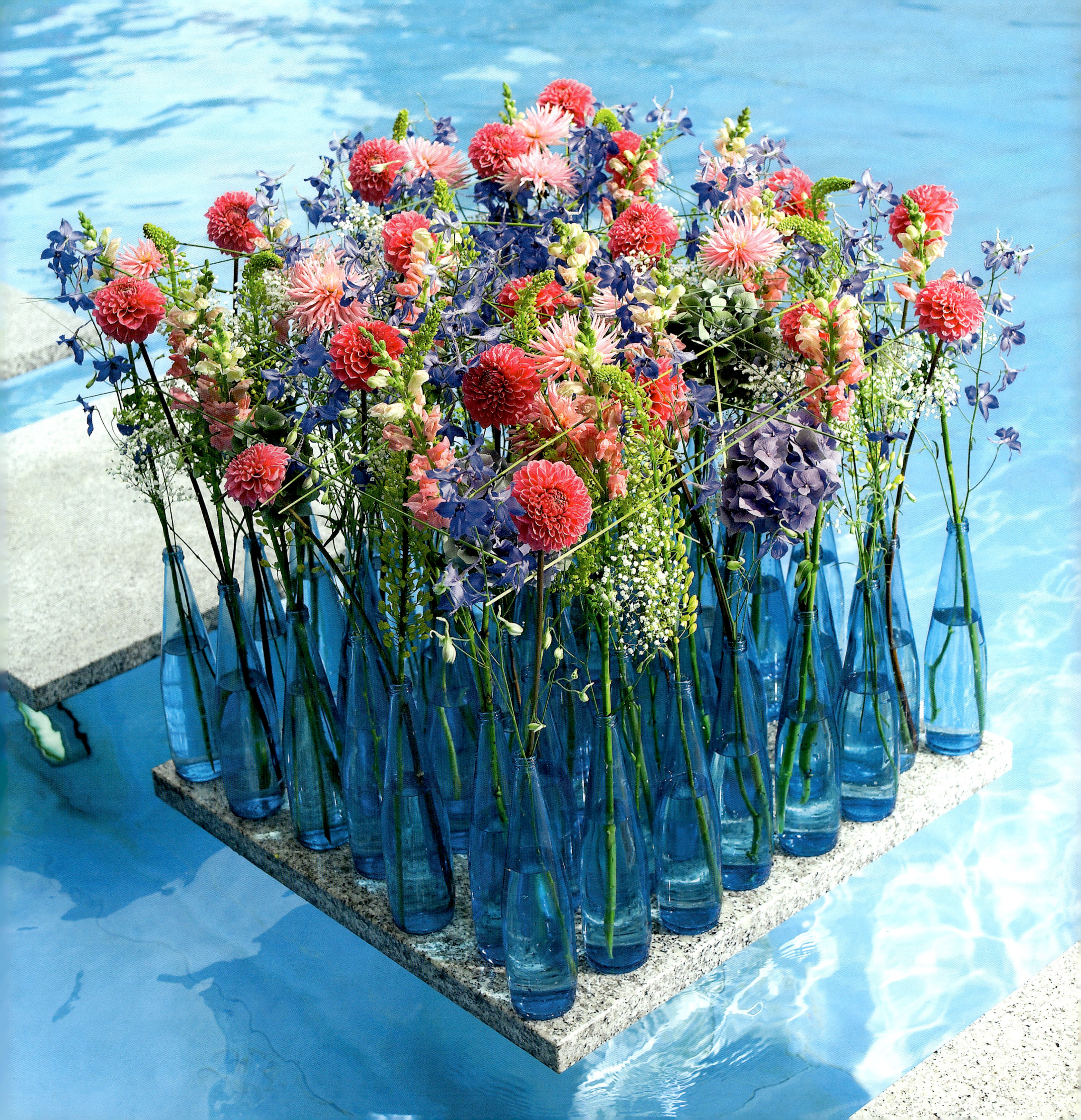

Sommerlich-frisch

WAGENER | Ganz persönliche Gefühle Very private Emotions

Wenn die Schwüle eines Sommertages die Luft zum Flimmern bringt, wenn lastende Wärme und bleischwere Füße jeglichen Aktivismus erlahmen lassen, bringt kühles, klares Wasser ersehnte Erquickung und Belebung. Was in den Kindertagen der Sprung in den Baggersee oder das Waten im gurgelnden Waldbach war, sind jetzt für mich die coolen Töne sommerlichen Blütenallerleis. Erfrischende Blickfänger, die Geist und Körper neue Kraft verleihen.

Summer Breeze

When the closeness of a summer day makes the air go flicker, when burdening heat and lead-like feet stop any activation, fresh, clear water brings refreshment and activation, which we were longing for. Whereas in childhood, I was thrilled to jump into the quarry pond or wade in the gurgling beck, today cool tinges of summer's bloomy sundries fascinate me: refreshing eye-catchers giving new energy to mind and body.

Frühlingshaft-verspielt

Am Frühling mit seiner zu neuem Leben erwachenden Natur fasziniert mich die Leichtigkeit und das lichte Helle. Karges bedeckt sich mit einem zarten, flattrigen Blütenkleid. Die sich mehr und mehr dazu gesellenden Farben umwehen die Natur wie ein zauberhaftes Band. Ein Gefühl der kindlichen Unbeschwertheit, in den Blumen tanzen zu wollen, drängt sich mir auf. Blütenträume werden zu Tagträumen, Erschöpftes erfrischt sich am erstarkenden Grün, das Rad des Lebens erhält neuen Schwung.

Spring-like Plays

Spring with its revitalized nature has a special fascination for me due to its lightness and brightness. Meagre elements are covered with a delicate, volatile flower dress. Colours joining gradually fan the nature with a magical ribbon. A feeling of childish light heartedness drives me to dance in the flowers. Dreams of blossoms become daydreams and exhausted flowers get refreshed by a strong green. The wheel of life is getting a new drive.

WAGENER | Ganz persönliche Gefühle *Very private Emotions*

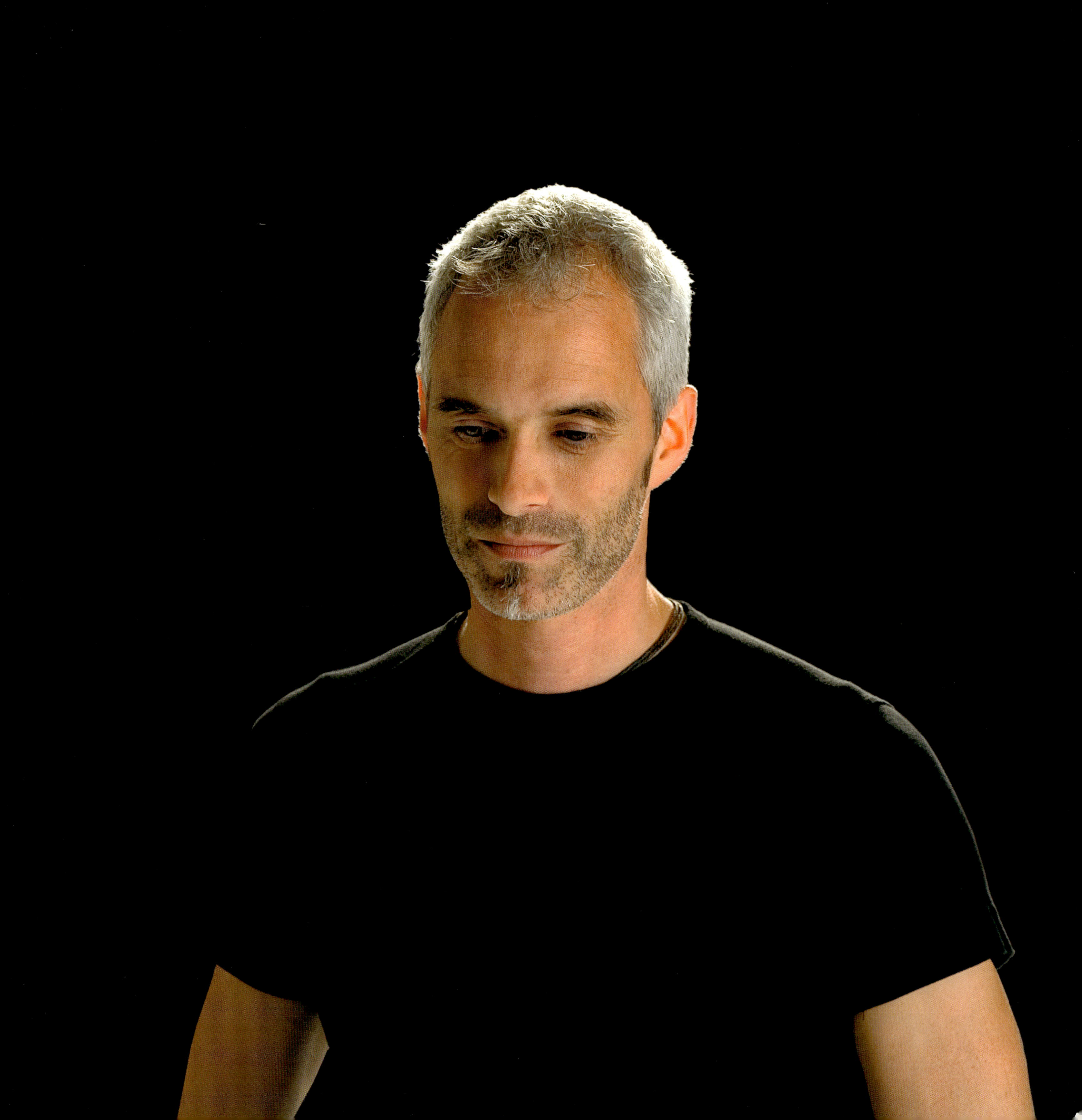

# Ganz persönliche Gefühle

Florale Gestaltung wird stets beeinflusst von ganz persönlichen Empfindungen und Emotionen. Diese immer wieder aufs Neue zum Ausdruck zu bringen, ist für mich als Kreativer eine ständige Herausforderung. Meine stärksten Emotionen und damit meine floralen Welten fußen auf meiner Wahrnehmung meiner geliebten Heimat, mit ihrer typischen Landschaft aus Wald, Wiesen, Feldern und Hügeln, mit ihrer jeweils charakteristischen Vegetation und im spannungsvollen Wechsel der Jahreszeiten.

Very private Emotions

Floral designs are always influenced by very personal feelings and emotions. As a creative person, I feel permanently challenged to express myself through my senses. My strongest emotions and thus my floral world are based on the perception of my beloved homeland with its typical landscape of forests, meadows, fields and hills and its respectively characteristic vegetation with an exciting change of seasons.

Klaus Wagener lebt mit seiner Familie in der Nähe eines kleinen Dorfes im westfälischem Weserbergland, umgeben von einem wunderbaren Garten und ländlicher Idylle.

Klaus Wagener is living with his family outside a small village in Weserbergland, North Rhein-Westphalia, surrounded by a wonderful garden and a rural landscape.

Bunte, farbenfrohe Darstellungen repräsentieren ein Dolce Vita, aus dem Leidenschaft und Esprit, Lebensfreude und Emotion pur sprechen. So eine Farbwelt ist sich selbst genug. Hier bedarf es keiner Zusätze. Die Gestaltung mit Form und Linie hält sich bewusst zurück, ist geradezu puristisch einfach. In der Wahl der warmen, leicht pastelligen Töne verbindet sich Avantgardistisches mit zeitgemäßen Anspruch und ein sommerlicher Naturlook voller Schlichtheit und Raffinesse.

Coloured Passion

Colourful demonstrations represent a dolce vita-like way of life, which shows pure passion and wit, vitality and emotions. Such a world of colours is sufficient, no other additives are needed here. The design with forms and lines is consciously conservative, almost puristic. In the context of warm, slightly pastel colours an avant-garde style is combined with contemporary needs creating a natural summer look full of simplicity and finesse.

Bunte Leidenschaft

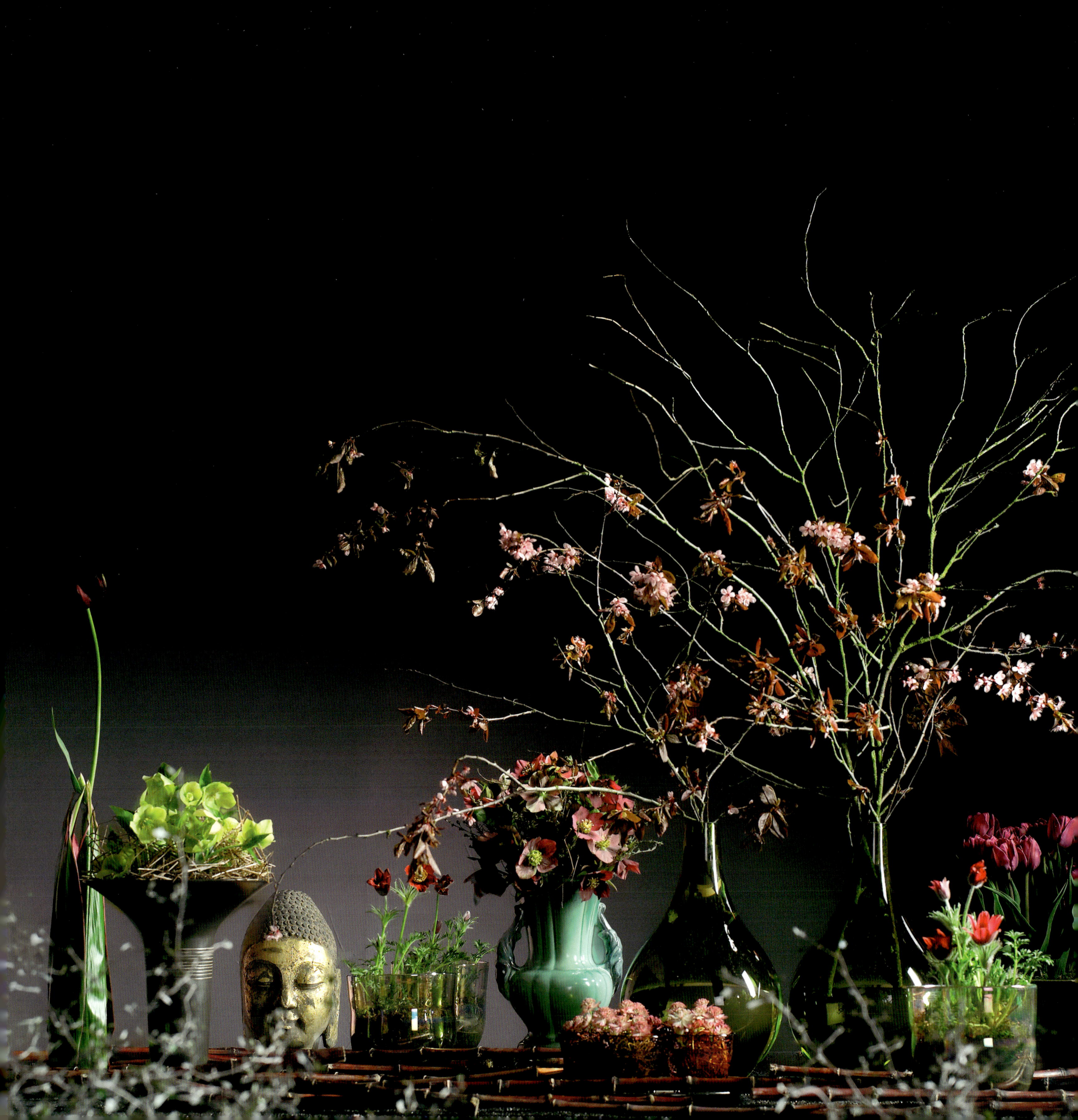

Farbige Lust

Farben stehen für Emotionen, für Lust und Freude. Farben sind sinnlich. Eine Farbwelt, die sich zwischen Traum und Wirklichkeit bewegt, stellt für uns Europäer Asien dar. Von ungewöhnlichen Farbkombinationen und einer subtilen Farbstimmung umgeben, lebt dieses Bild von vielen winzigen Farbbrücken, die höchsten Einsatz des Gestalters fordern. Jede Nuance erfüllt einen Zweck im Gefüge des Ganzen. Am Ende entsteht ein vollendetes, lustvolles, leidenschaftliches Farbenspiel, in dem jedes Teil seine Bestimmung hat.

Colourful Delight

Colours represent emotions, fun and delight. Colours are sensual. As Europeans we consider Asia as a world of colours, which is placed between dreams and realities. Surrounded by unusual combinations of colours and a subtle colour matching, this image is created by many tiny colour bridges, which require the designer's full implication. Each nuance fulfils its purpose within the framework of the whole arrangement. In the end, a complete, delightful and passionate play of colours in which any component has its own designation is created.

Die Vielfalt der Eintonigkeit wird hier zum gestalterischen Prinzip, denn Weiß ist nicht gleich Weiß. Abhängig von Material und Oberfläche, von Licht und Blickwinkel präsentiert sich das hellenistische Weiß in unendlich vielen Nuancen. Bewusst unterschiedliche Oberflächen, von natürlich bis artifiziell, unterstützen diese Differenzierungen. Weiß bekennt sich in gebleichtem Holz, geschlämmtem Ton, in cremefarbenem Porzellan, im Naturweiß der Eierschalen, im Perlmutt der Muscheln, im Kristallinen von Marmor, in der Transparenz von Papier, im Rein weißer Blüten.

Monochromatic Finesse

The diversity of monochromacity becomes a creative principle since "white doesn't always mean white". Depending on material and surface, lights and perspectives, the Hellenistic white is presented in an endless variety of nuances. The deliberate selection of different surfaces, from natural to artificial ones supports this differentiation. White is showing its colour in bleeched wood, a cream of clay, in a cream ware porcelain, in the natural off-white of egg-shells, in the pearls of mussels, in crystalline marble, in the transparency of a paper and in the pureness of white blossoms.

Monochrome Raffinesse

Floristen sind Formgeber und ständig auf der Suche nach der innovativen, zeitgemäßen Ausdrucksform. Bewusst oder unbewusst suchen wir nach Einmaligkeit und Individualität, in dem was wir schaffen. Ein Reiz, der mich persönlich stets fordert und antreibt. In der Reduktion von Form und Farbe entstehen skulpturengleiche Körper. Ihre Proportionen müssen aufeinander abgestimmt sein, wollen sie sich zum Bild eines neuen poetischen Purismus vereinen. Wie selbstverständlich muss die eine Skulptur zur Form der anderen passen oder sie ergänzen. Ausgewogen stehen sie nebeneinander und sind doch jede für sich individuell.

Innovative Objects

Florists give their work shape and are always looking for innovative and contemporary forms of expression. Whether consciously or not, we are searching for singularity and individuality in all our creations. This is an impulse that always challenges me personally and gives me power. While reducing forms and colours sculpture-like bodies are created. If they need to be unified to an image of a new poetic purism their proportions must be adjusted to each other. One sculpture must of course match the form of the other one or complete it. They are standing balanced next to each other, yet each of them is an individual.

Innovative Objekte

WAGENER | Gestalterische Bekenntnisse Creative Confessions

50 | 51

Texturen prägen die Wirkung einer Arbeit. Sie beeinflussen das Spiel mit Licht und Schatten, verändern Farben, übernehmen eine Eigenwirkung. Einige Texturen sind brav und sanft zurückhaltend. Andere wirken aufreizend und geradezu provozierend. Besonders dort, wo sie auch ein haptisches Erlebnis erwarten lassen, erzeugen sie ein Verlangen nach Berührung. Vom Floraldesigner durchaus gewollt, warten dann überraschende und lohnende Erfahrungen.

Impressive Textures

Textures influence a design's effect. They have an impact on the interaction between light and shadow, change colours and have their own effects. Some textures are brave and softly restrained while others seem to be infatuating, almost provocative. They engender a longing to touch, especially there, where a haptic adventure is to be expected. Then surprising and profitable experiences are waiting according to the floral designer's wish.

Beeindruckende Texturen

Mut zum Wagnis gilt auch für den Floraldesigner, wenn Ungewöhnliches entstehen soll. Dennoch darf Wagemut nicht zu Lasten einer soliden Technik und durchdachten Konstruktion gehen. Die Kunst ist der Balanceakt zwischen einer stabilen Statik und der scheinbaren Überwindung der Schwerkraft. Bei dieser Aura müheloser Eleganz stellt sich beim Betrachter von selbst die Frage nach der Wasserversorgung der Blüten und Zweige.

Risky Constructions

If unusual work is to be created, a floral designer must also be courageous to adventure. Nevertheless, daringness should not weigh on a firm technique and a deliberated construction. Realizing a balancing act between firm statics and an apparent surmounting of gravity is a key element. With this aura of effortless elegance, the observer himself will instinctively ask for the water supply of blossoms and branches.

Gewagte Konstruktionen

WAGENER | Gestalterische Bekenntnisse Creative Confessions

Wie ein Architekt entwickelt der Florist zunächst eine Grundkonstruktion für ein Arrangement. Dieses ist verdichtet oder lockerer gebaut, es wirkt entweder nur oberflächlich oder lässt tiefere Einblicke in ein Innenleben zu. Wie auch immer das gestalterische Prinzip sein mag, wirkt es stets bestimmend auf das gesamte Werk.

Insightful Structures

Like an architect a florist develops at first a basic construction for an arrangement. This is compressed or loosely constructed and has either a superficial effect or gives a detailed insight of its interior life. Whatever the design's principle may be, its impact will always affect the whole work.

Einsichtige Strukturen

WAGENER | Gestalterische Bekenntnisse Creative Confessions

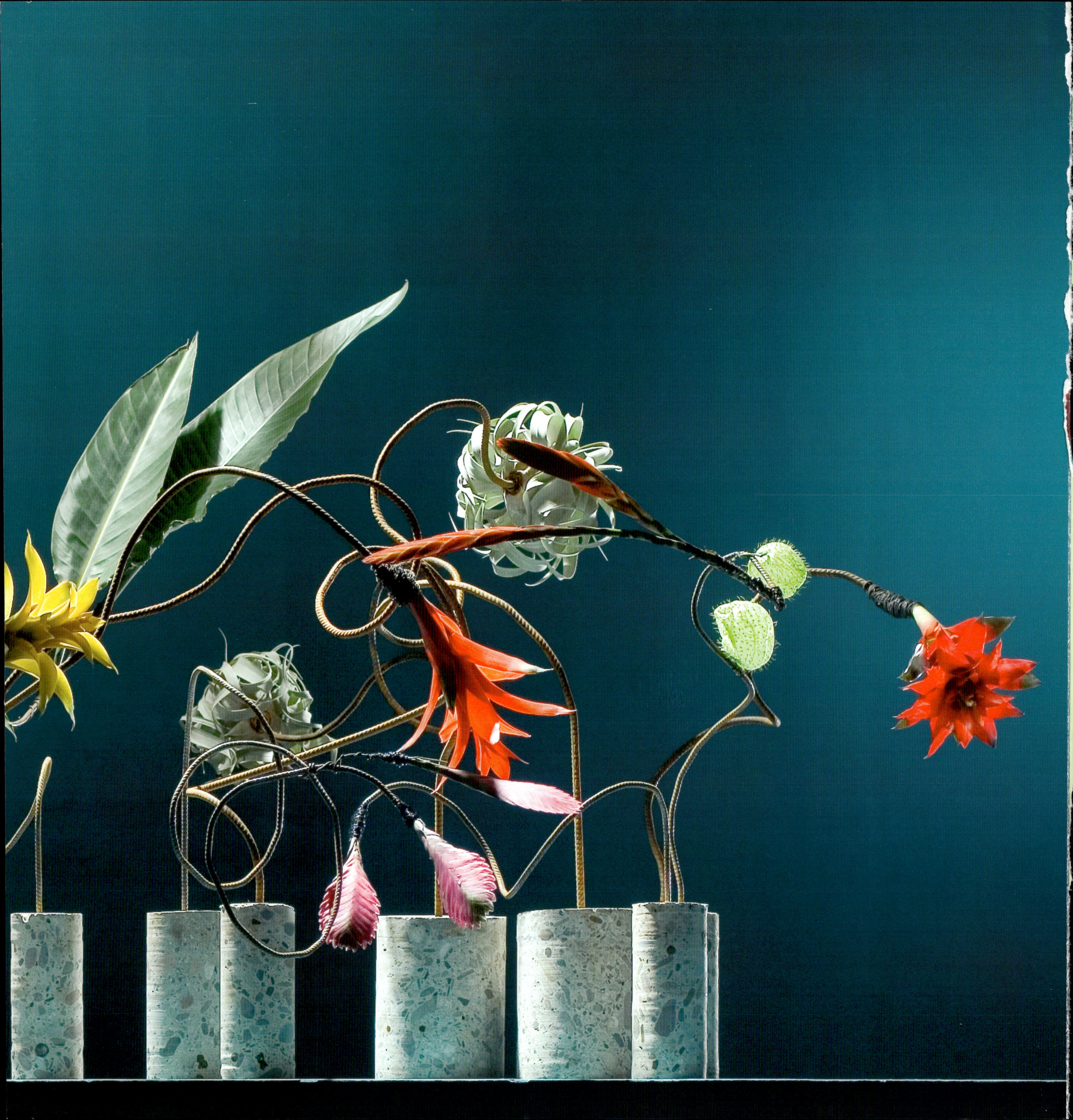

Der Florist und Floraldesigner muss Fantasie haben, den kreativen Freiraum geradezu bis zum persönlichen Stilbruch auszureizen. Erst die individuellen Ideen geben dem Designer Identität. Für mich liegt der Schlüssel der fantasievollen Botschaft in Reduktion und Plakativität. Beide Instrumente eingesetzt, prägen sie ein reizvolles Bild aus Linien, Formen, Farben und Materialien. Tänzelnde Bewegungen erheben sich über statischen Formen, leuchtende Blütenfarben kokettieren mit der Zurückhaltung des Betons, industrielle Materialien ergänzen sich mit Pflanzlichem. Stilistische Blüten meiner künstlerisch-schöpferischen Fantasien.

Formally linear Fancies

The florist and the floral designer must have the inspiration to exhaust the creative freedom almost to a form of personal stylistic incongruity. It's the individual ideas that give the designer an identity. In my eyes, the key to the imaginative message lies in reduction and focusing methods. By implementing both methods, a charming image of lines, forms, colours and materials is produced. Dancing movements rise over static forms, bright colours of blossoms flirting with the abstinence of the concrete and industrial materials complete the plant. Stylistic blossoms of my artful, creative visions.

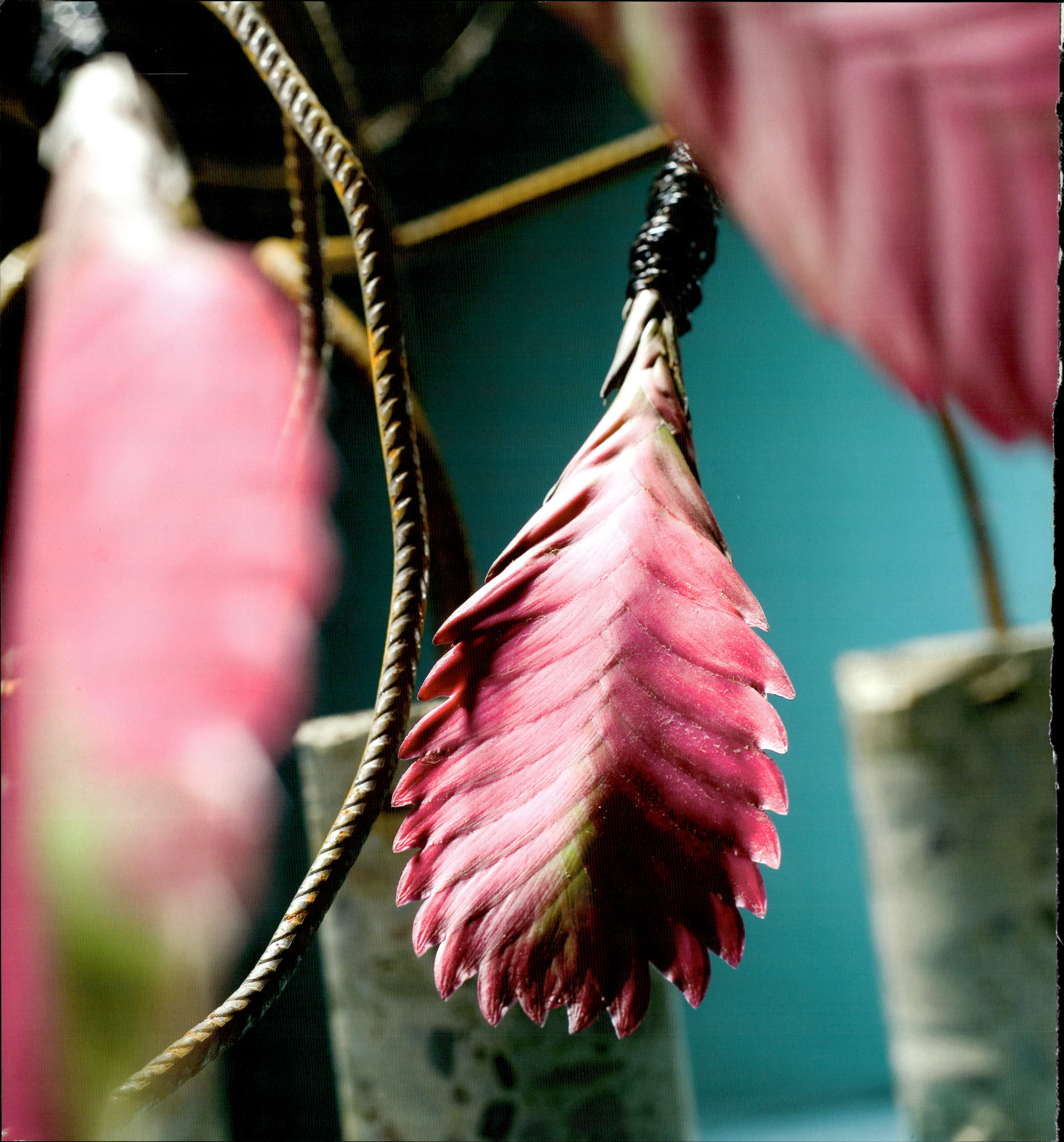

Formal-lineare Fantasien

WAGENER | Gestalterische Bekenntnisse Creative Confessions

42 | 43

Die Natur nachzuempfinden, stellt an den Floraldesigner die höchsten Ansprüche. In dem scheinbar Ungeordneten, Zufälligen und Natürlichen das Regelwerk Schöpfung zu spiegeln, liegt die besondere Herausforderung. Die vegetative Gestaltung lebt von der perfekten und raffiniert ausgeführten Bodenmodulation. Steine, Moose, Wurzeln wollen auf kleinstem Raum exakt positioniert, Höhen und Tiefen natürlich übertragen sein. Und weil alle gestalterischen Gesetze der Natur entnommen sind, gelten sie gerade auch hier. Erst wenn alles wie selbstverständlich wirkt, ist die Naturinterpretation gelungen, das Werk des Gestalters vollendet.

Vegetative Insights

The highest requirement for a floristic designer is to understand nature. A special challenge is to reflect creation as a regulator by the apparent disorder, coincidence and naturalness. The vegetative design benefits from a perfectly and cleverly completed modulation of the floor. Stones, moss and roots need to be exactly positioned in the tiniest place, heights and depths to be transmitted naturally. Since all designing laws are adopted from nature, they are valid especially here. Only if everything appears in self-evidence, nature's interpretation and thus the designer's work will be considered as a success.

Vegetative Erkenntnisse

WAGENER | Gestalterische Bekenntnisse Creative Confessions

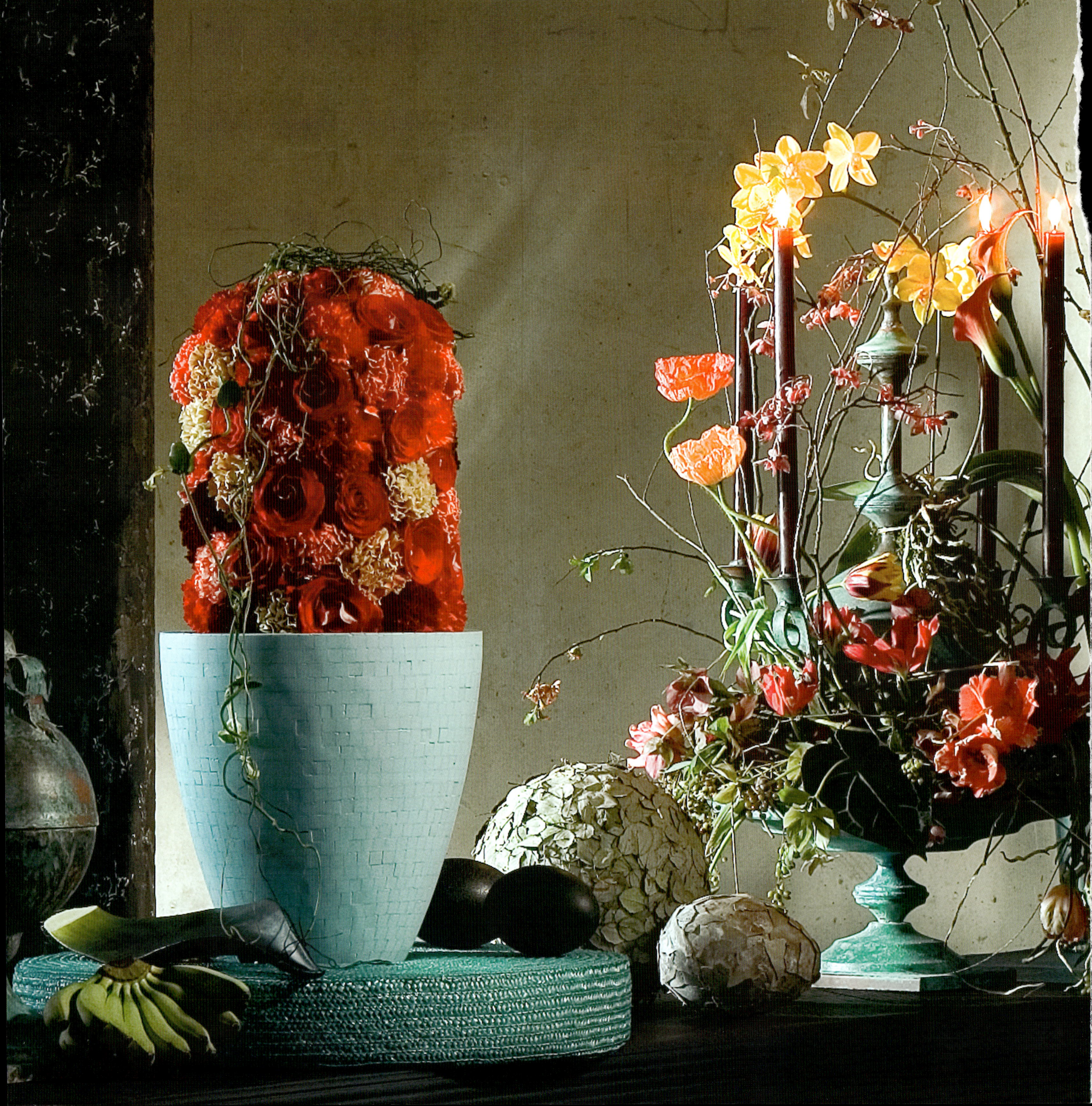

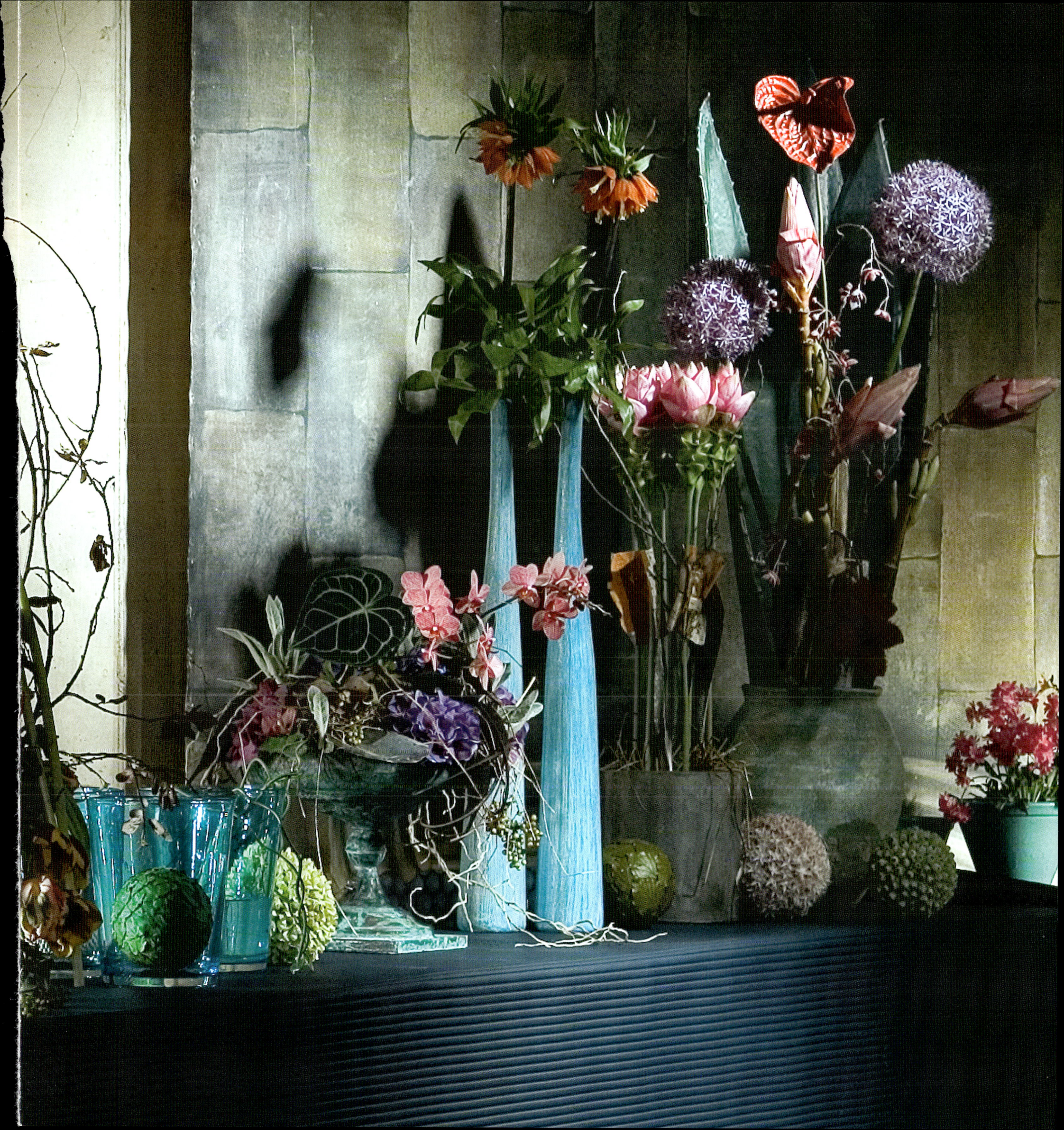

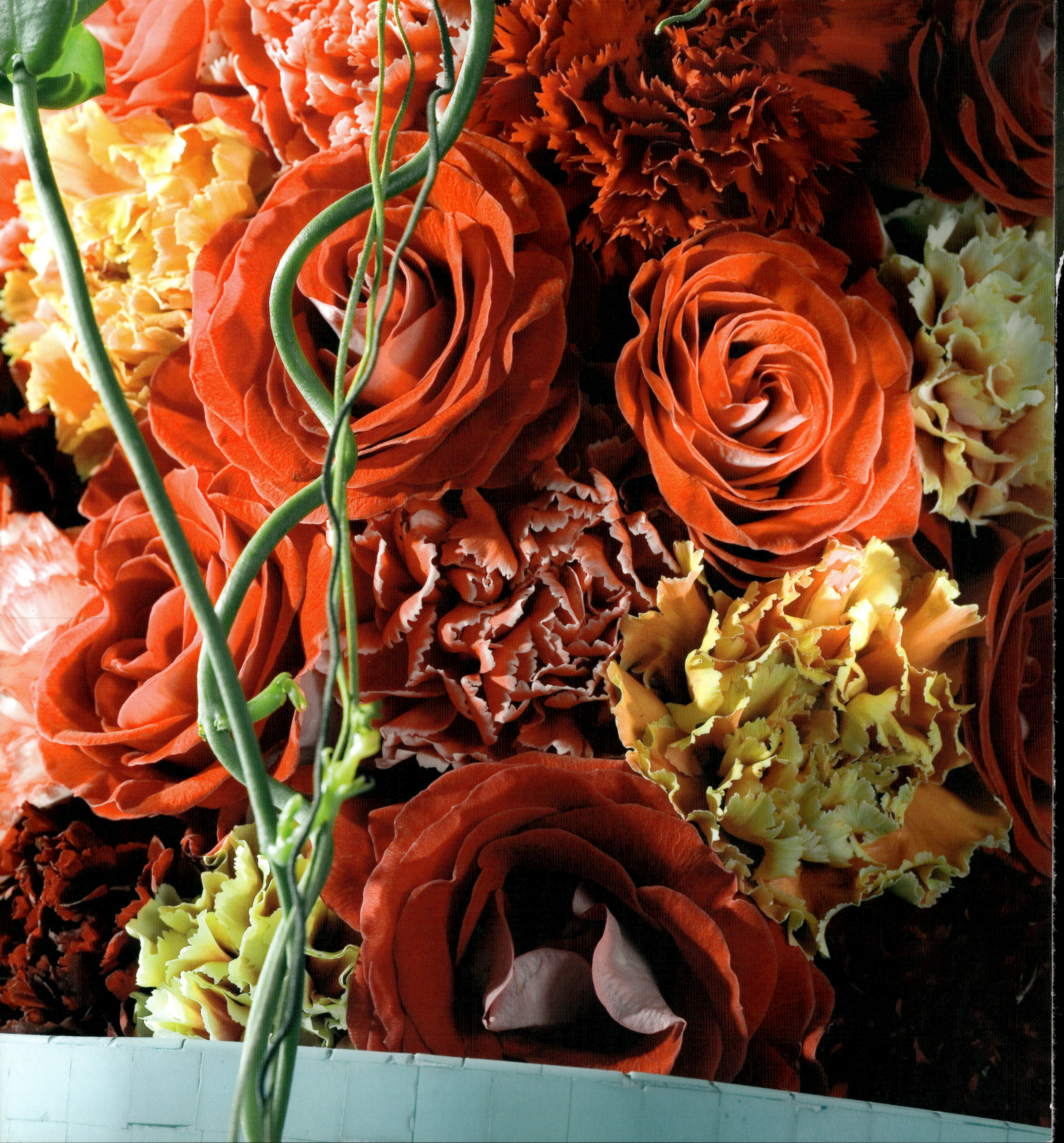

Dekorative Ansichten

Das Unterschiedliche kultivieren, den Mix zelebrieren. Darin liegt die Botschaft alles Dekorativen. Im vielgestaltigen Miteinander begegnen sich Klassik und Moderne, Üppiges und Schlichtes, Alt und Neu. Wie in einem Stillleben werden Zeit- und Raumbezüge aufgelöst, die Elemente stehen unvoreingenommen und gleichberechtigt nebeneinander. So finden sich exotische Pflanzenschönheiten neben schlichten, heimischen Werkstoffen, Grenzen werden aufgehoben, der Generationensprung vollzogen. Mich fasziniert, was die Alten Meister so genial inszenierten: eine idealisierte Realität. Im Dekorativen wird weder moderner Lifestyle negiert noch die Vergangenheit überhöht. Es existiert einzig um seiner selbst willen.

Decorative Views

Cultivating the difference, celebrating the mixture. This is the message of all decorations. In a multiform cooperation, classicism meets modernity, lusciousness meets simplicity and the old meets the new. Like in still lives the feeling for time and place vanishes, the elements are placed impartially and equally next to each other. Thus, exotic floral beauties are found next to simple and homelike materials. The division of generations has been fulfilled. I am fascinated by what the old masters produced ingeniously: an idealized world, which neither denies a modern lifestyle nor adores the past. Its only purpose of existence is for its own sake.

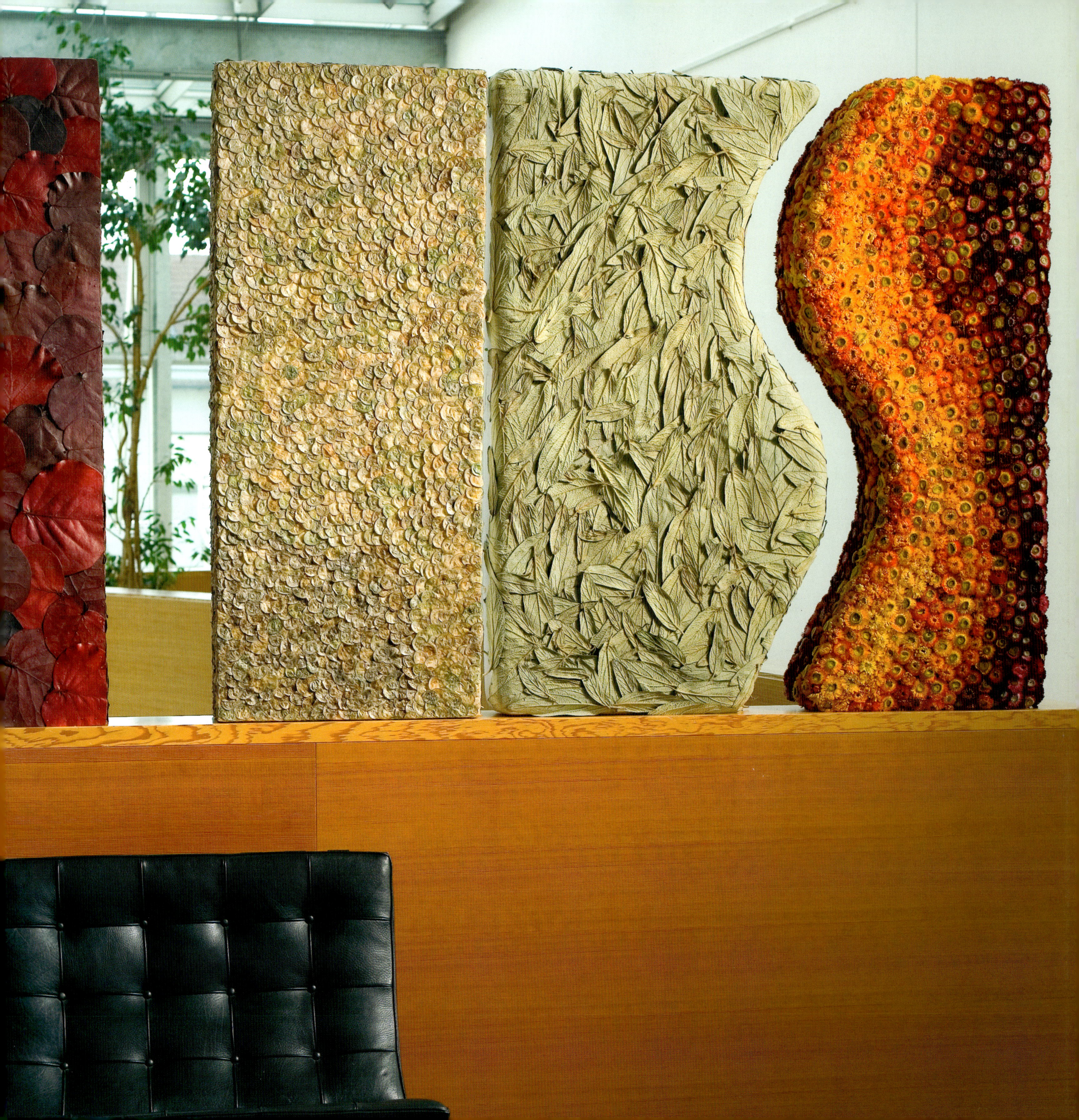

Asymmetrische Spannung

Gegensätzliches, Ungleiches erzeugt Spannung. Aber auch Kontraste von Form, Farbe und Struktur schaffen Reize, die vom Unterschiedlichen ausgehen. Im Spiel variierender Abstände, differierender Oberflächen und Farben liegt für mich die Spannung einzelner Elemente. Gleichzeitig bilden sie einen gemeinsamen übergeordneten Gleichklang, der aufgrund der klaren äußeren Umrisse harmonisch und perfekt wird. Die Form bändigt Gegensätzliches, die Harmonie wird zum Ziel der Gestaltung

Asymmetric Tension

Opposites and inequalities create tension. But also contrasting forms, colours and structures create impulses, which derive form the difference. In my opinion, the tension between certain elements lies in the interaction of varying distances, surfaces and colours. At the same time they build a common superior consonance, which is balanced and perfect due to its clear external outlines. The form restrains opposites and harmony becomes the target of the design.

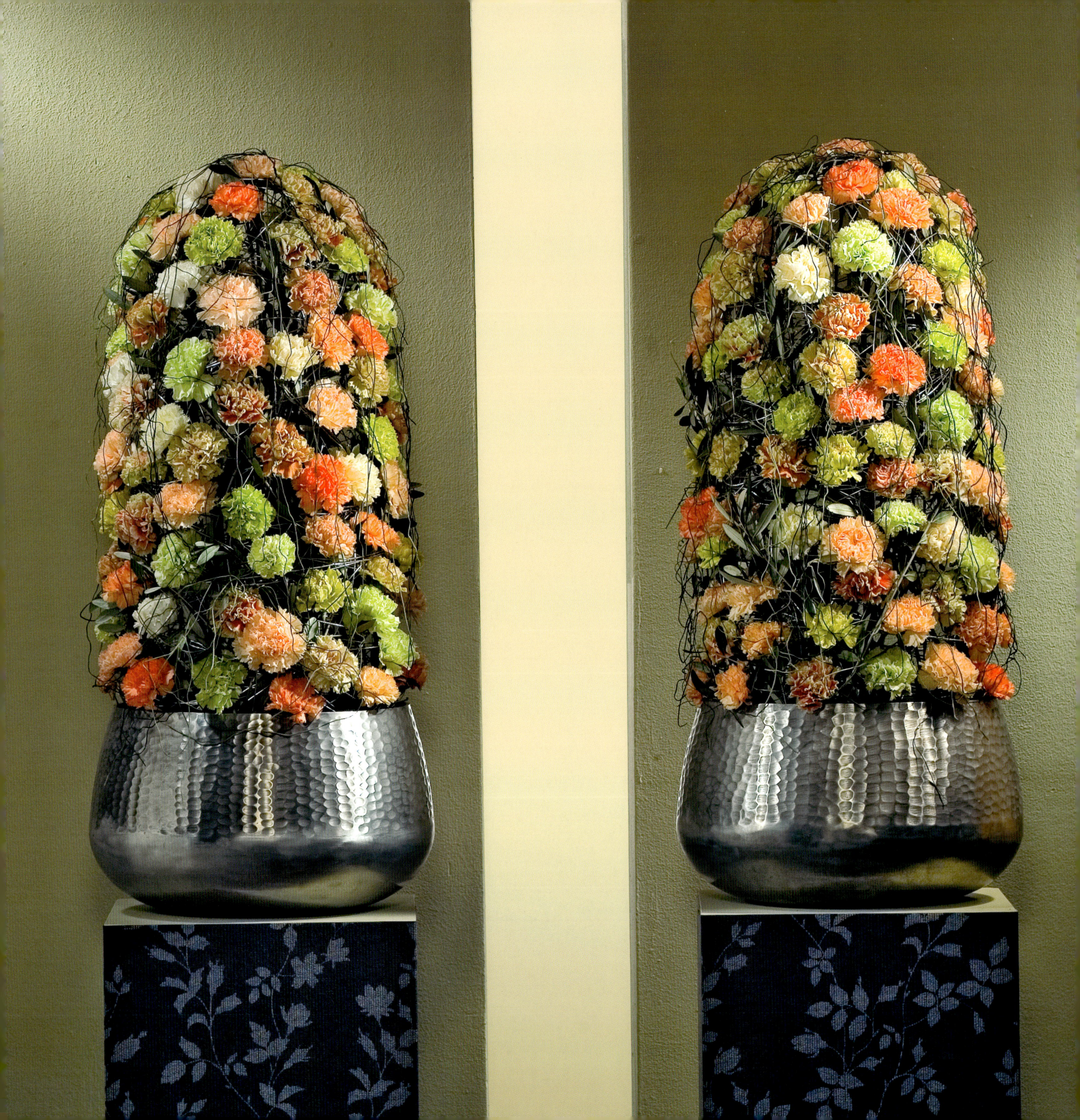

Symmetrische Ruhe

Brauche ich Ruhe und bin auf der Suche nach der schöpferischen Kraft, entscheide ich mich für die Symmetrie. In ihr begegnet mir eine Ausgewogenheit und Klarheit, scheinbar eine Zeitlosigkeit, geradezu wie für die Ewigkeit gemacht. Alles ist hier geklärt, alles hat seine Ordnung. Eine museale Erscheinung, die für Kontemplation und Gleichheit der Kräfte steht, unabhängig davon, ob es sich um eine paarige oder eine solistische Installation handelt.

Symmetric Silence

If I need some rest when looking for creative energy I opt for the symmetry. This is where I can find balance and clarity an apparent timelessness, almost made for eternity. Here, everything is clear and in order. A museal appearance representing contemplation and equality of powers, no matter if it is a paired or solo installation.

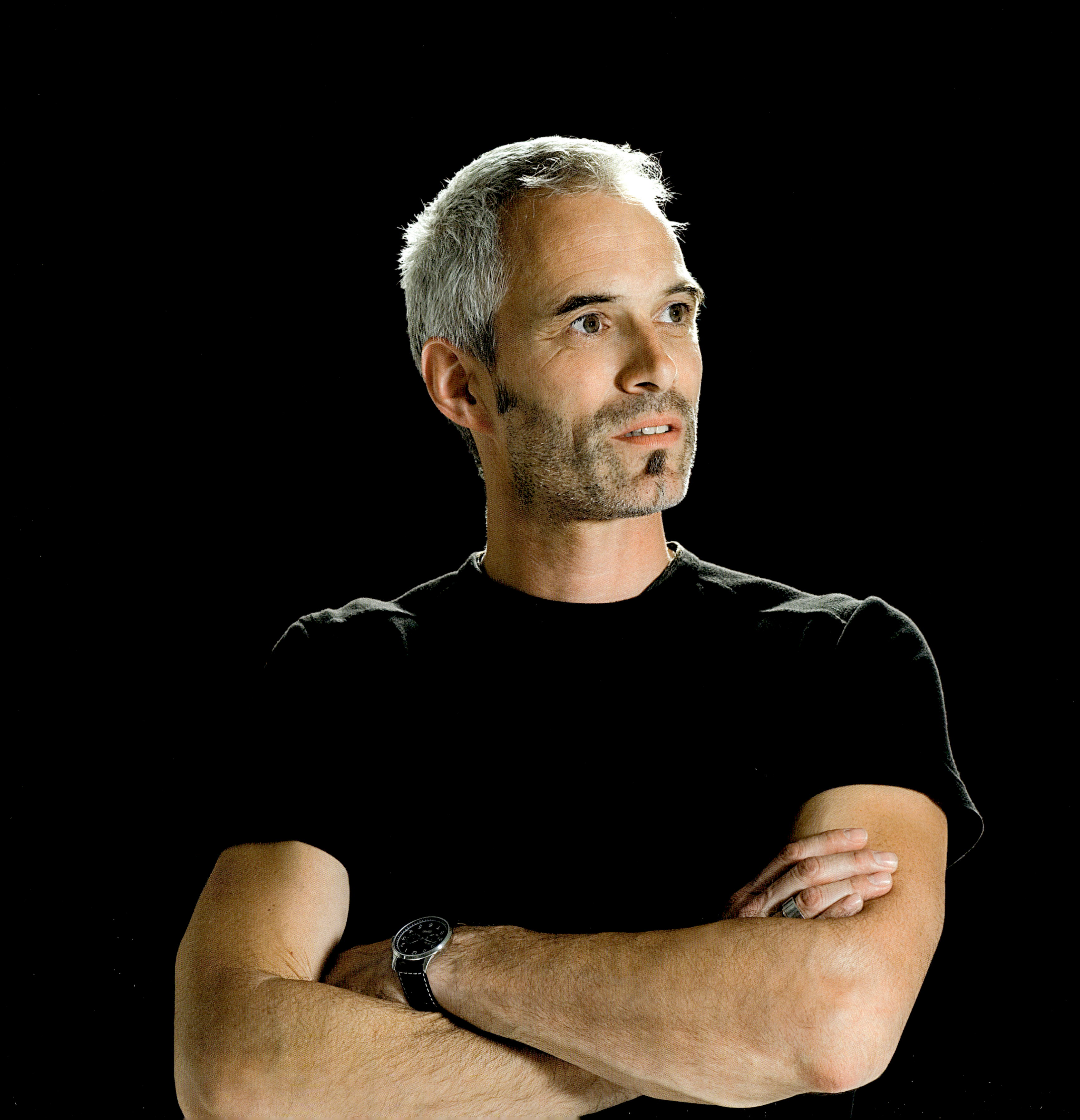

estalterische Bekenntnisse

Ich meine, nur wer eine Heimat hat, kann in die Welt hinauswandern. Das bedeutet, dass ich mich auf Basis einer klassischen, soliden Gestaltungslehre den aktuellen Trends und modischen Strömungen sowie meiner eigenen gestalterisch-kreativen Fantasie stellen kann. Meine floristische Herkunft ist mein Fundament, auf dem sich hervorragend bauen lässt. Die neuen beruflichen Impulse, die Veränderungen des Zeitgeistes und nicht zuletzt die eigene persönliche Weiterentwicklung halten mich schöpferisch wach und lebendig. Doch ausgestattet mit einem fundierten beruflichen Wissen und mit dem Respekt für unsere christlich orientierte, mitteleuropäische Kultur kann ich mich den kreativen Herausforderungen immer wieder aufs Neue stellen, ohne mir untreu zu werden oder mich gestalterisch zu verlieren.

Creative Confessions

I think that only those, who have a home, can leave into the whole wide world. This means that I can face the current trends and fashion flows and realize my own creative visions thanks to a classic, solid designing know-how. My floristic background is the foundation on which I can perfectly start building. New professional incentives, the change of the spirit of the age and of course my personal development keep me creatively awake and alive. However, due to my firm professional know-how and the respect for our central European Catholic culture I can keep on facing creative challenges again and again without becoming unfaithful to myself or loosing my creativity.

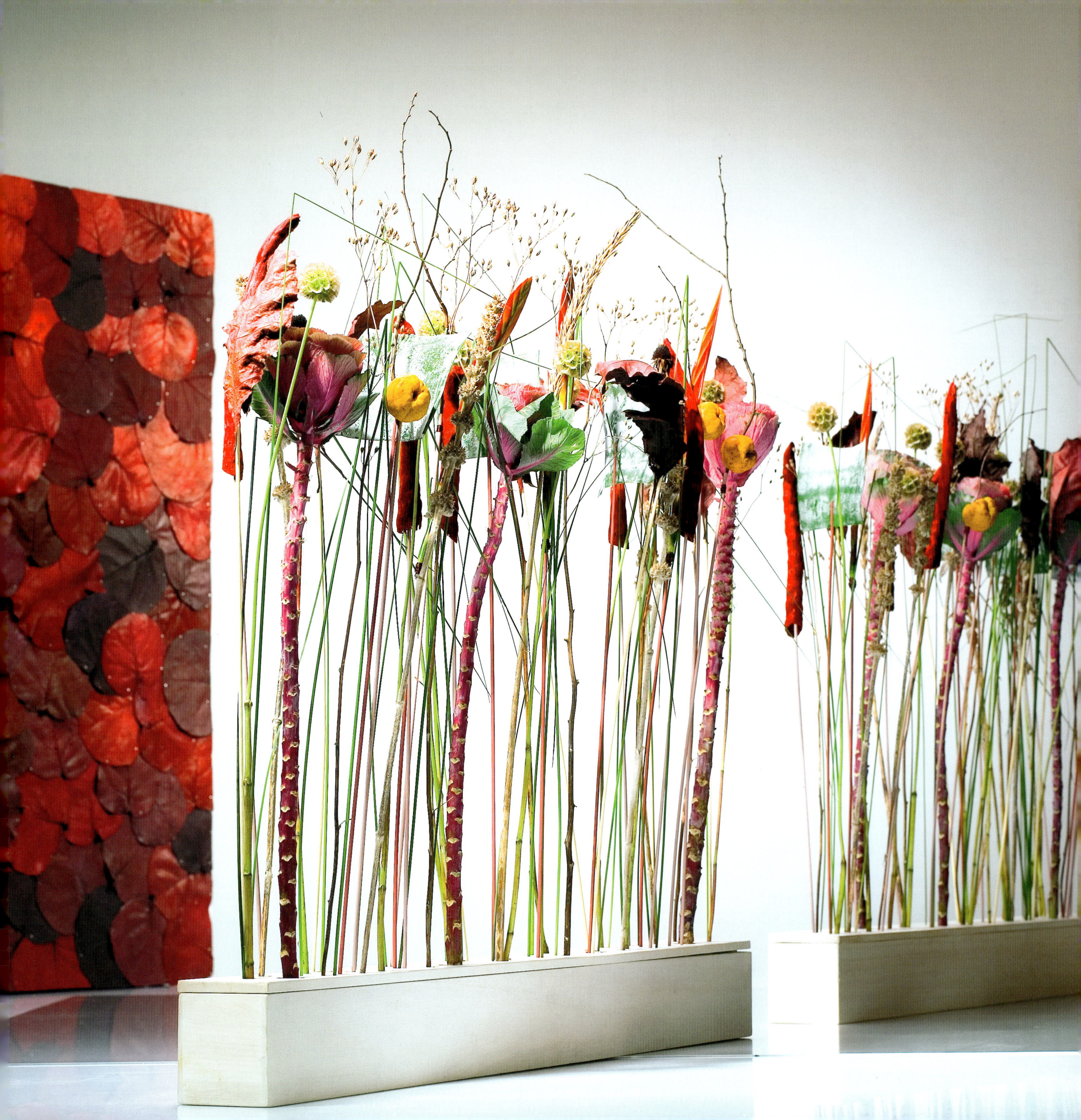

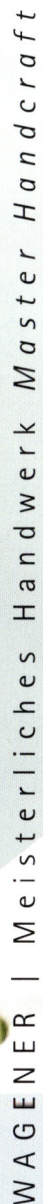

Eine Aufgabe als Florist ist es auch, scheinbar Unbedeutendes ins Blickfeld zu rücken. Reihung und Parallelität kommen in der Natur ganz selbstverständlich vor, bei den senkrecht wachsenden Bäumen im Wald oder den nach oben sich erstreckenden Grashalmen auf der Wiese. Dies wirkt geradezu unauffällig und selbstverständlich. Gereihtes jedoch zum floristischen Gestaltungsprinzip zu erheben, macht die Strukturen und rhythmischen Kerben entblätterter Stiele zu etwas Besonderem. Das Gereihte vermittelt neue Ansichten und damit vielleicht auch neue Einsichten.

Ranked to Alliances

One of the florist's duties includes also the focusing of apparently unimportant things. Rows and parallelism are quite certainly to be found in nature: with vertically growing trees in the forest or with blades of grass extending upwards in the meadow. And this with an almost inconspicuous and natural impact. However, ennobling rows as a floristic designing principle makes the structures and notches of defoliated stems become something special. Ranking conveys new views and thus maybe even new insights.

Gereiht zu Allianzen

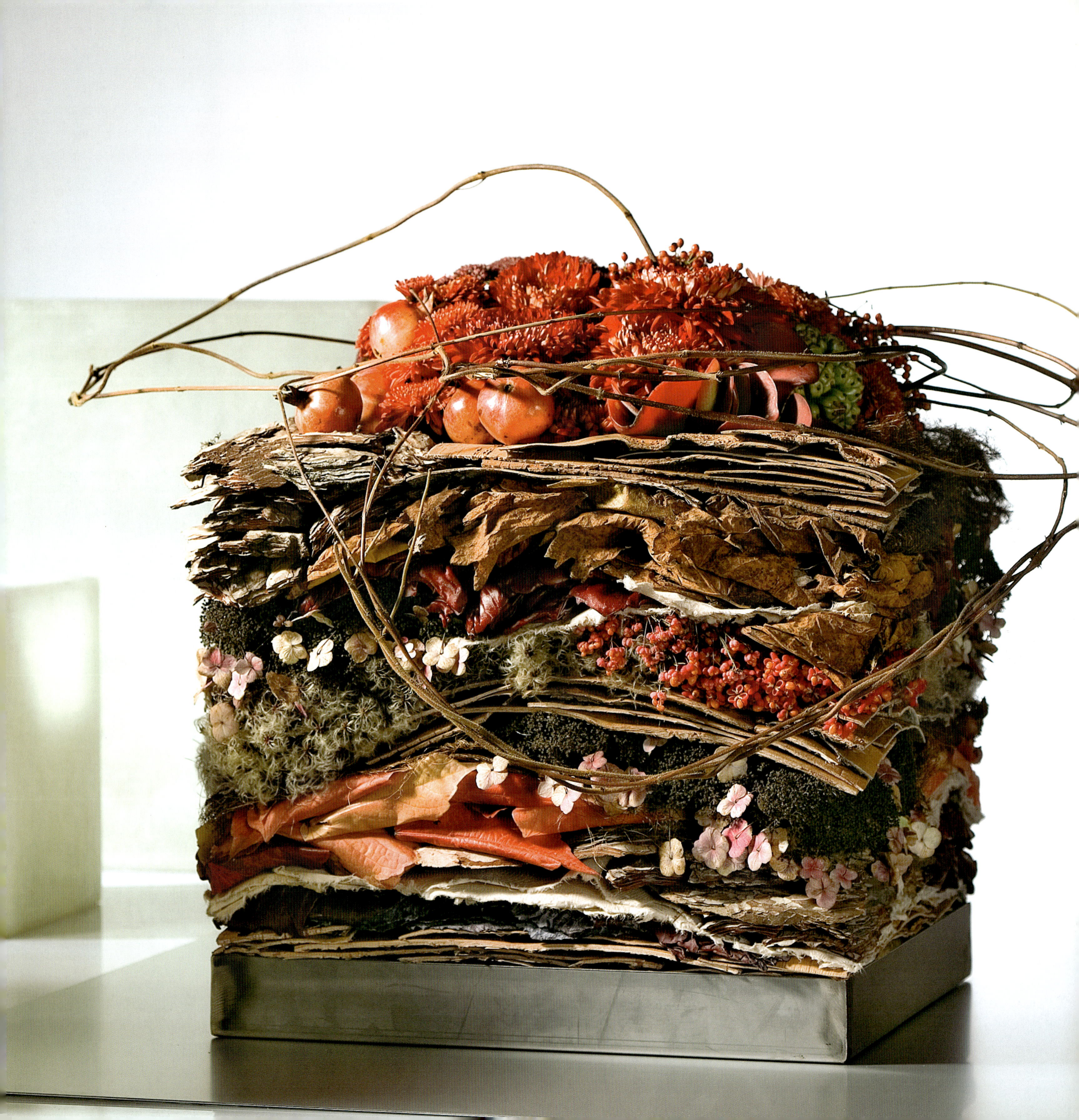

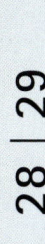

Wie in der Natur, wo sich abfallende Blätter und Nadeln auf den Boden legen, zu Humus werden, um bald darauf wieder von einer neuen Lage bedeckt zu werden, gestalte ich gerne Schichtungen. Dabei entstehen kastige, statische Formen mit einer ruhigen, schweren, lagernden Wirkung. Um so auffälliger ist eine einzige, hiervon abweichende Bewegungslinie. Die perfekte Silhouette ist das Ziel, deren Schichten aus Farben, Materialien und Strukturen faszinieren und die es wert sind, genau betrachtet zu werden.

Coated to new Dimensions

Like in nature, where leaves or needles falling down on the floor, become mould in order to be covered again by a new layer, I like to create superpositions. Thereby, box-like, static forms with a silent, heavy and encamping form emerge. The more striking is a single, deviating movement line. The perfect skyline is the target, whose impressive layers of colours, materials and structures are also worth being precisely contemplated.

Geschichtet zu neuen Dimensionen

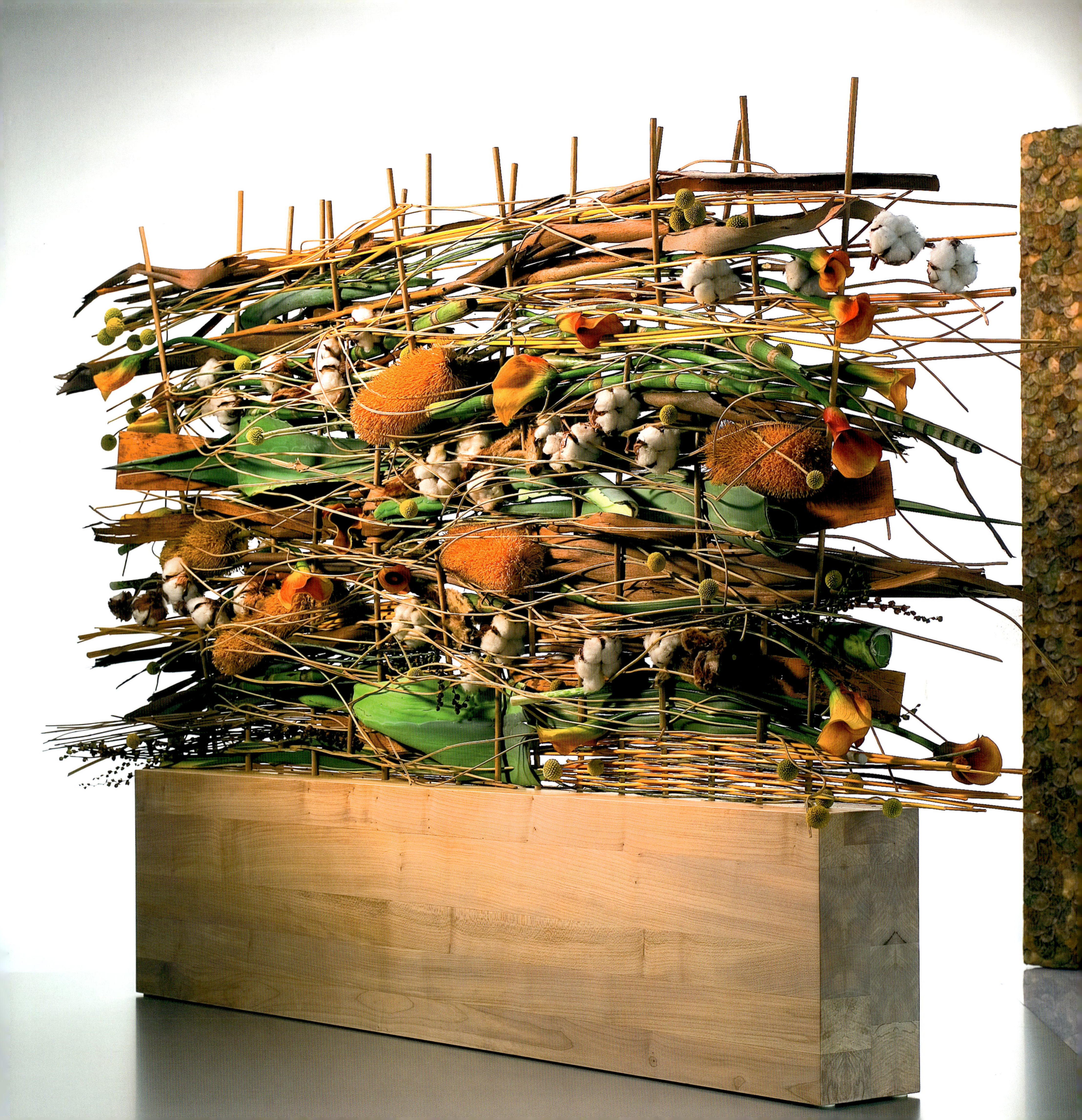

Texturen und Strukturen entstehen in dem bewegten Auf und Ab oder im spannungsvollen Kreuz und Quer der verschiedenen Materialien. Die kunsthandwerkliche Textiltechnik auf Florales übertragen, führt zu lebendig erscheinenden Flächen, die zu einem haptischen wie optischen Erlebnis werden. Bei der floralen Weberei reizt mich vor allem der Kontrast: Trockenes zu Frischem, Farbintensives zu Farbzurückhaltendem, Artifizielles zu Natürlichem, Strukturiertes zu Glattem. Farben, Materialien, Oberflächen verweben sich zu einem eigenständigen Neuen. Das Einzelne gibt sich und seine Identität zugunsten eines neuen Gesamten auf.

Woven into Textures

Textures and structures are created by up and down or strong criss cross movements of the different materials. Used within a floristic context this artisan textile technique apparently makes lively spaces appear, creating a haptical as well as optical adventure. In floral weaving I am mostly attracted to the contrast: what is flavourless becomes fresh, what is colourful becomes neutral, artificial becomes natural, and what is structured gets even. Colours, materials, surfaces interweave to become an independent new form. Single forms give up their identity in favour of a new collective form.

Gewoben zu Texturen

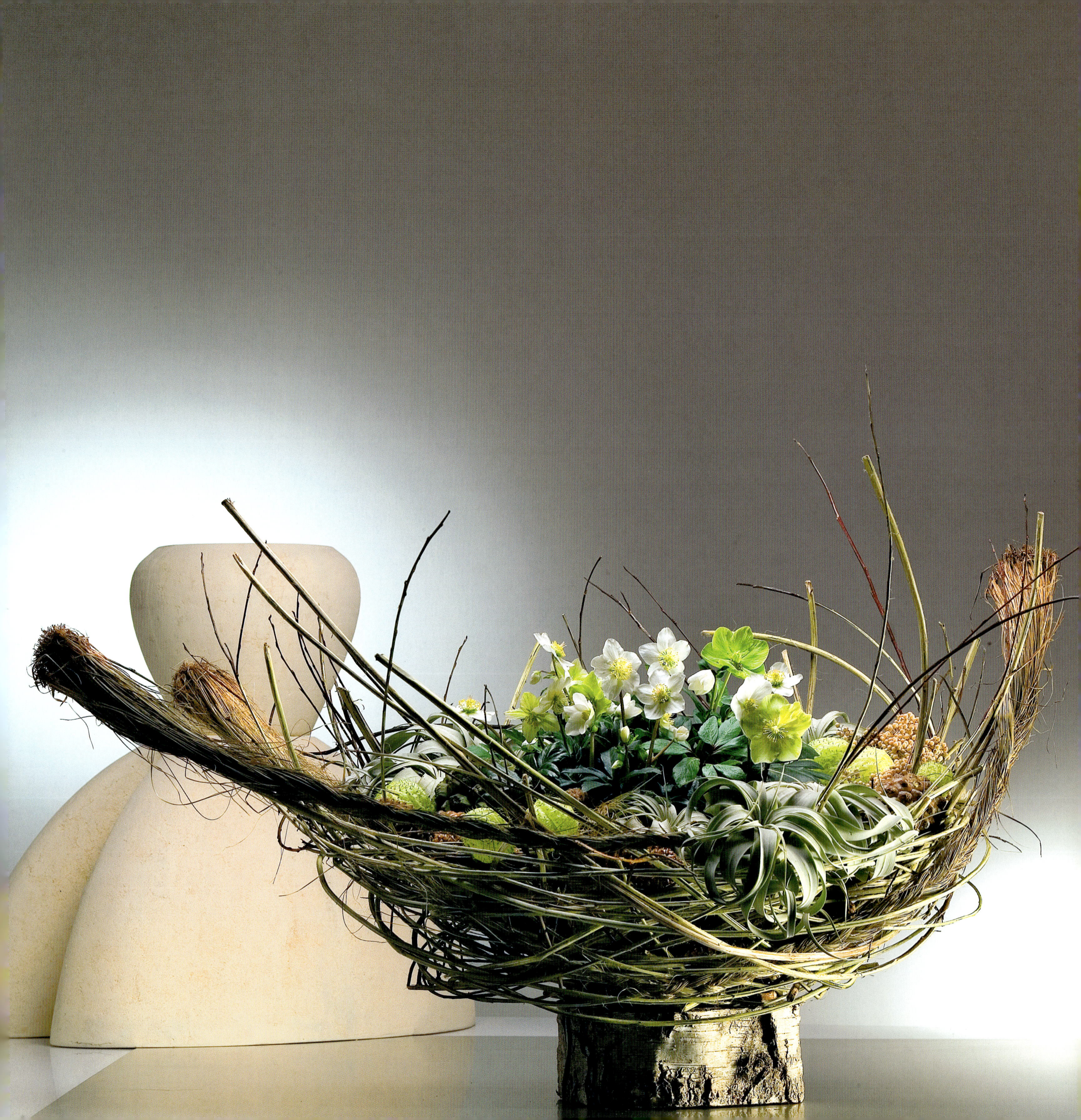

Voraussetzungen für das Flechten bilden langfaserige, biegsame Werkstoffe. Diese archaische Technik machten sich bereits die Urmenschen zu Nutze, um aus Schilf, biegsamen Zweigen oder Ranken Behältnisse zu schaffen, Areale einzufrieden oder Behausungen zu schaffen. Ich liebe diese Technik, gestaltet aus einer Vielzahl unterschiedlicher Triebe. Ob regelmäßig im Hin und Her der Bewegungen oder lieber ungeordnet, nahezu chaotisch im Ineinanderverwundenen der gewählten Werkstoffe, ist eine Frage des schöpferischen Prozesses. Das Ergebnis kann eine Basis sein, aus der eine sensible Floristik erwächst, wie ein schützenswertes Kleinod.

Braided for Protection

The basis of braiding is composed of flexible materials of long fibres. This archaic technique was already utilised by prehistoric men in order to create boxes, enclose areas or build housings with the help of reed, flexible twigs or twines. I love this technique, which is formed by a variety of shoots. It depends on the creative process whether it is carried out regularly according to the movements (up and down) or rather unstructured, almost chaotically through the twining of the selected materials. The result could be the basis for the growth of a sensible floristry, like a gem worth to be protected.

Geflochten zu Schützendem

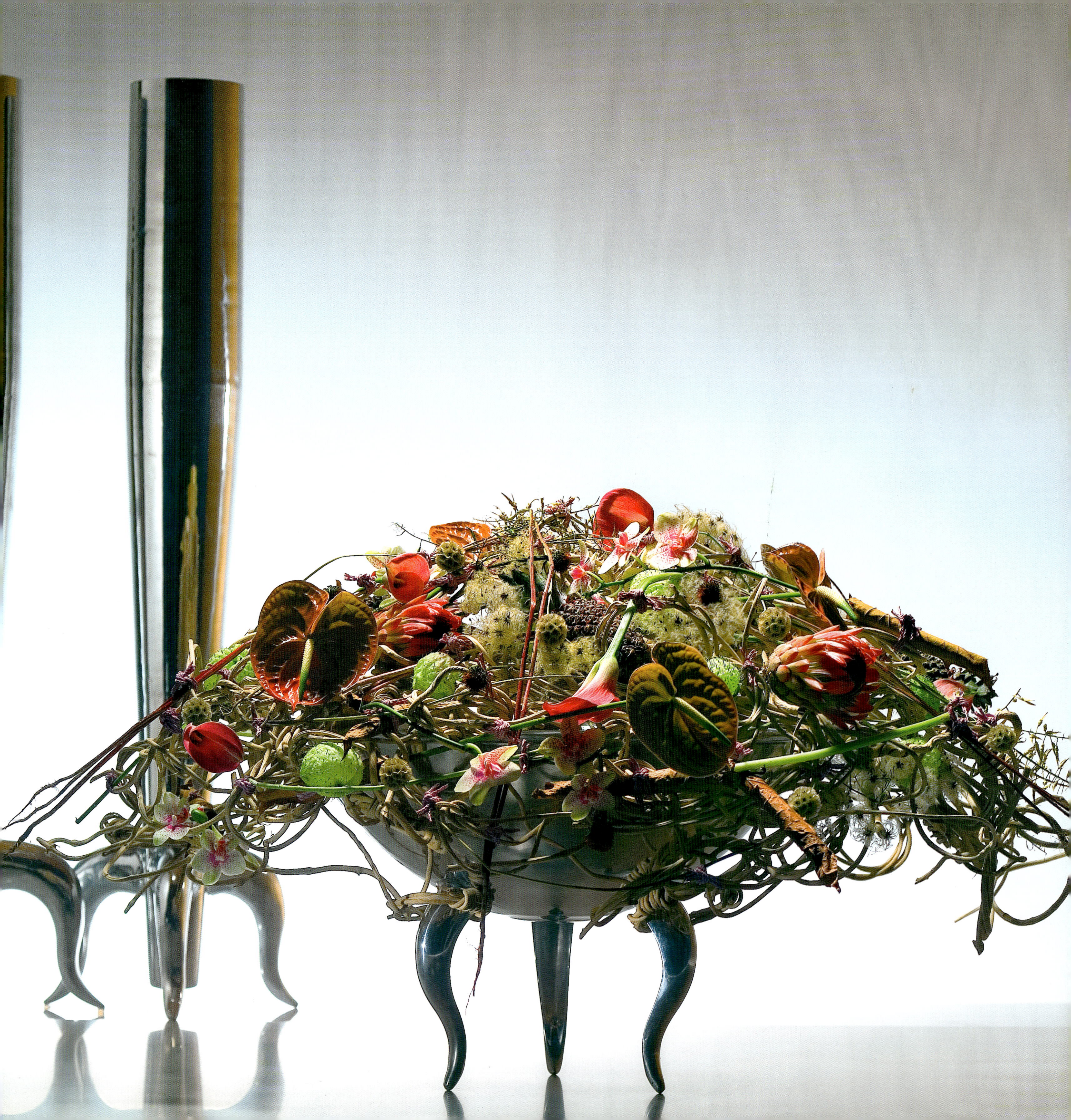

Bewusstes Gestalten unter Einsatz bestimmter und gezielt verwendeter Techniken schafft eine neue Art der Kreativität. Das Knoten verbindet Einzelnes zu einem Ganzen, integriert Formen, Linien und Flächen. Aus verknoteten Verbindungen von Ranken und Zweigen, Stielen und Wurzeln lassen sich ganze Netzwerke erstellen, deren scheinbares Wirrwarr zu einer spannenden Entdeckungsreise einlädt.

Knotted to Networks

With the help of certain specifically used techniques targeted designing forms a new way of creativity. In knotting techniques single parts are combined to a whole; forms, lines and spaces are integrated. Knotted combinations of twines, twigs, stems and roots can create whole networks whose apparent gallimaufry invites us to an exciting expedition.

Geknotet zu Netzwerken

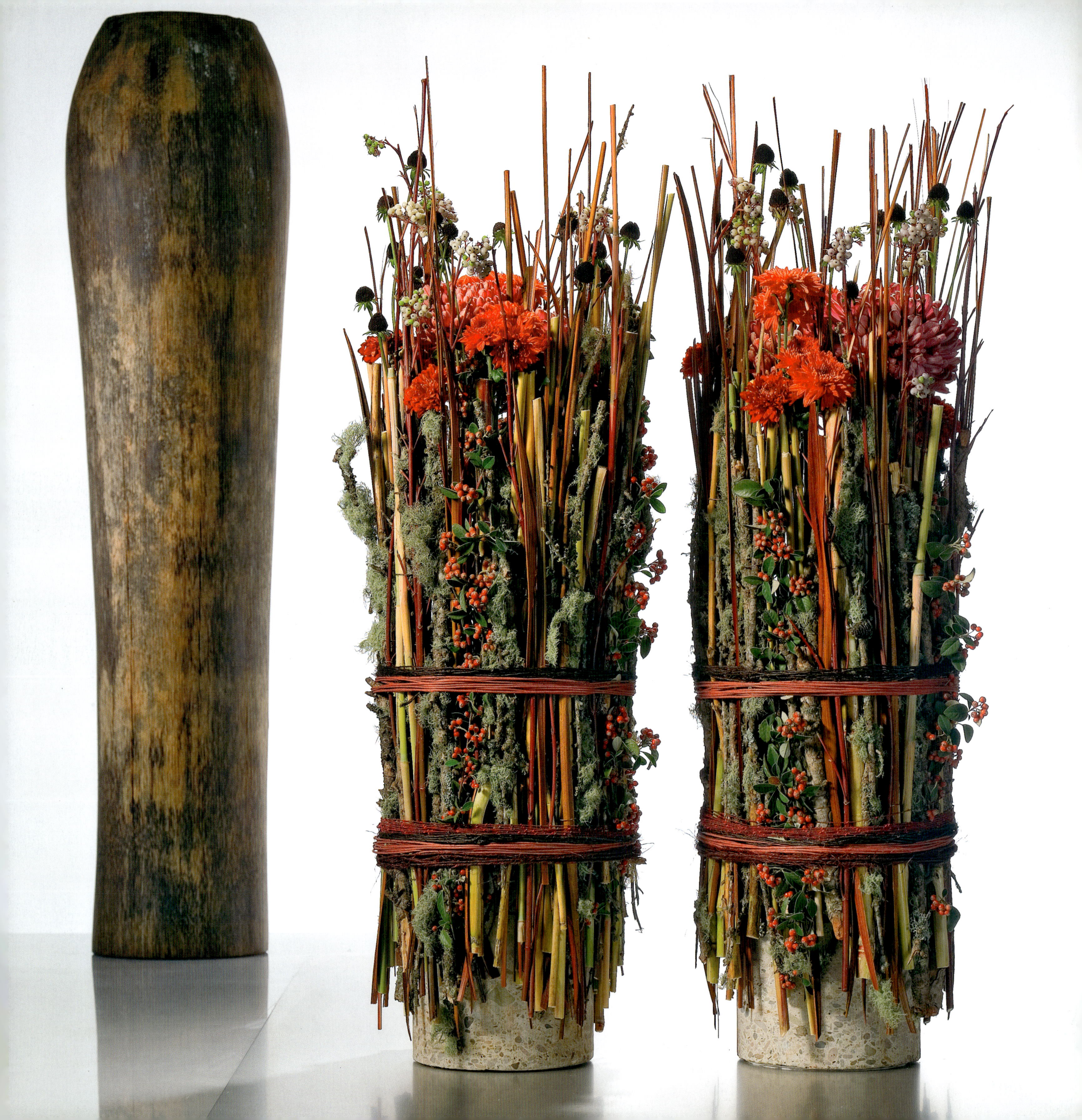

Das Bündeln zählt zu den ältesten und wesentlichsten Techniken in der Floristik. Floralien, die zusammen kommen und zusammen zur Geltung gebracht werden sollen, müssen gut aneinander befestigt sein. Mit stabilen Stricken sichtbar umwickelt, umschlungen und umwunden, gewinnt die Bündeltechnik selbst an gestalterischer Attraktivität. Moderne Floristik macht das Bündeln somit durch geschicktes Betonen und durch Wiederholungen zu einem aktuellen und eigenständigen Gestaltungsaspekt.

Bundled to a Solid Basis

Bundling is one of the oldest and most essential techniques in floristry. Flora, which is combined to accentuate, must be well attached. Firm cords being visibly encircled and twined support this technique and thus its creative beauty. Thanks to modern floristry, bundling becomes a current and independent designing aspect through skilful emphases and repetitions.

Gebündelt zur soliden Basis

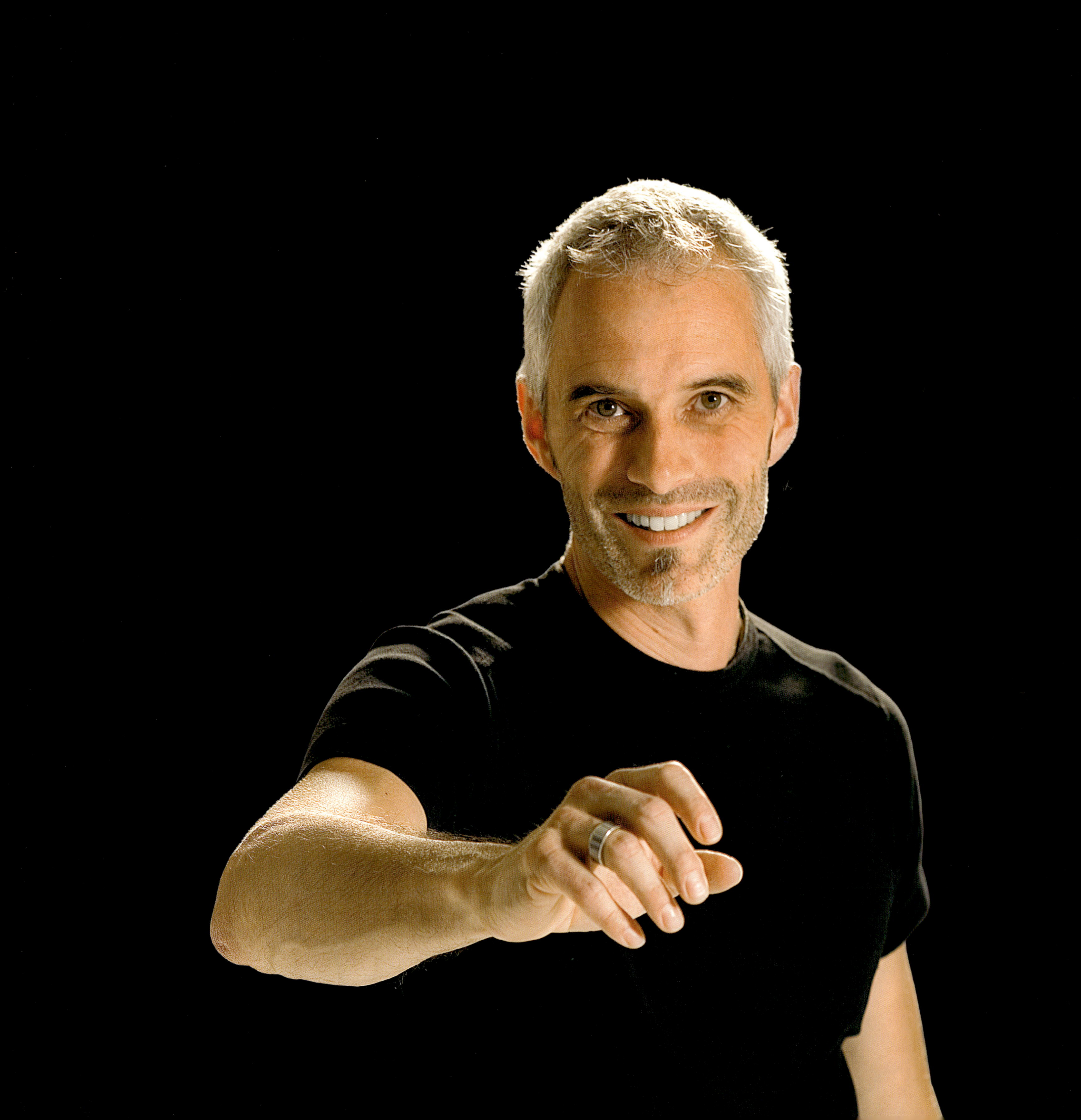

Meisterliches Handwerk

Floristik ist ein komplexes Gebilde. Hinter aller Kreativität und gestalterischer Idee steht eine konsequente Technik. Sie ist die Grundlage für echtes Handwerk und das schöpferische Tun. Sowohl Technik als auch Gestaltung wollen erlernt sein, wenn auch Talent und die Begeisterung für die Natur bereits in uns Floristen angelegt sein sollten. Sie müssen stets aufs Neue den Veränderungen, die sich durch neue und andere Werkstoffe und Materialien ergeben, angepasst werden. Gute Floristik ist Handwerk. Und Handwerk, so meine ich, ist das höchste Gut unseres Berufsstands. Es ist respektvoll zu achten, pfleglich zu kultivieren und sinnvoll zu modifizieren. Das ist unsere Aufgabe und Verantwortung als Floristen.

Master Handcraft

Floristry has a complex structure. Besides all creativity and artistic ideas it has a consequential technique. It is the basis for real handcraft and creative working. Both, techniques and design, need to be learnt even though skills and enthusiasm for nature must be a part of our personality as a florist. They must be constantly adapted to changes, emerging due to new materials. Good floristry is a trade. And trade is the highest good of our profession- that's what I think. It must be treated with respect, carefully cultivated and reasonably modified. This is our duty and responsibility as florists.

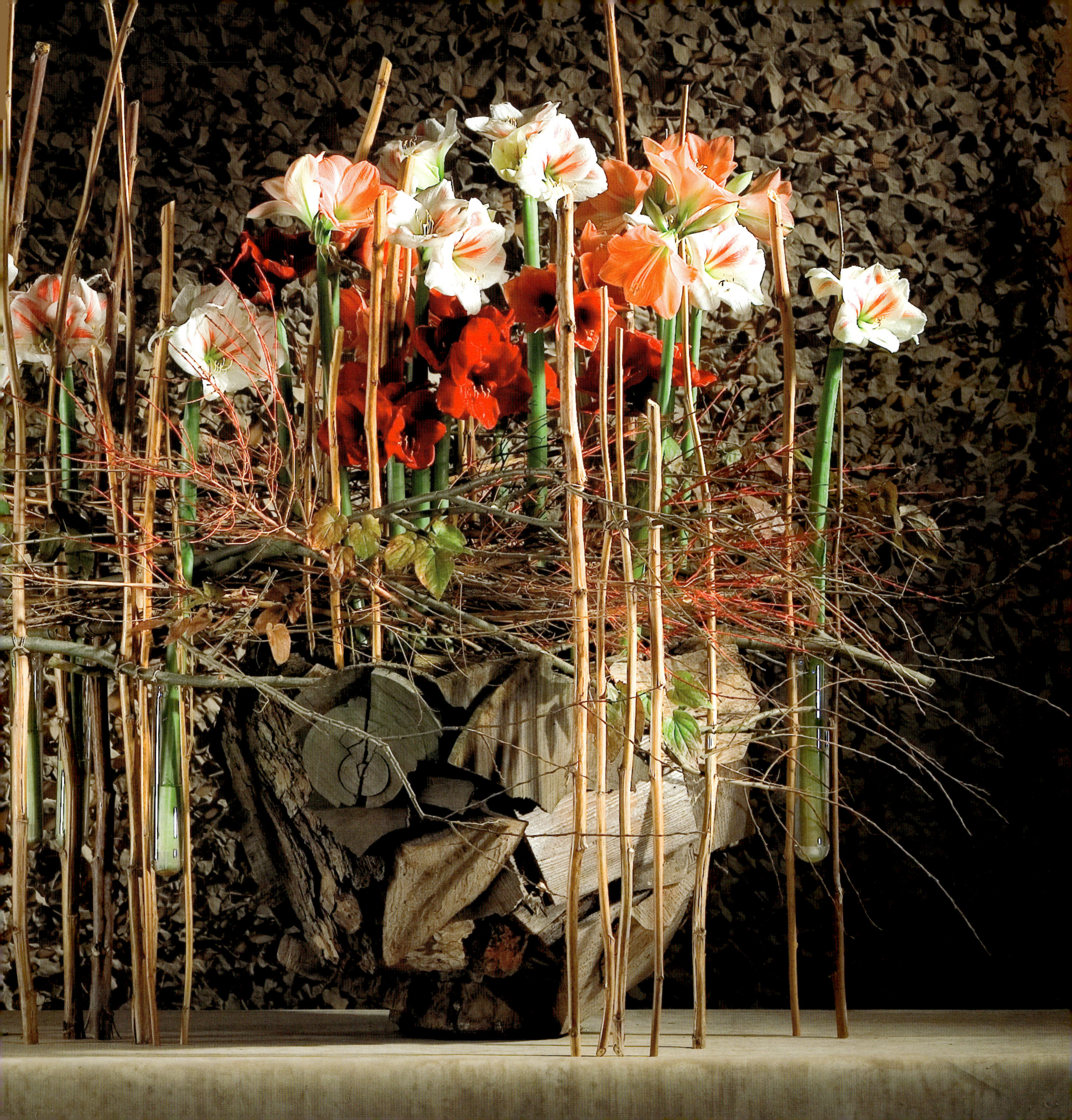

Faszinierende Blüten

Floristik bedeutet Vielfalt. In der Mitte des Lebens stehend und auf eine gesunde, fröhliche Familie, ein großes Unternehmen mit Partnern und Mitarbeitern blicken zu dürfen, von seiner Umwelt geschätzt und international bekannt zu sein, erfüllt mich mit Dankbarkeit und Freude. Aus kleinen Anfängen ist Erfolgreiches erblüht, das habe ich vielen Wegbegleitern zu verdanken. Eine Zukunft mit weiteren Aufgaben und Herausforderungen liegt vor uns allen. Meine Erfahrung lehrt, dass wenn Gewohntes verlassen und Grenzen überschritten werden, Neues entsteht. Doch geerdet, immer mit beiden Füßen auf dem Boden zu bleiben, ist meine Maxime. Mit der Sicherheit der eigenen, gesunden Wurzeln, mit der Begeisterung für alles Schöne und der sich immer wieder erneuernden Faszination für das Leben kann florale Kreativität ihre Knospen treiben und zum Erfolg erblühen. Dazu möchte ich Mut machen.

Fascinating Blossoms

Floristry means diversity. It gives me great satisfaction and gratitude to look back on what I have achieved so far at this stage of my life after almost half a century: a healthy and happy family, a big company with partners and employees, appreciation by the environment and an international reputation. Thanks to many companions I was finally successful after my first modest steps. A future with further duties and challenges is laid down for all of us. During my experiences I learnt that anytime you leave your habits and cross borders, something new is created. However, staying a down to earth person is my principle. With the security of one's own healthy roots, with the enthusiasm for all beauty and a permanent revitalized fascination for life, floral creativity can bud to a blooming success. Therefore I want to encourage people.

Mehr über Klaus Wagener unter www.klaus-wagener.com

For more information about Klaus Wagener see www.klaus-wagener.com

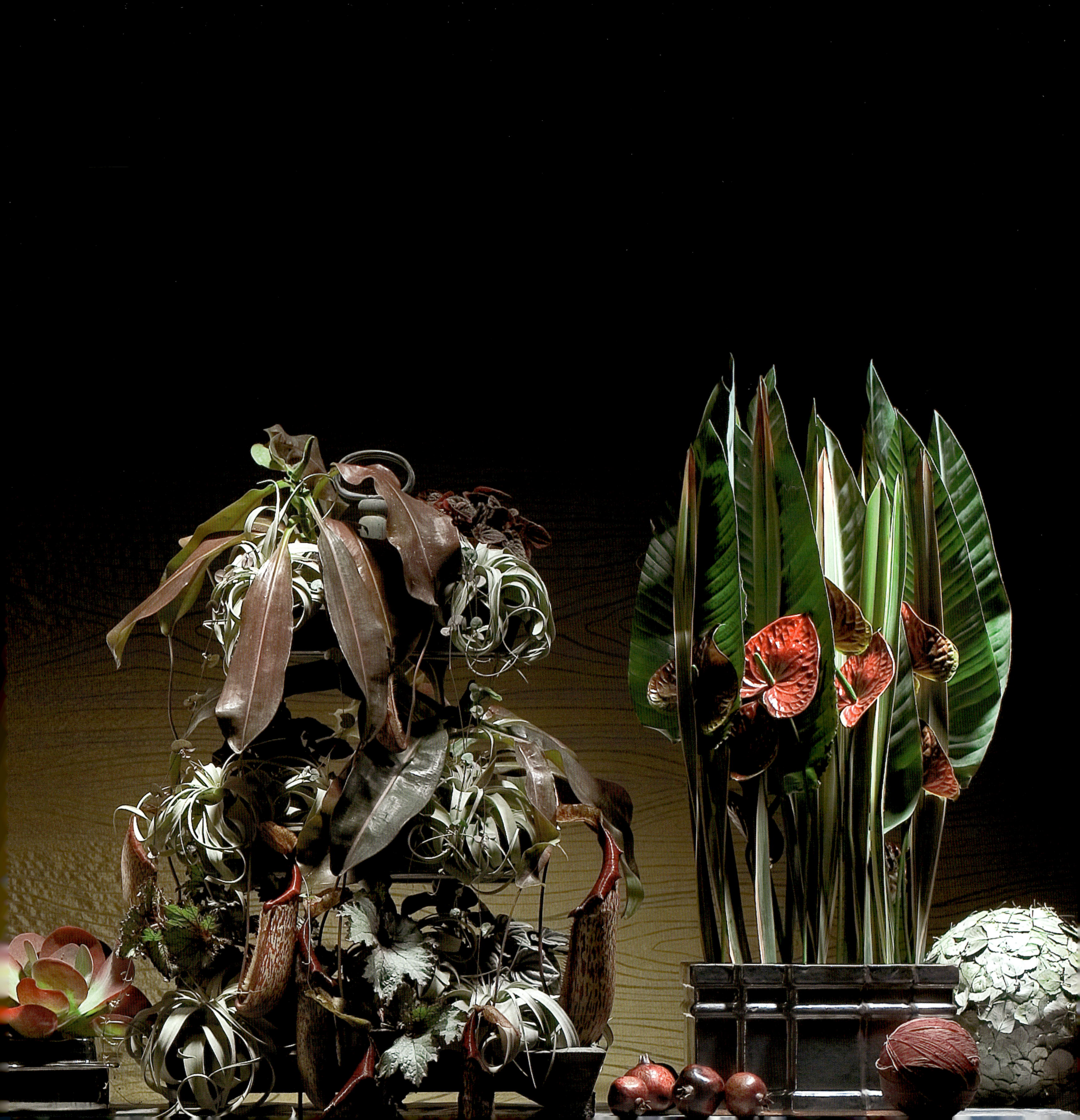

Aufregende Blätter

Floristik braucht Inspiration. Das kreative Leben ist eine ständige Herausforderung. Viel Unterschiedliches entsteht gleichzeitig und parallel, jedes für sich eigenständig und individuell. Aus anfänglich einem floristischen Fachmagazin entwickelt sich eine Vielzahl an Publikationsreihen, es folgen Bücher, Shows, Seminare, mediale und florale Netzwerke – das Unternehmen wächst. Mein Leben als Florist hat sich vom Floraldesigner zu einem Medienproduzenten und Unternehmer gewandelt. Viele junge, engagierte Menschen, die noch an der Schwelle zum Aufbruch und am Beginn ihrer individuellen beruflichen Entfaltung stehen, begleiten mich. Ich bin ihnen ein erfahrener Mentor und Wegweiser, sie sind mir erfrischender Quell für neue Ideen.

Exciting Leaves

Floristry needs inspiration since creative life is a permanent challenge. A lot of different ideas develop simultaneously; each of them individually and independently. A range of publications, followed by books, shows, workshops, floral and media-related networks have been created from an initially floristic magazine – the company grows. My life as a florist has changed from a floral designer to a media producer and entrepreneur. Many young motivated people who stand on the threshold of setting off and at the beginning of their individual professional evolvement are at my side. For them I am an experienced mentor and guide, for me they represent a refreshing source of new ideas.

2003 wird Klaus Wageners Name in die Personenenzyklopädie „Who is Who" aufgenommen. Rund 15 international verbreitete Fachbücher tragen seinen Namen, er tritt im Fernsehen auf. Die BLOOM's GmbH hat inzwischen über 50 Mitarbeiter.

In 2003 Klaus Wagener is added to the „Who is Who". Around 15 internationally distributed reference books bear his name and he gets on TV. Meanwhile BLOOM's GmbH counts over 50 employees.

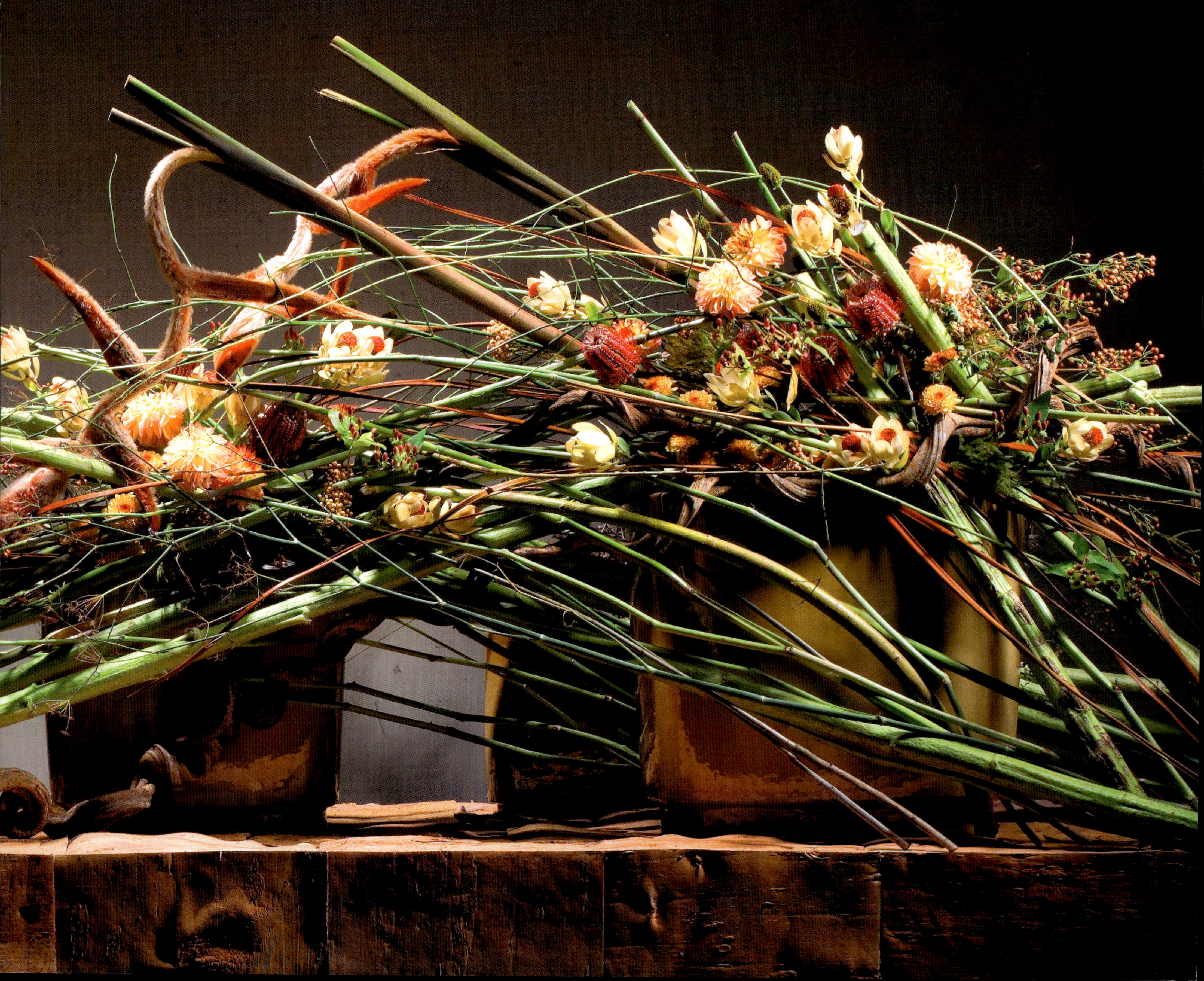

Dynamische Stiele

Floristik ist grenzenlos. Nach dem Gewinn der Weltmeisterschaft bin ich in vielen Ländern der Welt zu Gast. Ich lerne interessante Menschen, fremde Kulturen, andere Sitten und Lebensweisen kennen. Mein Wissen trage ich in die Welt hinaus und nehme im Gegenzug Fremdes auf. Es ist eine Zeit des intensiven Wahrnehmens, des Experimentierens und einer unerschöpflichen Kreativität. Ich stehe auf bedeutenden floristischen Bühnen dieser Welt, arbeite im Auftrag führender Industrieunternehmen an der Entwicklung neuer Produktsortimente. Im Netzwerk dieser internationalen Verflechtungen pflocke ich den zweiten wichtigen Meilenstein meines beruflichen Daseins ein: Zusammen mit drei kompetenten Partnern gründe ich einen Fachverlag, der zu einem der renommiertesten mit internationalem Ruf werden soll.

Dynamic Stems

Floristry is boundless. After having won the world cup, I started visiting many countries in the world. I get to know interesting people, foreign cultures, other customs and ways of life. I provide the world outside with my knowledge and learn in return things I haven't known so far. It is a period of intensive percipience, experiments and inexhaustible creativity. I have been on important floral stages of the world and I have been working on behalf of leading industrial companies to develop new product ranges. The second important milestone of my professional existence lies within this international complexity: together with three skilled partners I found a publishing company, which is supposed to become one of the most renowned with an international reputation.

1993 Gründung von Floristik Marketing Service GmbH, der heutigen BLOOM's GmbH. 1994 erscheint das erste floristische Trend-Magazin `profil floral`, das schon in kurzer Zeit weltweit zu einem anerkannten Designmagazin avanciert.

1993 founding of Floristik Marketing Service GmbH, today's BLOOM's GmbH. The first floral trade magazine, `profil floral` is published in 1994 and advances since then to a worldwide accredited trend and design magazine within a very short time.

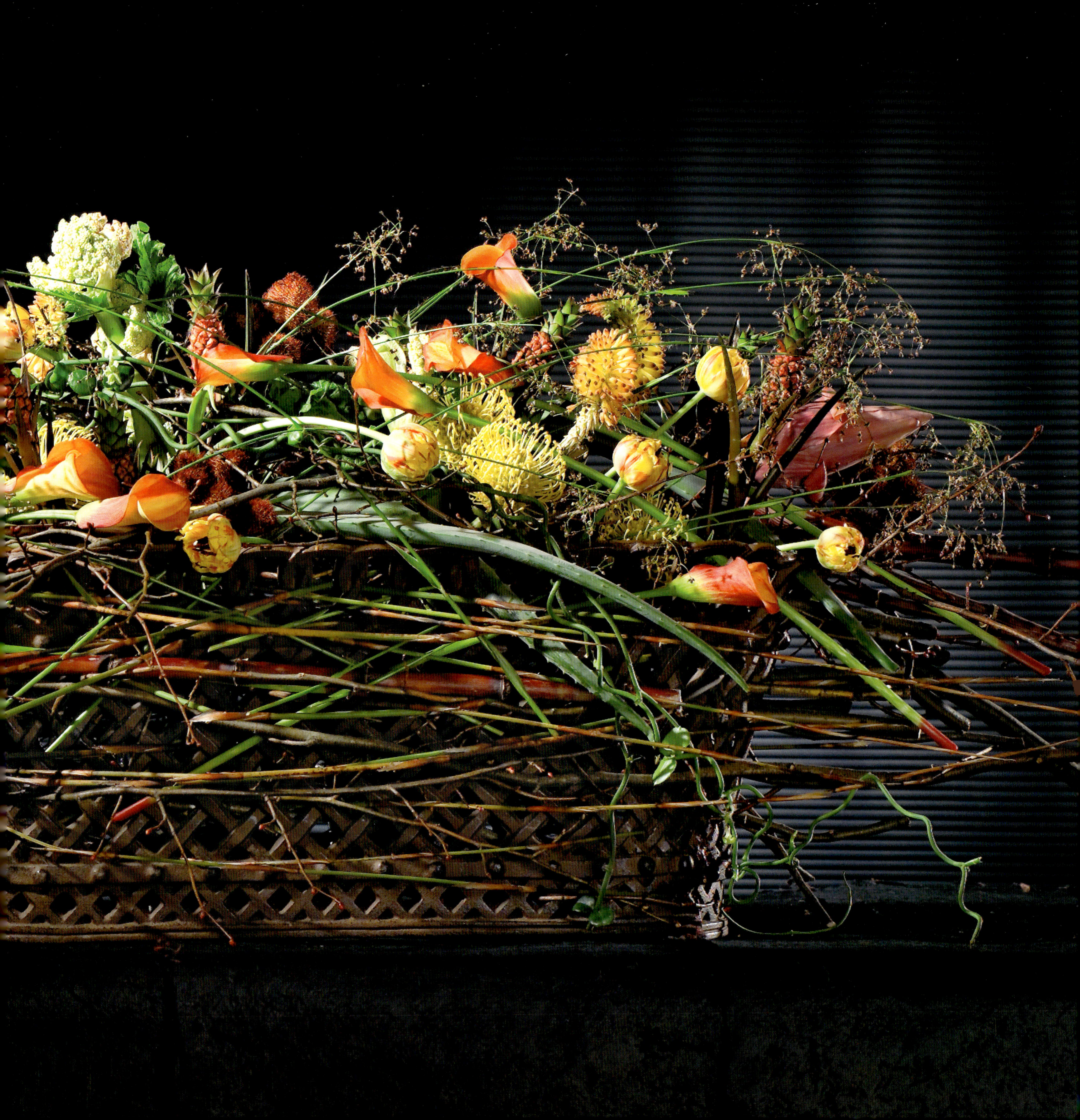

Erstaunliche Triebe

Floristik muss sich entfalten. Nach behüteter Jugendzeit folgt die Zeit der beruflichen Findung, der Lösung vom Elternhaus. Das Bisherige wird zu eng, der Blick in die weite Welt geworfen. Es schließen sich die Jahre der Lehre mit dem Besuch der Floristmeisterschule an, wo ich auch meine spätere Frau kennenlerne. Aus den Berufswettkämpfen, erst auf Bezirks-, dann Landes- und schließlich Bundesebene, gehe ich jedes Mal erfahrener und gereifter hervor. Immer wieder ergibt sich überraschend Neues, eingeschlagene Wege werden schon bald aufgrund neuer Kontakte und Chancen überdacht. Ein Meilenstein, der mein ganzes Leben prägen soll, ist der Gewinn der Weltmeisterschaft der Floristen in Detroit/USA.

Astonishing Shoots

Floristry must evolve. After a careless childhood and sheltered youth a period of professional finding and liberation from my parents' house begins. Everything I had known so far appeared to be too narrow to me. Then I stepped out into the wide world. During the following years I complete an apprenticeship, and then attend the master school for florists where I meet my later wife. Anytime I participated in a professional competition, at first at regional then at land and finally at federal level I gained more experiences and maturity. There is always something new to my surprise, decisions already made are reconsidered because of new contacts and opportunities. A milestone, which is supposed to influence my whole life, is the moment I won the world championship for florists in Detroit, USA.

Klaus Wagener besucht 1983/84 die Floristmeisterschule Friesdorf. Sein wichtigster Fachlehrer, der ihn auch nachhaltig prägt, ist Hermann Bömeke. 1984 gewinnt er die Deutsche Meisterschaft der Floristen, 1985 den Worldcup in Detroit/USA. 1985 heiratet er Bernhild Wagener, mit der er einen Sohn und eine Tochter hat.

Klaus Wagener attends the master school for florists in Friesdorf. His most important technical instructor is Hermann Bömeke. In 1984 he wins the German championship for florists, in 1985 the world cup in Detroit/USA and gets married the same year to Bernhild Wagener with whom he has a son and a daughter.

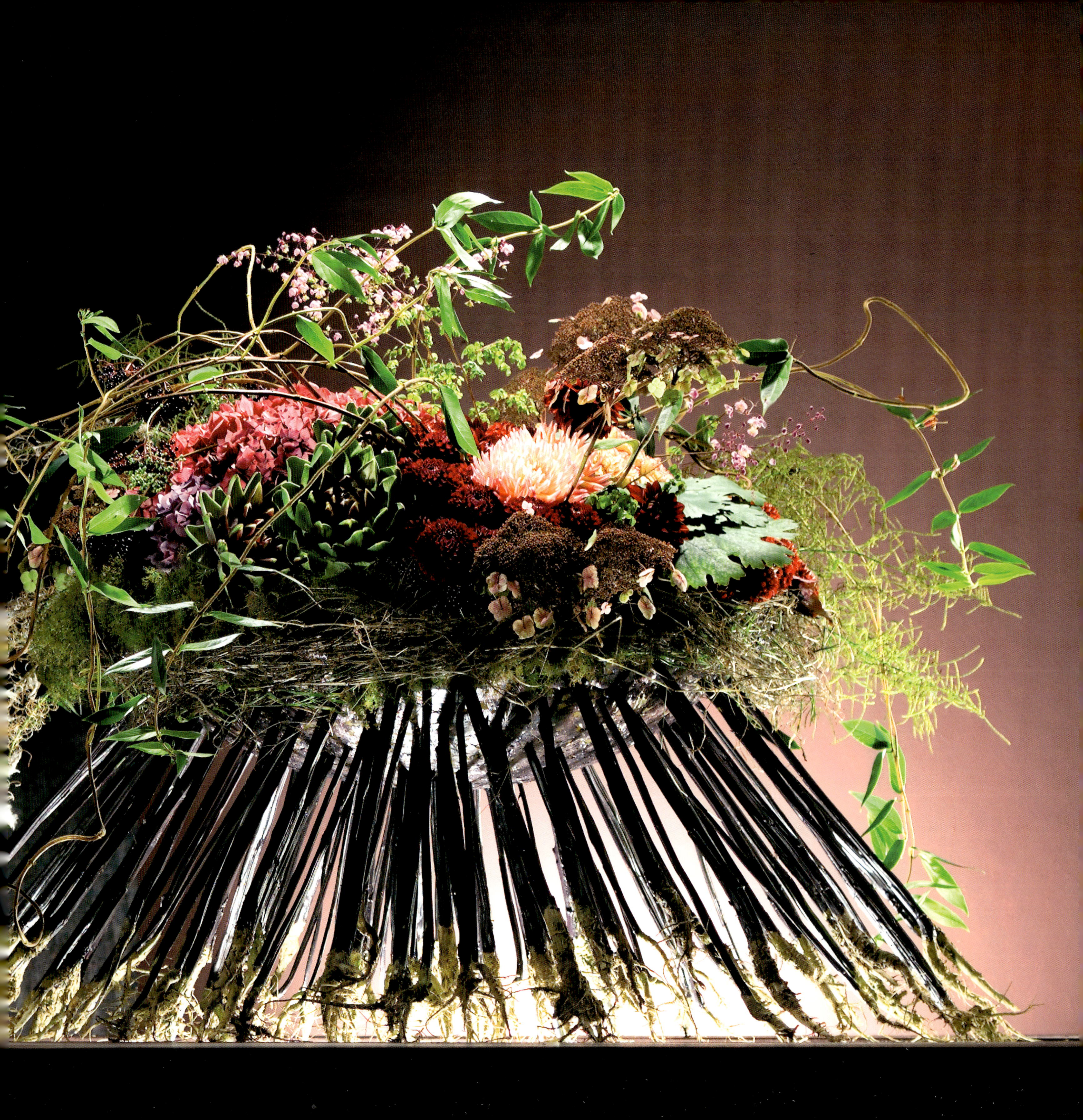

Floristik braucht Wurzeln. Ende der 50er Jahre geboren, sind für mich die wilden 70er Jahre des vergangenen Jahrhunderts die prägendsten auf dem Weg ins Erwachsenwerden. Es sind die Jahre des Aufbegehrens, des Widerstands einer mündigen Jugend gegen verkrustete Konventionen sowie der politischen Umwälzungen. Meine unbeschwerte Kindheit, die mir auch heute noch im Rückblick vom Licht überstrahlt erscheint, bildet meine Wurzeln, die mich auf der Bahn halten. Sie verankern mich trotz bewegter Zeiten, intensiven Wahrnehmens und vielseitigen Ausprobierens fest in den mir vermittelten Werten, die mir seitdem immer wichtiger geworden sind.

Mysterious Roots

Floristry needs roots. Born at the end of the 50s, the wild seventies of the past century strongly influenced my growing up. It was a period of protesting, antagonism of a mature youth against crusted conventions. But it was also a time of political changes. My carefree childhood, which still appears like a fairy tale to me when looking back today, constitutes my roots, which keep me on the right way. They function as a firm anchor of the values I was taught and have become more and more important for me since then despite eventful periods of intensive percipience and trials and errors.

Klaus Wagener wird 1958 als der ältere von zwei Geschwistern im westfälischen Minden geboren. Seine Eltern sind beide Floristen. Seine Spielwiese ist somit das elterliche Blumengeschäft, wo er von klein auf mit Blumen konfrontiert wird.

Klaus Wagener is born in 1958 in Minden, North Rhine-Westphalia as the elder brother of his sister. His parents are both florists. Thus, his parents' florist shop became his playground to which he was confronted since he was a little boy.

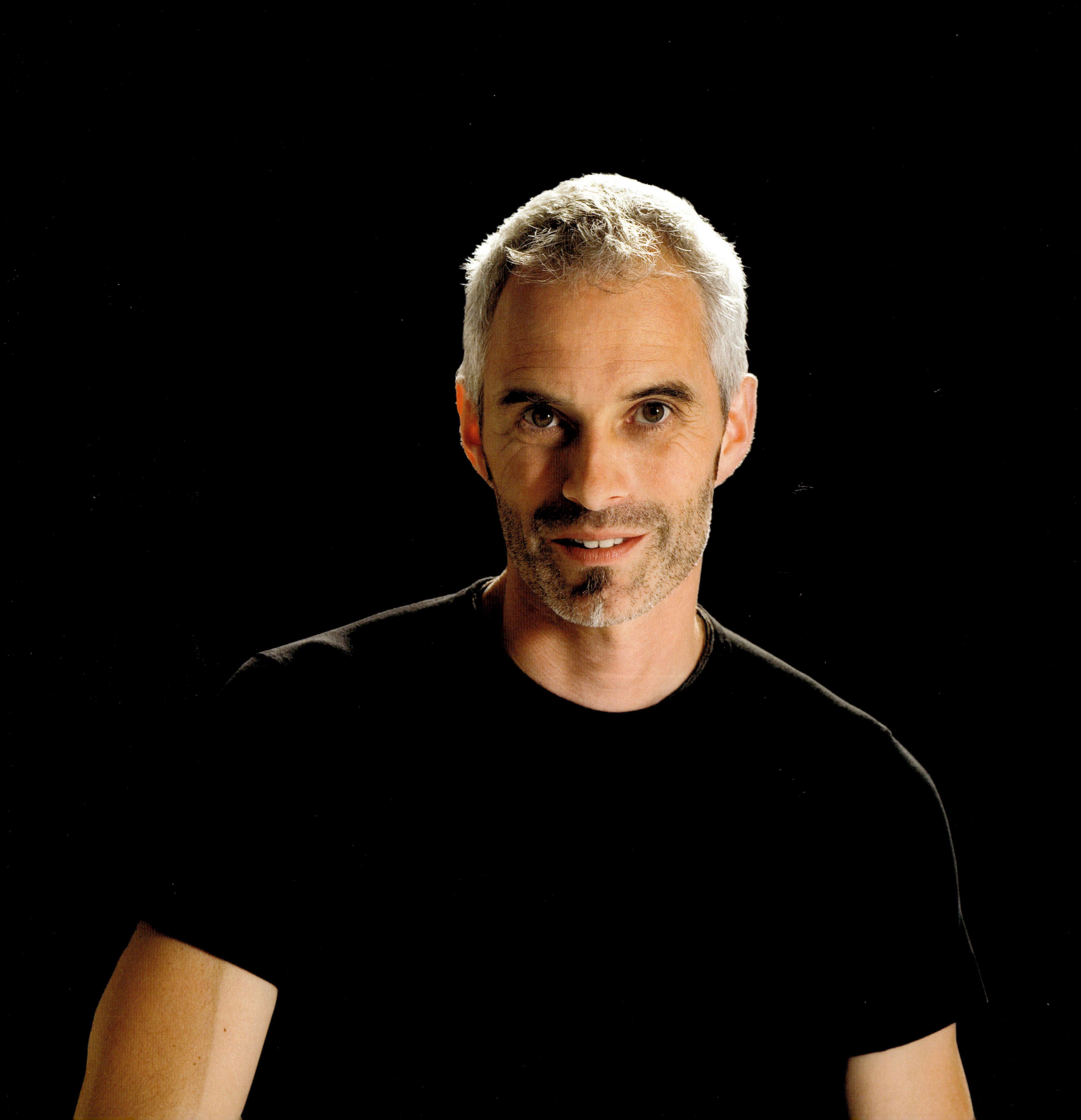

Professionelle Leidenschaft

Jede Profession bedarf der emotionalen Basis. Können, Leistungsbereitschaft, Arbeiten auf ein Ziel hin, sind nur möglich, wenn neben dem Kopf auch der Körper, neben dem Geist auch das Herz, neben Vernunft auch die Emotion den Taktschlag geben.

Dies gelingt, wenn Profession bereits in Kindheitstagen keimen, erstarken und in späteren Jahren wie Früchte zu beruflichem Erfolg heranreifen kann. Die Symbiose eines behüteten familiären Umfelds und einer wunderschönen Landschaft, in der ich aufwachsen durfte, haben diesen Keim einer frühen Begeisterung für die Natur und alle ihre Geschöpfe in mir zum Wachsen gebracht. Dafür bin ich heute sehr dankbar und weiß den Wert dessen zu schätzen, was mich zu dem gemacht hat, was ich heute bin und für was ich stehe.

Professional Passion

Any profession needs an emotional fortification. Skills, motivation, purposeful working to achieve something are only useful if there is harmony between head and body, mind and heart and also between rationality and emotion. The basis for this is laid down back in childhood, where the roots of a certain professional idea are put down, concretized and later in adolescence developed to a professional success. The symbiosis of a sheltered family background and a wonderful landscape in which I was grown up created an early enthusiasm in me for nature and all of its creatures. Today, I am very thankful for this and I appreciate everything I am and stand for.

Wagener | Impressum | Imprint

Herausgeber | *Publisher*
profil floral by BLOOM's GmbH, Ratingen | Germany
und | *and*
FloralDesign Edition
by kriener-potthoff communications | Germany

Konzept und Floristik | *Conception and Floristry*
(Seiten | *Pages* Wagener)
Klaus Wagener

Fotografie | *Photography*
Jörg Manegold
c/o Patrick Pantze Werbefotografie, Lage | Germany
(Seiten | *Pages* Wagener 1 - 131 und | *and* Portraits)

Redaktion und Text | *Editor and Text*
(Seiten | *Pages* Wagener)
Hella Henckel

Übersetzung | *Translation*
Fatiha El Mokrani

Grafikdesign | *Art Direction*
(Seiten | *Pages* Wagener)
Marion Hennig

DTP | *DTP*
(Seiten | *Pages* Wagener)
Gordian Jenal
Britta Baschen
Bettina Münch

© Copyright 2006
BLOOM's GmbH – Medien, Marketing, Events
40885 Ratingen | Germany
T +49-2102-9644-0
F +49-2102-896073
Email: info@blooms.de
www.blooms.de

in Zusammenarbeit mit | *in cooperation with:*
Floraldesign Edition
by kriener-potthoff communications

48155 Münster | Germany
Das Werk ist urheberrechtlich geschützt. Jede Verwertung ist ohne Zustimmung des Verlages oder des Herausgebers unzulässig und strafbar. Das gilt insbesondere auch für Vervielfältigungen, Übersetzungen, Mikroverfilmungen sowie die Einspeicherung und Verarbeitung in elektronischen Systemen.

All rights reserved. No part of this publication may be reproduced, stored in a retrieval system, or transmitted, in any form by any means, electronic, mechanical, photo-copying, recording or otherwise wihout the written permission of the publisher.

ISBN 13   978-3-9810443-6-2
ISBN 10   3-9810443-6-3

ISBN 13   978-3-938521-17-5
ISBN 10   3-938521-17-1

Danke | *Thank You*

Herzlich danken möchte ich folgenden Unternehmen und Personen, die uns bei der Erstellung dieses Buches in besonderer Weise unterstützt haben:
I would like to thank the following companies and people for having supported us in a special way in making this book:

Für das Zurverfügungstellen von Produkten und besonderen Pflanzen:
For providing us with products and special plants:

Anthura B.V. www.anthura.nl
Altefrohne-Messebau
www.messebau-altefrohne.de
Auroflor GmbH & Co KG www.auroflor.de
ASA Selection GmbH www.asa-selection.de
Bell`Arte bell-arte@t-online.de
Di Franco Bonturi Casa www.bonturicasa.com
Buco - vom Braucke GmbH & Co. KG
www.buco-wire.com
Decorama GmbH www.decorama.info
Kunstgewerbe Drescher www.drescher-sw.de
Edelman B.V. www.edelman.nl
Försterei Porta Westfalica, Achim Büscher
www.wald-und-holz.nrw.de

Försterei Porta Westfalica, Achim Büscher
www.wald-und-holz.nrw.de
Christrosengärtnerei, Josef Heuger
www.heuger.com
Haans www.haans.com
Halbach Seidenbänder Vertrieb GmbH
www.halbach-seidenbaender.com
Friedrich Hohmeier, Landwirtschaft und Landhandel in Porta Westfalica
Inge's Christmas Decor GmbH www.inge-glas.de
Kayak Wohnaccessoires Handelsgesellschaft mbH
www.kayak-GmbH.de
Konert Wohnart GmbH www.konert-wohnart.de
Koziol Ideas for Friends GmbH www.koziol.de
PTMD Collection by Pot & Mand b.v.
www.ptmd.nl
Poldermans + Artz B.V. www.poldermans-artz.nl
Smithers-Oasis Germany GmbH
www.smithersoasis.com
O-Living Interior Design GmbH
www.o-living.de
Mobach Keramiek b.v. www.mobach-keramiek.nl
Jens Ruhe, Dahlien-Gärtnerei
Sandra Rich GmbH www.sandrarich.de
H. U. Scheulen GmbH & Co. KG www.scheulen.de
Spang GmbH www.spang-online.de
Vivant www.vivant.nl
Woestijnroos BVBA www.woestijnroos.be

Für die Nutzung als Fotolocations:
For using the locations for our shootings:

Energie-Forum-Innovation, Bad Oeynhausen
Gemeinschaftskraftwerk Veltheim, Porta Westfalica
Katholische Kirche Skt. Walburga, Porta Westfalica
Melitta Hauptverwaltung, Minden
Sparkasse Minden-Lübbecke, Hauptverwaltung Minden

Den Mitarbeitern und Kollegen für die floristische, organisatorische und technische Unterstützung, bzw. für das Einbringen als Modell, für die grafische Realisation, Betextung und Übersetzung:
The collaborators and colleagues for their floristic, organisational and technical support or their contribution as the basis for the graphical realisation, editing and translation:

Marion Bauer, Maike Bruder, Dany Eschenbüscher, Carolin Fischer, Andrea Gerecke, Alexander Hafke, Dorothea Hamm, Hella Henckel, Marion Hennig, Jan-Dirk von Hollen, Norbert Knapp, Britta Kroggel, Gordian Jenal, Steffen Laible, Karen Meier-Ebert, Viola Nikić, Anna Nickel, Stephan Pantze, Britta Peters, Markus Reinhold, Andreas Regalar, Inga Santen, Anna Wagener, Bernhild Wagener

Das Fotografenteam für die kreative Arbeit hinter und mit der Kamera:
The team of photographers for their creative work with and behind the camera:

Patrick Pantze-Werbefotografie, Lage (Jörg Manegold, Stephan Röcken, Freddy Peterburs, René Deppe, Patrick Pantze, Sebastian Harms)

Gedankt sei auch den vielen anderen, hier nicht im Einzelnen genannten Personen, die uns aus ihrem privaten Fundus Requisiten zur Verfügung gestellt oder in anderer Weise unterstützt haben.
Sincere thanks also to all the persons, not particularly mentioned here, who have provided us with their personal props or have helped us in another way.

Klaus Wagener

Wagener | Inhalt | Content

2 | 3	Vorwort / *Preface*	36 | 37	Asymmetrische Spannung / *Asymmetric Tension*	70 | 71	Sinnlich-körperlich / *Sensual Material*	104 | 105	Leben & Sterben / *Life & Death*
4 | 5	Inhalt | Impressum / *Content | Imprint*	38 | 39	Dekorative Ansichten / *Decorative Views*	72 | 73	Sexy-provokant / *Sexy Provocations*	106 | 107	Ordnung kontra Chaos / *Order versus Chaos*
6 | 7	**Professionelle Leidenschaft** / ***Professional Passion***	40 | 41	Vegetative Erkenntnisse / *Vegetative Insights*	74 | 75	Opulent-dekadent / *Abundant Decadence*	108 | 109	Mono kontra Masse / *Mono versus Mass*
8 | 9	Geheimnisvolle Wurzeln / *Mysterious Roots*	42 | 43	Formal-lineare Fantasien / *Formally linear Fancies*	76 | 77	Reduziert-pointiert / *Trenchant Reductions*	110 | 111	In der Stadt – hoch hinaus / *In the City – starting up*
10 | 11	Erstaunliche Triebe / *Astonishing Shoots*	44 | 45	Einsichtige Strukturen / *Insightful Structures*	78 | 79	Heimat: Wiese / *Homeland: Meadow*	112 | 113	Auf dem Land – buntes Treiben / *In the Countryside – life full of colours*
12 | 13	Dynamische Stiele / *Dynamic Stems*	46 | 47	Gewagte Konstruktionen / *Risky Constructions*	80 | 81	Heimat: Sonnenblume / *Homeland: Sunflower*	114 | 115	Bei der Arbeit / *At Work*
14 | 15	Aufregende Blätter / *Exciting Leaves*	48 | 49	Beeindruckende Texturen / *Impressive Textures*	82 | 83	Heimat: Buche / *Homeland: Beech*	116 | 117	Feier: Mit Freunden / *Celebrating: With Friends*
16 | 17	Faszinierende Blüten / *Fascinating Blossoms*	50 | 51	Innovative Objekte / *Innovative Objects*	84 | 85	Heimat: Zuckerrübe / *Homeland: Sugar Beet*	118 | 119	Bühne: Im Rampenlicht / *Stage: In the Limelight*
18 | 19	**Meisterliches Handwerk** / ***Master Handcraft***	52 | 53	Monochrome Raffinesse / *Monochromatic Finesse*	86 | 87	**Individuelle Ansichten** / ***Individual Views***	120 | 121	**Engagierte Synergien** / ***Committed Synergies***
20 | 21	Gebündelt zur soliden Basis / *Bundled to a solid Basis*	54 | 55	Farbige Lust / *Colourful Delight*	88 | 89	Elementar wichtig / *Basic Importance*	122 | 123	Kopfstand der Kontraste / *Contrasts upside down*
22 | 23	Geknotet zu Netzwerken / *Knotted to Networks*	56 | 57	Bunte Leidenschaft / *Coloured Passion*	90 | 91	Heiß geliebt / *Precious Treasures*		122 Werkstück | *Work* Lersch / 123 Werkstück | *Work* Wagener
24 | 25	Geflochten zu Schützendem / *Braided for Protection*	58 | 59	**Ganz persönliche Gefühle** / ***Very private Emotions***	92 | 93	Neu entdeckt / *New Discoveries*	124 | 125	Erkennbare Parallelen / *Visible Parallels*
26 | 27	Gewoben zu Texturen / *Woven into Textures*	60 | 61	Frühlingshaft-verspielt / *Spring-like Plays*	94 | 95	Natürlich gewachsen / *Natural Growth*		124 Werkstück | *Work* Lersch / 125 Werkstück | *Work* Wagener
28 | 29	Geschichtet zu neuen Dimensionen / *Coated to new Dimensions*	62 | 63	Sommerlich-frisch / *Summer Breeze*	96 | 97	Architektonisch konstruiert / *Architectural Constructions*	126 | 127	Harmonie der Gegensätze / *Harmonie of Contrasts*
30 | 31	Gereiht zu Allianzen / *Ranked to Alliances*	64 | 65	Herbstlich-melancholisch / *Autumn's Melancholy*	98 | 99	Themen – Trends – Tendenzen / *Topics – Trends – Tendencies*		Werkstück | *Work* Lersch / Wagener
32 | 33	**Gestalterische Bekenntnisse** / ***Creative Confessions***	66 | 67	Winterlich-erstarrt / *Winter's Freeze*	100 | 101	Feuer – Wasser – Erde – Luft / *Fire – Water – Earth – Air*	128 | 129	Verbindung von Kompetenzen / *Combination of Competencies*
34 | 35	Symmetrische Ruhe / *Symmetric Silence*	68 | 69	Romantisch-ländlich / *Rural Romanticism*	102 | 103	Natur & Technik / *Nature & Technology*	130	Zusammenspiel der zwei Gesichter / *Interaction of the two faces* / Werkstück | *Work* Lersch / Wagener

Sie können es drehen und wenden, wie Sie wollen,
aber dieses Buch ist einfach nicht normal. „two faces of Floral Design" präsentiert die Arbeiten von zwei Designern an gleichen Themen. Gleiche Seitenzahlen – gleiche Themen. Auf der einen Seite die Werke von Gregoer Lersch, auf der anderen Seite die von Klaus Wagener. In der Mitte des Buches treffen sich dann beide zu immer intensiveren gemeinsamen Arbeiten. Also ein Buch zum Drehen und Wenden, zum Blättern und Vergleichen, zum Vorwärts- wie Rückwärts- und Querlesen.

You can turn it the way you want,
but this book is simply not a usual one. In "two faces of Floral Design" two designers present their work concerning the same topics. Same number of pages – same topics. On the one hand, the works of Gregor Lersch, on the other hand those of Klaus Wagener. In the middle of the book, you can find their common work. Well, a book to turn, compare, browse, and to read forwards as well as backwards and crossways.

Seine Vita:

Klaus Wagener wurde 1958 geboren und wuchs in einer Floristen-Familie auf. 1983 erlangte er an der Floristmeisterschule in Bonn-Friesdorf sein Floristmeisterdiplom. Es folgten die Jahre der beruflichen Wettkämpfe und Herausforderungen. 1983 gewann er die „Silberne Rose", die Landesmeisterschaft des Bundeslandes Nordrhein-Westfalen. 1984 folgte der Gewinn der „Goldenen Rose", die Meisterschaft der deutschen Floristen. Als Deutscher Meister trat Klaus Wagener dann 1985 beim „World Cup", der Weltmeisterschaft der Floristen in Detroit/USA an und trug auch hier als bislang einziger Deutscher den Sieg davon. Danach war er weltweit als freiberuflicher Florist und Designer gefragt.

1992 gründete er zusammen mit drei Partnern das Unternehmen FMS-Floristik Marketing Service GmbH, in Minden/Ratingen, einen Fachverlag und eine auf Gartenbau und Floristik spezialisierte Marketing-Agentur. Das Unternehmen machte sich mit seinen in mehrere Sprachen übersetzten Büchern, Fach-, Design- und Lifestylemagazinen schnell auch international einen Namen. 2006 firmierte es um in BLOOM's GmbH und beschäftigt mittlerweile über 50 Mitarbeiter. Klaus Wagener ist als geschäftsführender Gesellschafter für das International Design Center in Minden zuständig. Er leitet dort das BLOOM's-Kreativ-Team, ist Herausgeber und Autor diverser Fach- und Endverbraucherbücher, recherchiert als Trendscout für Industrie und Handel die aktuellen Strömungen in Design und Lifestyle und tritt als Dozent weltweit bei Fachvorträgen, Seminaren und Design-Shows auf.

2003 wurde sein Name in die deutsche Ausgabe der Personenenzyklopädie „Who is Who" aufgenommen. Klaus Wagener ist verheiratet und hat zwei fast erwachsene Kinder. Sein persönliches Credo: „Nach vorne blicken und die Herausforderungen der Zeit leidenschaftlich nutzen!"

His Vita:

Klaus Wagener was born in 1958 and grew up in a family of florists. In 1983, he obtained his diploma as a florist master at the Florist Master School in Bonn-Friesdorf, Germany. Then, the years of professional competitions and challenges followed. In 1983, he won the 'Silver Rose', the regional championship of the federal state of North Rhine-Westphalia, in 1984 the 'Golden Rose', the championship of German florists, and finally in 1985, Klaus Wagener, the then reigning German champion, participated in the world championship for florists in Detroit, USA. Even here he won the cup as the so far only German. Afterwards he was worldwide demanded as a freelance florist and designer.

In 1992 he founded together with three partners the company, FMS-Floristik Marketing Service GmbH, in Minden/Ratingen, a publishing house and a Marketing agency specialized in horticulture and floristry. The company rapidly obtained an international reputation with its books and trade-, design- and lifestyle magazines being translated in several languages. In 2006 the company was renamed BLOOM's GmbH with a number of meanwhile 50 employees. Klaus Wagener is responsible for the International Design Centre in Minden as the executive partner. He leads the BLOOM's-Creative-Team, is the publisher and author of various reference and end-user books, makes investigations as a trend scout for the commerce and industry about current flows in design and lifestyle, and gives lectures, workshops and presents design shows all over the world.

In 2003 his name was added to the German edition of the 'Who is who'. Klaus Wagener is married and has two almost grown-up children. His personal credo: 'Look forward and passionately benefit from the time's challenges!'

Zu diesem Buch
Ein Stück von mir

Wir haben den schönsten Beruf, den es gibt! Diese Feststellung treffe ich nach 30 Jahren professionellen Schaffens, in denen ich den Beruf des Floristen von allen Seiten kennen gelernt habe. Voller Dankbarkeit und Freude blicke ich auf das, was gewesen ist, auf meinen Werdegang und das, was ich geschaffen habe. Dazu zählen viele Wegbegleiter, glückliche Umstände, aber vor allem auch eigene Motivation, innerer Antrieb und stete Bestätigung von außen.

Jede Zeit hat ihre eigenen Gesetze. So stelle ich fest, dass die Rahmenbedingungen heute für unseren Beruf ganz andere geworden sind. Oberflächlich betrachtet könnte man meinen, dass wir damals mehr kreativen Freiraum hatten als die jungen Floristen von heute. Zum Beispiel die zahlreichen beruflichen Leistungswettkämpfe oder auch die intensiven grundlegenden Diskussionen über neue Gestaltungsformen, die unter anderem die Plattform für unsere Entwicklung und Findung darstellten.

Solche Möglichkeiten scheinen heute in dem Maße nicht mehr zu bestehen. Allerdings bietet die moderne Zeit andere Impulse zur beruflichen Entfaltung. Heute prägen eher Schnelligkeit, Flexibilität und Technologie die jungen Menschen. Sie wachsen bereits mit den Einflüssen von Internationalität, Mode und Design auf, weltweite Vernetzung und Medien sind ihnen von klein auf vertraut. Beste Voraussetzungen für einen kreativen Beruf. Allerdings sehe ich bei ihnen auch eine gewisse Unsicherheit, was in dieser von Eindrücken überfluteten Zeit der richtige oder beste Wege sein kann.

Diese Einschätzung teilt auch Gregor Lersch. Auch er ist der Meinung, dass neben aller Vielseitigkeit und dem besonderen Potenzial der neuen Generation das Wahrnehmen von Erfahrungen vonnöten ist – ein Durchdringen dessen, was unseren Beruf ausmacht, mit all seinen Tiefen, seinen handwerklichen Ansprüchen und vielgestaltigen Möglichkeiten.

So kam es zu diesem Buch! Dass wir beide, Gregor Lersch und ich, nach Jahren der unterschiedlichen Zielverfolgung gemeinsam ein Buch herausgeben, zeigt, dass es noch Ideale gibt. Wir wollen ein Stück unserer Lebenserfahrung abgeben, wollen das vielgestaltige Gesicht der Floristik präsentieren. „Two Faces" ist ein visueller Extrakt unserer beruflichen Erfahrung. Wir wollen Mut machen, Kreativität rund um die Blume und Pflanze auszuleben. Wir wollen lebende Blumen und Pflanzen wieder mit einer Aussage versehen, die Menschen zur Auseinandersetzung mit Natur und Natürlichkeit herausfordert. Wir wollen Grenzen überschreiten, zum Hinschauen, Entdecken und Nachdenken anregen, vor allem in einer Zeit der gesichtslosen Massenware, der zunehmenden weltweiten Uniformität von Design und Anspruch. Wir wollen kreieren um zu konfrontieren, profilieren und polarisieren, anstoßen und anregen. Wir wollen uns den jungen Floristen stellen und zum Diskurs herausfordern.

Nur wenn ein Berufsstand lebt und sich stets von innen und aus sich selbst heraus agil hält, kann er auch nach außen hin kreativ und motivierend wirken. In diesem Sinne soll das Buch, das auch Gregor Lersch und mich gefordert und aus dem Trott des Alltages herausgerissen hat, ein Stück gelebte Identifikation mit unserer Profession sein. Unser Tun und Handeln ist nach wie vor geprägt von einem lustvollen Schaffen für den Berufsstand. Der Nachwuchs ist unser höchstes Gut. Ihm widmen wir dieses Buch!

Herzlichst Ihr

In reference to this book
A part of me

We have the most beautiful job in the world! After 30 years of professional working during which I have learned all aspects of the florist's profession I finally come to this conclusion. I'm so grateful and happy when looking back on the past, my career and everything I have achieved so far. This concerns many companions, lucky circumstances but mostly my own motivation, initiative and a steady confirmation by others.

Each era has its own rules. Thus, I realize that today's guidelines for our profession have meanwhile completely changed. From a superficial point of view, you might assume that earlier we had more freedom for our creativity than the young fellow florists have today. There were, for instance, various professional competitions or intensive, basic discussions about new designing forms, which among others determined the basis for our evolvement and professional orientation.

Today, such opportunities do no longer seem to exist. Yet, the modern time offers other impulses for a professional evolvement. Young people are nowadays characterized by speed, flexibility and technology. They grow up in an environment being influenced by a world of globalization, fashion and design and are familiar with the internet and the media from their childhood. These are the best conditions for a creative profession. However, I see a certain uncertainty, which they have, concerning the right or best solution for them, caused by this time with its endless flow of impressions.

Gregor Lersch also approves this assessment. He also thinks that, besides all diversity and the particular potential of this new generation, looking for experiences is necessary – i.e. exploring intensively all aspects of our profession including all its depths, manual requirements and various possibilities.

That was the reason for this book! The fact that we both, Gregor Lersch and me, publish a book together after having pursued different objectives for years, shows that ideals still exist. We want to share our experiences of life with others and present the multifaceted image of floristry. Two Faces is a visual extract of our professional experience. We want to encourage people to live out their creativity around flowers and plants, to transmit a message again with the help of vital flowers and plants challenging people to have a look on nature and naturalness, cross borders, incite people to look, discover and think about especially in a time stigmatized by faceless mass-produced articles and a growing worldwide uniformity of design and demand. We want to confront, to profile and polarize, to initiate and incite with our creations as well as to face the young florists and invite them to a discussion.

Only if a profession is active and steadily kept in motion from the interior and out of itself it may obtain a creative and motivating appearance. In this way, the book that challenged Gregor Lersch and me and tore us away from the routine of the everyday-life should serve as a part of a lived identification with our profession. Our actions are still characterized by a joyful creation for the sake of our profession. Young people in the profession are the most precious good. To them we dedicate this book!

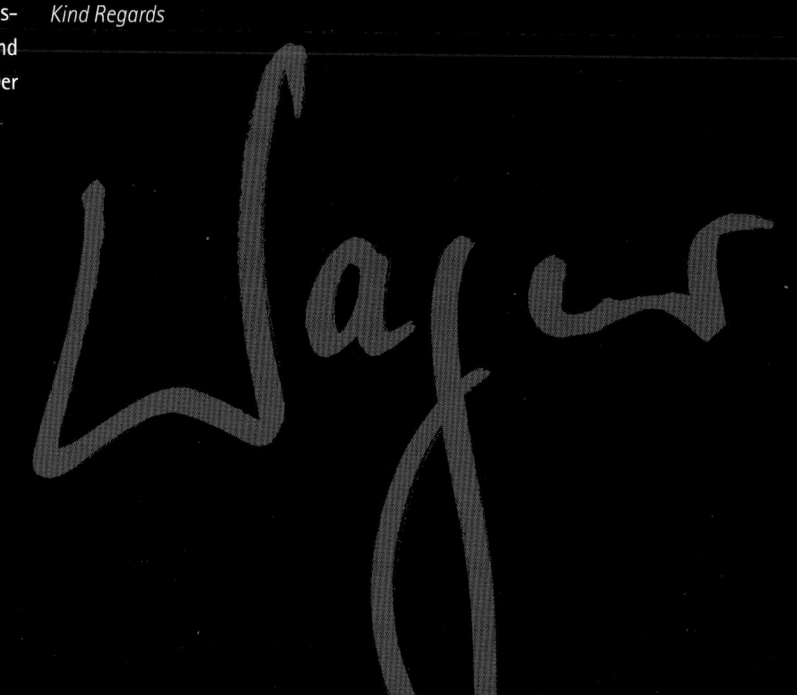

Kind Regards

Klaus Wagener